ALSO BY NEIL SIMON

Rewrites

The Play Goes On

A MEMOIR

NEIL SIMON

A TOUCHSTONE BOOK
PUBLISHED BY SIMON & SCHUSTER
NEW YORK LONDON TORONTO SYDNEY SINGAPORE

TOUCHSTONE
Rockefeller Center
1230 Avenue of the Americas
New York, NY 10020

First Touchstone Edition 2002

TOUCHSTONE and colophon
are registered trademarks of Simon & Schuster, Inc.

For information about special discounts for bulk purchases,
please contact Simon & Schuster Special Sales:
1-800-456-6798 or business@simonandschuster.com

Manufactured in the United States of America

10   9   8   7   6   5   4   3   2   1

The Library of Congress has cataloged the Simon & Schuster edition as follows:

Simon, Neil.
    The play goes on : a memoir / Neil Simon.
        p.   cm.
    Continues the author's Rewrites.
    1. Simon, Neil.   2. Dramatists, American—
20th century—Biography.   I. Simon, Neil.
Rewrites.   II. Title.
PS3537.I663Z473   1999
812'.54—dc21
[B]   99-36449   CIP
ISBN 0-684-84691-8
        0-684-86980-2 (Pbk)

ACKNOWLEDGMENT

My enormous gratitude to Michael Korda, for his willingness to go to bat with me again; to Charles "Chuck" Adams, Editor Extraordinaire; Gypsy da Silva, Copy Supervisor Extraordinairess; Victoria Meyer and all those supporters at Simon & Schuster, and to my invaluable assistant, Terry Oxford, and to my good friend Morton Janklow.

To Elaine Joyce—

who turned my life around.

The Play Goes On

LIFE REVISITED

1

EVERYTHING STOPPED. The sun came up, the clocks ticked on but nothing moved. I was always a morning person: the first one up in the house, the first one dressed, the first one down in the kitchen, the first one at breakfast.

But now I was still in bed, without a clue as to what time it was. I could hear the hum of the air conditioner, feel a chill in the room and yet my pajama tops were drenched through with perspiration. Were the girls upstairs in their rooms, silently waiting for me to come up to tell them what we would do with this, the first day of our lives on our own? I was fighting the act of awakening. I kept my eyes closed in hopes that sleep would overtake me once more, buying me more time before I would have to take a deep breath and then release it, acknowledging that I was alive. The future was a totally unpleasant prospect and I wasn't quite ready to deal with it. We had buried my wife, Joan, the day before at the Pound Ridge Cemetery in New York. She had just turned forty and had died of cancer, the most surprising thing she had done in a life filled with surprises.

I clung tenaciously to the darkness behind my closed lids, trying to keep the daylight at bay, much as I had as a boy when it was time to leave the local movie house, knowing that I left Humphrey Bogart or Errol Flynn still battling villains on the screen, while outside I squinted at the glaring harshness of the four o'clock sun and faced the heat of another endless summer's day.

Nancy was ten and Ellen was fifteen. It was July 12, 1973. Eight days before, on the Fourth of July, I had turned forty-six. It might as well have been sixty-six for all the lethargy and despondency I felt in my aching mind and body on that dreary morning. I pushed myself out of bed and crossed to the closet, looking for a robe that I almost never wore. Robes always made me feel either sick or old or both. Mine was a gift from Joan's mother, and I had feigned delight and pleasure when I opened it in front of her at an earlier birthday, knowing that I would never wear it, that it would only take up valuable space in my small closet. How ironic that I would be putting it on today, the day after her daughter died. But I needed a robe that morning because I did not want to face the girls in sweaty pajamas, although I had neither the strength nor inclination to get out of those pajamas, nor could I imagine myself doing so in the foreseeable future. What for? There was nothing outside that small town house on East 62nd Street that I wanted or needed to see. Nor *anyone* besides my daughters. I neither asked for nor invited friends or family to pay us a condolence call. At least not on that first day. The few really close friends I had would call later that morning, but they understood when I said, "Not yet. Give me today alone with the girls." Despite the fact that I had been aware for the past year and a half that Joan was going to die, I was unprepared for what I experienced on that first morning. It was not exactly grief, because, in a sense, I had been grieving those last few months of her life. This was a feeling of numbness, inertia and confusion, leading to a frightening inability to make a decision, trivial or otherwise. I have no memory of when I first saw the girls that morning, but Nancy told me recently that for some inexplicable reason, what she pictures in her mind today was the three of us in semi-darkness, sitting on the steps leading from the kitchen down to the basement. An implausible place to meet, and yet, for that morning, as plausible as any.

The thought uppermost in my mind was to distract the girls from dealing with the past, and to get them busy with getting on with life, making some small attempt at normalcy. I am always amazed at the resiliency of the young. They looked at me, waiting to hear what my plans were, ready and eager to comply. Neither girl had intended to be home that summer, both having made plans, not fully realizing the graveness of Joan's condition. Nancy was summoned back from camp when Joan passed away sooner than I ever imagined, and Ellen had canceled a student trip to Europe to be with her mother for her last few months. I suggested getting away from New York, as far away as possible, distancing ourselves from loss and sorrow. The summer house in Pound Ridge, New York, that I had bought expressly as a gift to Joan, where I hoped she would recover from her illness, was just a marginal choice to revisit. I offered to take them both to Europe, reasoning that traveling and being together would be, if not a fun-filled vacation, at least a chance to heal ourselves in new surroundings, in a place with fewer memories. Nancy surprised me when she opted to return to camp. It also gave me a sense of relief to know that this ten-year-old knew what was best for her. Ellen and I left together for Europe a week later.

I made the mistake of returning to all the same hotels that Joan and I had stayed in, something that proved harder for me to deal with than for Ellen. But slowly, day by day, I began to see a change in Ellen, a maturing, perhaps growing up faster than she normally would have if Joan were still alive. She started to point out things in shops in London and in Paris that might go nicely in our house. As it had been with Joan, who always brought home pretty and useful items from our trips, it was now with Ellen, who kept her eye open for unusual pieces I never thought remotely interested her before. In a sense, she was emulating Joan, perhaps not consciously, but in the normal way that a child takes on some of the traits of the parent of the same gender. By the time we returned home in late August, Ellen walked into our kitchen, opened the cabinets and said, "You know what, Dad? We need new dishes." Nancy came home a few days later, taller, tanner and a good deal happier than when she left. We were all so glad to see each other, and our conversation that night was about what we had done that summer and not about the tragedy we left behind. But it was certainly not gone from their minds; I noticed that clearly as Nancy climbed the steps that night and glanced quickly in my bedroom to see the made-up bed which Joan had occupied for so many months during her illness.

Later I heard laughter from their rooms and then the sound of tapes playing the Broadway musicals they loved so much, and their singing the lyrics to their favorite songs, loudly and slightly off-key. Eventually they switched to television and called down to me, "Dad, come on up and watch with us." I knew once I got in their room, they would bar me from leaving, forcing me to watch every fashion show, sitcom, summer rerun and old black-and-white movie. As I ascended the stairs, smelling the fresh popcorn they had just made, while scorching the bottom of the pot, I said to myself, "Thank you God for making daughters."

THE WANDERER
2

IN THE DAYS and weeks following, I walked through the streets of New York like a somnambulist, having to look up at corner signs to see where I was. Not that I was walking in any particular direction, or with any specific destination in mind. I walked through Bloomingdale's, fingering shirts or jackets without the slightest intention of buying anything. I was constantly looking at everyone who passed by, with the preposterously illogical hope that I might see Joan. There was always the possibility that the doctors had been mistaken about her death, or, just as unlikely, that I merely dreamt she died, which would explain the foggy, half-awake state in which I existed. The memory flashed in my mind how sometimes, before Joan ever got ill, I would be walking down a street and would glance up and see her looking in a store window. She would turn and see me, and we would both smile, thinking the same thing: "We just had a free one"—meaning an extra time of seeing each other, one we hadn't planned on.

I climbed the steps of the Metropolitan Museum of Art on Fifth Avenue, and wandered through the great exhibition halls, delving into Egyptian antiquity. Then I went up the stairs to the paintings of Matisse and Renoir, Van Gogh and Rembrandt; I stared at the John Sargents I loved so well, remembering when I first saw them with Joan. With her at my side, I had the added advantage of having her fill me in with minute details of the painter's art, most of which I might not have noticed on my own. For me she was like one of those tape-recorded talking guides you rent as you enter the museum, except with this one, you were allowed to hold the hand of this guide, or watch her hair bobbing up and down as she tried to peer over the crowd to see the museum's latest and most talked about acquisition.

On the day I chose to revisit the museum alone, I suddenly heard a voice directly behind me.

"Neil?"

I turned and looked.

"I'm Carol Mantz."

She said her name as though I should know it, but I didn't have a clue as to who she was. Or maybe I did know her, but like everything else in my life at that moment, I couldn't fit the pieces together.

"I think you knew my husband, Mark. He said you both grew up together in Washington Heights."

"Mark? Oh, yes. Mark. Of course." I had no idea who Mark was. Well, perhaps it sounded vaguely familiar, but if I was struggling with my own identity, I couldn't blame myself for not remembering a boy I knew thirty years before.

"I was sorry to hear about your wife. I read about it in the paper."

"Yes. Thank you." Wanting to get off the subject, I went back to hers: "So, how is Mark these days?"

"He died six months ago. Heart attack."

"Oh, God, I'm so sorry. Was he ill?"

"Never sick a day in his life. Just keeled over in his office."

"Oh, no. How terrible for you."

My words of comfort seemed as empty as the ones I had been hearing myself every day for the past three weeks. You appreciate them, but you don't quite know how to deal with them.

"When you started writing plays, Mark told me he was a friend of yours. He was so proud of you. I think we've seen all of them."

I could see the tears welling up in her eyes and I was suddenly jolted back to the past. A picture of Mark Mantz as a teenager came vividly into my mind: outgoing, funny, friendly; had to be about my age. I looked at her and this time I actually saw her. She was about thirty-six, a few years younger than Joan. She told me they had a little boy who was seven. Then, for no apparent reason, the conversation stopped. There was an awkward silence because neither one of us wanted to talk about death and losses. I wanted to walk on but didn't want to appear unsympathetic to her troubles nor self-involved by talking about mine.

"So, I guess we're sort of in the same boat, aren't we?" she said. I nodded, sensing what her next line would be.

"I don't know how you feel about it, but if you'd like to talk about—well, you know. If you'd like to have coffee or a drink or dinner, I could give you my number."

The mood changed in an instant. We had moved from tragedy to new beginnings. In a sense, whether it was coffee or a drink or whatever, it was still a date, and I was not only unprepared for a date at this time, I was also not sure I knew my way home from the museum.

"Thank you," I said. "That's very kind of you. To tell you the truth, I'm not quite—"

"Oh, I understand. I wasn't either at first."

"Then you know what I'm—"

"I do. Honestly, it was just an offer. If you change your mind, my number's in the book. Take care of yourself. Your girls are going to need you now."

She turned and walked away. Interesting that she even knew about my girls. Here was a date that was being contemplated by her, not necessarily by mutual attraction, but by mutual tragedy. By the rules of natural selection, people have been bonding that way since the beginning of man's time on earth. However, the thought of moving on with my life as yet hadn't even occurred to me.

She had six months of mourning behind her. I was hardly out of my first three weeks.

I realized I could no longer find refuge in department stores, bookstores, movies or museums. My only salvation was to get back to work. Throughout my career, whether in moods of quiet despair, painful back spasms, a high-grade flu and, amazingly, even during Joan's illness, I was able to continue working, albeit only a few hours a day. I had the ability to block everything else out of my thoughts and focus completely on the

work at hand. By picking up a pen and gazing at the blank pages of the spiral notebook in front of me, I suddenly lost sight of my surroundings and
circumstances, and entered the world in which the characters I created
were living out their own problems or good fortune. They had no interest
in *my* immediate woes, no knowledge they even existed. Which led me to
think: Did they know I was there, in *their* place, *their* room, sitting in a dark
corner witnessing the most personal moments of their own inner conflicts?
Did these characters even care that I was committing their words, their
thoughts, their actions to paper? Were they oblivious to the fact that I
might one day share their lives with total strangers, who were privy to this
information only by my invitation? Since they never brought it up, I didn't
bother mentioning it to them.

In the year and a half of Joan's illness, I had completed the screenplay
of *The Prisoner of Second Avenue,* which was to start filming in Hollywood
in a matter of weeks. It was to star Jack Lemmon and Anne Bancroft. I also
had completed a new play, *The Good Doctor,* based on short stories by
Anton Chekhov. Warner Brothers and director Mel Frank wanted me to
attend two weeks of rehearsals in Los Angeles to do any last-minute
rewrites on *Prisoner,* the kinds of changes that would inevitably be needed
once the actors started digging into their roles. *The Prisoner of Second Avenue,* although a critical and commercial success on stage, worried me as
film material. It was a serious comedy or a funny drama, a sort of hybrid
form of play, atypical for most playwrights in the 1970s. Eugene O'Neill
wrote drama/tragedies. George S. Kaufman wrote comedies. Samuel Beckett wrote poignant humor laden with a sense of anguish and loss, while
Eugene Ionesco wrote abstract farces with strong social overtones. Tennessee Williams wrote poetic tragedies that managed to have a great deal of
ironic humor. What they all had in common was that they did their work
masterfully. These were the greats that I wanted to emulate. The problem
was that I wanted to emulate them all at the same time, and often, all in the
same play. What was odd about my plays was that when they were funny,
they were true comedies, and when they were dramatic, they dealt with
everyday people faced with serious dilemmas. What was confounding and
somewhat annoying to many critics was that I was attempting to do both
things in the same play. They felt I was being neither true to the comedy

nor true to the drama. Since most audiences seemed to like what I was doing, however, there was the paradox of my having a great many hits that critics did not praise. It's hard to sell tickets to plays that critics frown on, yet the audiences came anyway. Since I was committing the cardinal sin of being popular without their stamp of approval, the critics (not all, but a lot) banished me to the Devil's Island of the Arts by designating me "Not Important."

In the case of *Prisoner,* I worried that the moviegoing audience wouldn't be as accommodating as a theater audience. *The Odd Couple* and *Barefoot in the Park,* both true comedies, were successes in both mediums. The darker my plays became, however, the more lackluster the results when they were transferred to the big screen.

Despite my eagerness to get back to work, I soon realized I was in no emotional shape to handle two projects at one time, no mind to do rewrites and little desire to fly to Hollywood for two weeks, leaving the girls behind. Yet I needed to occupy myself before the girls became caretakers to the one person in the world who should be taking care of them. Foolishly or not, I plunged into work, hoping somehow to keep my head above water.

As for the new play, I left that in the hands of my more than capable producer, Manny Azenberg. He started the wheels in motion, prepping *The Good Doctor* for production late in the fall. We hired a director, scenic designer and costume designer and began casting. I sat through auditions with director A. J. Antoon in a darkened theater, wondering what I was doing there, unable to concentrate on the actors, while I played mind games with myself, something in the order of "I'd give two years of my life if I could make just one phone call to Joan wherever she was in the universe that day."

Christopher Plummer accepted the starring role playing both Chekhov as narrator and as principal actor in Chekhov's creations, as interpreted by Neil Simon. Other fine actors like Barnard Hughes, Frances Sternhagen and Rene Auberjonois were soon added to the cast. What we were missing was one young, attractive, funny, touching, serious, seasoned and delightful new actress who could play five completely different roles in one evening. You could search for three years and still not find someone like that. We didn't have years; I was to leave for California in two weeks, and in that time we auditioned thirty or forty actresses. Many of them could do one, perhaps two of the roles, but not a single one could come close to doing all five roles, being convincing in each one of them.

I was worried about not being able to ever find the right actress, and being in the fragile state I was in, I wouldn't have minded if we canceled the entire production either forever or, more reasonably, until I became something more than just the shadow of my former self.

A few days before I was to leave for California, I received a call from actor's agent Phyliss Wender. She said she was representing someone very special and asked if I could see this actress in the next day or so. Phyliss was someone I respected and liked, and the fact that she called me personally and avoided going through the normal channels of calling our casting director first was a signal to me that this person was someone I should pay attention to. I told her I was about to leave for Los Angeles and asked if I could see her client when I returned in two weeks.

"She'll be gone in two weeks," Phyliss answered. "She'll be gone in two *days.* She has to be in Seattle to start a new film. Neil, I'm asking you to trust me on this one. This is someone you should really see."

"Phyliss, I trust you, but I don't trust me right now. I don't think I'm clearheaded enough to make a good judgment." I paused while I tried to force reason through the cementlike block of protection that the mind sets up while one is healing. "When is the last day I could see her?" I finally asked.

"Tomorrow. I feel terrible about pushing this, but after this movie, I may never be able to get her out of pictures."

In my silence, we could both hear my brain trying to fight through to a decision. She tried to find a way around it: "Would you leave the decision up to Manny and A. J. Antoon?"

"I would, but Manny would never sign anyone if I didn't see them first. Do I know her?"

"I'm not sure. Her name is Marsha Mason."

"No. Not familiar to me."

"She did *The Indian Wants the Bronx* off-Broadway with Al Pacino. She got great reviews. I could send them to you."

"I can't audition reviews. I can't even remember if I saw the play.

Probably not." I trusted Phyliss too much to pass and I knew she wasn't just trying to get a client a job. She was too earnest and smart for that.

"All right. What about tomorrow afternoon? About four."

"Could we make it at two? Actually, she's leaving tomorrow night."

I smiled. "You really love pressure, don't you? And there's going to be a lot of it, if we all come down to audition just one girl."

She was ready for that one. "I thought of that. I'm bringing another girl as well. She's good, but this part belongs to Marsha."

"Phyliss, you should be running MGM and Paramount."

"No, thanks. I love New York, and I've got my kids in a good school. I'll see you tomorrow at two."

Tomorrow sounded like a thousand years away. I hung up and took Ellen and Nancy out to the same Chinese restaurant for the third night in a row. I had no idea it was the third night until Ellen opened up her fortune cookie and read aloud, "Hello Simon family. We were expecting you." Nancy laughed before I realized it was a joke. I was glad that someone in the family still had a sense of humor.

NIGHT VISITS
3

I BEGAN PERFORMING a ritual each night before I went to bed. I had read a good deal about meditation but found it very difficult to keep my mind and thoughts still enough to receive any benefit from it. With Joan's passing, I now had a reason to go back to meditation, not for quieting my restless mind, but to somehow find a way of keeping Joan's positive and reassuring qualities still alive within me. I was afraid if I lost contact, not with her, but what she meant to me, I would lose an important part of myself. I believed in our marriage so firmly—the give-and-take between two loving people, the bolstering of one's spirits when the other one's were flagging—I desperately needed to keep the memory of what she contributed to my life, some way, somehow, always there beside me.

Each night, after the girls were asleep, I put my favorite picture of Joan on a small table and lit a candle on each side of it. Then I sat on the carpeted floor, my back against the small sofa in the room in which I worked; with all the lights off and the shades drawn, I stared deeply at the face of Joan as I remembered her best. I was trying to burn the image of her face into my mind, burn it so deeply that it would never fade and always be there at any time of the day or night that I summoned it. After a while, I began to talk to the picture in a whisper, although low enough not to be heard by anyone (including myself) for fear I would feel foolish, embarrassed and self-conscious. Hence the drawn shades. It even occurred to me that Joan might be watching this ritual from the place in the room that she still inhabited, and that she was surprised to see a part of me she never knew existed. For that matter, neither did I. I wasn't sure if she was amused by it or simply appreciated the fact that I was making a kind of person-to-person call to her each night.

I was not looking for help to assuage my pain: I counted on the pain to assure me she was still in my thoughts. What I wanted was guidance in becoming both a father and a mother to my two daughters. I needed someone to show me the ropes, to whisper in my ear those things girls growing up needed to hear. It soon occurred to me that it wasn't Joan that I was talking to at all, but rather it was me appealing to and sum-moning up the best parts of me, using the image of Joan, who knew me so well, as a guide to help me to find my own answers. These sessions be-came such a habit that I couldn't fall asleep without them. If I had for-gotten somehow, I'd get up in the middle of the night, like a fan devoted to his favorite program, cross into the "session" room and tune her in. After a while, the sessions became lighthearted and conversational chats rather than the earlier solemn, ceremonial and reverentially clandestine meetings. Sometimes they began with, "Hi, Joan, and how was your day today?"

Miraculously, it worked for me. If I had a problem at night, then sat down for a quiet midnight tête-à-tête with my deceased wife, more often than not I awoke in the morning having resolved the problem while I slept. For example, as I woke up early one morning, I answered my own question: "You can't be a mother to your daughters. Just be a better father." I never had to deal with that one again. The days were slowly getting bet-ter, but the improvement rested on the premise that I was looking forward to chatting with Joan that night—and every night. Without my realizing it, the more I held on to Joan through our talk sessions the more I was im-peding my own recovery from the grief, a situation that was to remain constant for a very long time.

I ARRIVED at the theater for the audition promptly at two o'clock. I am almost never late for anything. Actors generally get there earlier than their appointed time to go over the pages they're going to read and to try and settle their nerves. As I entered the stage door, I saw one actress sitting on the steps that led up to the dressing rooms. I had no idea if this was Marsha Mason or the girl that Phyliss sent along to read as a backup if we didn't like Ms. Mason. As I passed her, the actress looked up from her pages, smiled at me and nodded. I returned the nod. Not good to get too friendly with them, I always thought. Be polite, yes, but not amiable. It makes it that much harder when and if they got rejected, which was ninety percent of the time. I was never very good at this auditioning business anyway. I was always grateful that the director or casting agent was the one to say, often before they were through reading, "Thank you very much. We appreciate your coming in." That was the standard line for, "No. Not you." The actor knows it immediately and will either look up surprised or disappointed, or will just take it in stride and leave. I always found the longest and most difficult few seconds were when he or she walked off the stage, usually having to pass the other actors who were waiting their turn. Sometimes they made casual comments to each other in passing, other times it was a quick walk out the door in silence, and if they were lucky, off to another audition. Twenty-five years ago, when the New York theater had an abundance of new plays, an actor could go to two or three auditions a day. Today they're few and far between.

Very often an actor I knew, liked and had worked with before came out to read. When it was clear that he or she was not quite right for this role, the thank-yous and goodbyes were more pleasant. There might be some funny exchange about the good times we remembered on that other play. Oftentimes, they would remark as they left, "Good luck with this. It's a great play." A generous thing to say. This despite the fact the actor *always* thinks he's right for the part. They *should* feel that, otherwise why would they be there? And if he thinks he's not right for the part, he should believe that with enough work he could *make* himself right for it. Only once in my life did I hear an actor stop himself in the middle of his reading and say, "You don't want to hear any more of this, do you? I'm stinking it up." He did eventually go on to win an Academy Award as Best Actor in a film that also won as Best Picture. It was F. Murray Abraham and the film was *Amadeus* and his award was well deserved. And in case Murray wants to know, he did not stink it up that day. I think he decided he just didn't want to do that particular play.

This auditioning business works both ways, of course. Once, an actor who had just won the Tony Award as Best Actor in a Play a few weeks before he came to audition, sat in a room with us and thought carefully before he said, "Do you think the time will come when an actor who just won a major award doesn't have to audition?"

I said, "Tell me something, would you want to do my play if you hadn't had the opportunity to read it first?"

He smiled and said, "No. But you've seen my work."

"You've seen my work too," I added.

He decided to audition, but his heart wasn't in it. He took another job before we ever came to a decision about him. The truth is, yes, there comes a time when an actor doesn't have to audition. If he's Tom Hanks or Jack Nicholson or Barbra Streisand, ad infinitum. I *always* have to audition. No star will do my play until he reads it first. Jack Lemmon was the only actor *ever* who said yes to doing a film of mine after I gave him a mere five-sentence description of the story.

But back to the audition at hand. As I started for the door that led from back stage to the theater, I saw the second actress sitting on a chair, studying the pages. She looked up and smiled at me, as the first girl had, but there was something in this smile that was different. There was a warmth and intelligence and confidence in her face that left little doubt in my mind that *this* was Marsha Mason. It was also a face I had seen before—but where? In a play? A film? On television? Wait a minute. I think this is the girl in that commercial. Manufacturers Hanover Trust, I think. All she did was look straight in the camera and recite the copy the ad agency had written. About higher interest rates, more convenience, better locations. The usual boring patter that we, the viewers, dismiss out of hand. Until they show it often enough and you absorb it by repetition. But as I watched her in that commercial, the writer in me knew that the actress in her was adding a subtext to what she was saying merely by the way she looked at the camera. What was the subtext was *her* secret, and we could only guess. To me she was saying, "All else aside, if you come down to our bank, you'll have one hell of a time." Well, obviously the delivery was not that overtly sexual, but I found myself waiting for that commercial to come on again soon. And suddenly her name also seemed familiar. I had read it in a review. Now it was coming back. That movie with George Segal and Kris Kristofferson . . . Damn, what was the name of it? And as it came to me, I found myself blurting it out.

"Oh," I said in recognition. "You're that girl from *Love in Blume,* aren't you?"

"Blume in Love," she said, correcting me. "Yes, that was me."

Then she laughed and there was that smile again. I suddenly had an overwhelming desire to go down to a bank. Subliminal advertising had worked its powers on me again.

"Right," I said. "I thought you were terrific."

"Oh? Thank you," she said, surprised at the good review I had just given her. "I'm glad you liked it."

I had just made a mistake. I was being chatty. I was being amiable. I had told her she was terrific in the movie I had seen. Turning her down for the play after such a positive connection would be tantamount to saying, "Amazing. You were so good in that movie, but your reading for the play was lousy."

Inasmuch as she hadn't heard what I was thinking, I continued being chatty.

"Well, I'll see you again in a few minutes, won't I?"

She laughed in agreement. "Yes, I guess you will."

As I walked into the darkened theater, I remembered more clearly why I liked her performance in *Blume in Love.* She first appeared in the film coming out of an arrival gate at the L.A. airport. Coming from the opposite direction was a glum and recently separated Blume, played by George Segal. She sees him and calls out to him, an old friend she once dated. He turns, surprised and happy to see her. Strangely, so was I. What struck me most about her, aside from her being very pretty, warm and vivacious, was that she didn't seem like an actress at all. She wasn't acting. She was talking. When she started to talk to Blume, I thought to myself, "Oh, no. This woman is interrupting the movie. She must know George Segal. Maybe she's just a fan. She's not even aware there's a camera around. The director will probably shout 'Cut' and have her ushered away." But their conversation continued. Perhaps the director thought, "Say, this is good. This is like real life. I don't know who this woman is, but she's so good I'll just leave it in the picture."

Well, since I'm not a total dummy, I soon realized this *was* the movie and she was *in* the movie. And that's pretty much how I had felt when I saw Marsha Mason sitting back stage a few moments before. She's someone you connect with immediately, whether she's in a film, in a play or sitting in a chair preparing to audition. She'd even be nice to run into at a grocery store. She also had coloring I was very partial to. Reddish hair, light skin and a hint of freckles barely concealed by the small amount of makeup she was using that day. Anxiously, I took my seat next to A. J. Antoon and Manny. Manny whispered to me, "I was going to leave for the country last night. This better be good."

Good would have had a better chance if he had seen *Blume in Love,* but Manny spent less time in movie theaters than I did. And I knew I couldn't very well say, "Hey, have you seen that Manufacturers Hanover Trust commercial? She had a terrific quality in that." That quality would be fine if we were doing a play about high interest rates in a bank, but this was Chekhov, and for Chekhov, you'd do best by having a classically trained actress.

From the corner of my eye, I saw Phyliss Wender quietly take a seat about eight rows behind us, giving silent support to someone she truly believed in. The first actress, not Marsha, was introduced to us by our stage manager, who was going to read with her. We exchanged pleasantries. This young woman had the disadvantage of not being in *Blume in Love;* therefore, although she had my attention, she did not have the benefit of my anticipation. Before she began reading, she stopped for a moment to prepare. She paused, looked away and apparently moved her mental geography from 49th Street in New York to a dacha about two hundred miles north of Moscow, in the dead of winter, circa 1890. When she arrived there, she nodded to the stage manager, who spoke his first line, cueing her into her first speech. Surprisingly, it went well. She was good. Nice quality, warm and competent. Phyliss Wender was no fool. Even if this girl was just a setup for Marsha, she was in no way being sent out on stage as a human sacrifice. Phyliss did not represent anyone unless she thought they had quality. Perhaps this audition was going to turn out to be a head-to-head race to the finish line. Nevertheless, two thirds into the reading, my attention waned. She was playing one or two wonderful notes while we were looking for someone who could give us the entire concerto. I looked at Manny and A.J., who both shook their heads, "No," as did I. A.J. called out, "That's fine. Thank you very much. We appreciate your coming in." She smiled and nodded and as she turned to go, I called out, "That was very good. I really liked it." She looked pleased, even though I knew she wasn't counting on getting the part. She was seen by us and that was primarily what she wanted. Who knows? We might call her back when we were casting for understudies or possibly we'd remember her for another play we'd do in the future.

As the stage manager escorted her off, my mind momentarily went back to reality. I knew that once I left the theater after auditions, I would be back in a world that belonged to everyone else, but one that I did not feel a part of anymore. I also knew I would not be permitted back into it until I presented myself at the main gate, knocked on its door loudly and proclaimed that I was *ready* to enter again. When I got into that frame of mind, I would sometimes have to slap my thigh to remind myself to focus and attend to the business at hand. This time I didn't have to slap my thigh. I focused the minute the stage manager said from center stage, "Marsha Mason."

Almost as a reflex, I called out, "I told you we'd meet again soon."

She laughed and said, "Yes, I had a hunch we would."

I remembered that laugh from a scene in *Blume in Love*. George Segal's character had just said something to Arlene, Marsha's character, that could easily be construed as thoughtless and cruel. I expected an outburst from her, but instead, Marsha looked at him and laughed. It put him in his place more than any vitriolic words could have. It surprised me and it surprised George Segal. I wondered, was it Marsha who made this choice or was it the director? My hunch was that Marsha did it in rehearsal and the director loved it and told her to leave it in. She hadn't even read a word for *The Good Doctor* as yet, and already I knew more about her as an actress than I did when I entered the theater twenty minutes before. A.J. asked her a few questions to put her at ease before she tackled the first of the five shortened scenes we asked her to prepare. Very often actors will say to a director before reading, "Is there anything you want to tell me about this part?" in hopes of finding a clue to what we were looking for. I preferred it when they didn't. Marsha didn't.

Manny whispered to me before she began, "Interesting girl." "She's good," he said after she breezed through the first two scenes.

"This girl can act," he continued after the third scene. As far as I was concerned, she already had the part wrapped up and tucked in her pocket. But I let her continue through to the end of the last scene, not to make certain she could do it, but selfishly, because I got a free reading of the play so I could see what it was I wanted to rewrite later. In a sense, we were already in rehearsal. When she finished, Manny looked at us to corroborate his own feelings.

"Do we want her?" he asked.

"I want to marry her," said A.J., this coming from a man who recently left a Jesuit school where he was preparing to spend his life as a priest.

"Absolutely," I added my own vote. "She's wonderful."

"Unanimous," said Manny. He called out to Marsha and asked her if she could wait a few minutes as he walked back in the darkened theater to negotiate with Phyliss. I used the time to find out a little more about this young actress. She told me she had spent the last two seasons in San Francisco doing repertory at the American Conservatory Theater, one of the best regional theaters in America. She did everything from Ibsen's *A Doll's House,* to Rostand's *Cyrano* to Noël Coward's *Private Lives.* I breathed more easily. Besides being sexy doing a staid bank commercial, she was also a classically trained actress. Manny and Phyliss called me back to speak to them. Money and billing were not a problem, but we had a steadfast rule that all actors in featured roles had to sign on for a year's run, nine months in rare exceptions. "She'll only do six months," said Phyliss. "She has a contract with 20th Century Fox for seven pictures, and that's all the time they'd let her out for." Nine out of ten times that would be a deal breaker with us.

"Take her," I said to Manny, "I don't want to lose her." Neither did Manny nor A.J. The deal was made although I don't think Marsha knew until she left the theater. I had no idea what her reaction was. I was delighted that we finally had a cast, and I could now leave for California without having to think about the play for at least two and a half months.

As I walked home, *The Good Doctor* and Marsha Mason were no longer in my thoughts. I now had to focus on packing a bag and flying three thousand—or was it three hundred thousand or three million?—miles away from Nancy and Ellen. It would be the first time I'd been separated from the girls since Joan died, and I worried how they would be. I also wondered how I would manage on my own, and how I was going to rewrite a movie I barely had any recollection of writing in the first place.

THE STARK MAN
4

I ARRIVED in Los Angeles and took a cab to the Beverly Hills Hotel. This was a smart move on my part because if I had rented a car at Avis, I would have spent the next three days trying to find my way out of the airport. For anyone like myself, who has totally no sense of direction, getting around a city such as L.A. was unimaginable. Gertrude Stein, as I heard it, once aptly said of Los Angeles, "There is no there there." That, however, was not my problem. I knew it was there. I just couldn't find where where was. I like cities that are laid out in grids, cities like New York and Paris. They have a center which extends out to all points of the city. Los Angeles is laid out like laundry strewn about on a windy desert, which, when giving directions, makes about as much sense as saying, "Go left at the blue denim shirt, then make a right at the tan sock which turns into a gray sock and then when you get to the white pajama top, make a sharp right at the Calvin Klein undershirt, unless it's blown away."

Fortunately, the next morning Warner Brothers sent a car and driver to take me out to Burbank for the first rehearsal of *The Prisoner of Second Avenue* film. I slept badly due to jet lag and homesickness, two problems that never had bothered me before. Going up and over the hills and down the valleys, I felt queasy and had more than a touch of vertigo.

Starting a new project was usually exciting for me, but today it was the last thing in the world I wanted to do. My spirits took a turn for the better when I saw Jack Lemmon again, this being our third picture together, and I was thrilled at the prospect of working for the first time with the wonderful Anne Bancroft. Once we gathered around the table and listened to Jack and Annie read the script, I felt an enormous sense of relief and gratitude. I had two major stars who would carry the day even though I wasn't sure I could carry my weight. The vertigo and the queasiness continued and even increased as the day wore on.

Before we broke just after the reading, director Mel Frank gave me a list of cuts he thought necessary and asked if I could rewrite some speeches and add a few short scenes that would move the script further away from the play and more toward a film. I agreed to all his suggestions and intended to start doing the work that night, but as the car that drove me back to the hotel made the sharp twists, turns and coils that stretch out over Laurel Canyon, I felt I had been lowered into a lifeboat in the North Atlantic, the last male survivor of the *Titanic*.

I had no dinner that night and whatever attempts I made at rewrites were pitiful. I couldn't eat, I couldn't throw up and I couldn't stop the Matisse print over the sofa from floating around the room, barely missing the drifting Cézanne print that bobbed and weaved from the opposite direction. I had to hold on to the chairs in order to get to the telephone. I called a producer friend of mine and asked if he knew the name of a doctor I could see as soon as possible, because I didn't want to spend the night in a rolling bed, staring up at a chandelier that kept sliding around the ceiling, threatening to crash on me. He told me it would be hard finding a doctor at ten o'clock at night, but when I told him my symptoms, he said he once had the exact same thing and that one good massage cleared it up in an hour. He offered to send a masseur over to my hotel in forty minutes. I did not have the strength to say either no or yes and left my life in his hands, although as I lay there I wondered what kind of masseur comes out at twenty to eleven at night.

On the dot, forty minutes later, there was a knock on my door. So relieved was I that help was on the other side of that door that I braved getting hit by the flying Impressionist paintings that were now making sorties at my head like multicolored dive-bombers. Practically crawling along the ground, I finally made it to the door and opened it. I did not expect to see what I saw. It was a Eurasian girl, about twenty-six and beautiful. She walked into the room with a smile, a portable massage table and a face and a figure that would remain perfect even if Picasso painted three eyes on her head and gave her two extra arms. She told me her name was Yanna but that you don't pronounce the Js or the Ms. I hadn't heard any Js or Ms. She turned on her small tape player and I heard a flute and some strings playing music that was probably very popular in jungles.

As she opened her massage table, she asked in the friendliest terms if I would strip down to my shorts; then she headed for the bathroom. Two minutes later she came out with all the towels the Beverly Hills Hotel could supply, and considerably less clothes than she was wearing when she came in. She wore white denim shorts so brief and tight that I wondered if it was just an extra layer of her own skin. She wore a sheer scarf around her ample breasts and tied in the back. Taking into consideration her outfit, I soon had an inkling why she was available at twenty to eleven at night.

I sat on the sofa in my extra-long boxer shorts, shivering and clinging to two pillows from the sofa to keep me warm and my body less visible. I lay down on the massage table and for the next five minutes I was anointed with enough oil to burn a thousand lamps for a year. Yanna talked small talk as she rubbed my neck and back as gently as human hands could glide across the surface of a body. I never noticed when she had lit the incense, but as far as I was concerned, it wasn't half as pleasing as the aroma of her own skin.

I faded in and out of sleep and couldn't tell if I still had vertigo or if I was just wandering around in some benign jungle, soothed by the musical strains of its biggest hit single. About twenty minutes later, she turned me over on my back and I couldn't help notice that she was no longer wearing that sheer scarf across her breasts. As a matter of fact, her breasts were now rubbing across mine, as she was gently but rhythmically massaging my neck. It seemed pretty obvious to me by now that the massage was a prelude to sex, but what I didn't know was whether it was optional or mandatory.

I tried to make it clear without hurting her feelings that if she had planned going beyond the massage, I was neither physically nor emotionally capable of doing that; I even told her about my recent loss. She was not hurt and explained that all she cared about was giving me some relaxation, in whatever way was best for me. She then wrapped me in towels and dried me off as if I were her own baby. When she finally dressed and folded her table, I asked her how much the fee was. She said, "Oh, no. Your friend took care of all that. If you need to see me again while you're still out here, here's my card. Call me any time, night or day." And she vanished quietly somewhere into the Hollywood Hills, no doubt on to another errand of mercy. This was the kind of gift Hollywood producers often send. Had I been in New York and called a friend for help in a similar situation, he would have given me the number of a bald, sixty-two-year-old German chiropractor who loves to hear the sound of cracking necks.

I slept well that night. When I woke in the morning, I opened my eyes and looked at the ceiling. So far so good. I got to my feet and tried to stand. The room suddenly turned into a carousel. Whatever healing powers Yanna possessed, the cure for vertigo was not high on her list. I dressed slowly for fear of putting on everything backwards and getting hit by a car whose driver thought I was walking in the opposite direction.

I went out to Burbank one more time but the drive felt like sailing through a storm going around Cape Hatteras in winter. When I got out of the car, I realized I couldn't make it through the day, the rehearsal or the rewrites. I left early, making my apologies to Jack and Annie and told Mel Frank he was free to make any changes in the script as he saw fit. When I got back to the hotel and took two minutes to get my key into the trembling lock, I knew I was in trouble. I booked the first available flight out in the morning, hoping it would be a bumpy flight which might flatten out my vertigo. By seven-thirty that night I knew I couldn't even wait that long. I found another friend, more dependable than my gift-bearing producer, who gave me the number of a first-rate doctor, one who wore a white jacket instead of shortened jeans and a scarf across his breasts.

Dr. Robert Koblin met me about nine-thirty that night in the examining room of the Century City Hospital. He was a warm, friendly man, a few years younger than myself. After examining me, he said I was suffering from dehydration and gastroacidity, normally symptoms of emotional distress. Before I could get any words out, I burst into tears, giving vent and release to what I'd been holding back for almost a month. When I told him my wife had died about three weeks ago, he nodded and said with a great deal of empathy, "Well, there it is." He prescribed fluids and some pills, but suggested the best medicine for me was to go back to New York, rest and give myself time to deal with my feelings rather than filling up my days with work, which only diverted the pain that I kept bottled up.

Even as I sat on the plane the next morning, looking out on the clouds below me, knowing for the first time ever that I would have to give up control over one of my scripts, I slowly began to feel the vertigo lessening. I closed my eyes, leaned back and slept the entire way back home.

SIX MONTHS before all this happened, a man named Ray Stark had come soaring into my life like a comet. He reached down, grabbed me by the scruff of my neck and pulled me along on the wildest and most exhilarating ride I ever experienced. It lasted over twenty years. Ray Stark was an agent turned producer, whose only claim to fame, initially, was that he was married to the daughter of Fanny Brice, one of the great vaudeville and stage stars of the first half of the twentieth century. He certainly became one of the most successful and powerful producers in Hollywood, with films like The Way We Were and Funny Girl to his credit, along with dozens of others.

I received a call from him one day, without prior warning or introduction, asking if he could come over to my house to talk to me. He didn't say what it was about and I thought it was interesting that he wanted to meet me in my home rather than inviting me out to lunch in some showy restaurant. I think he did it knowing that if we met on my turf, I would not feel that he had the advantage and I would be more amenable to what he had to say. That was the day I found out how smart he was.

Minutes after he walked in the door on East 62nd Street, a big smile on his warm and very unmogul-like face, I liked him. And suddenly he had the advantage, which was probably what he had in mind all the time. He complimented me on everything in my house (all of which Joan had done) and from studying the few small paintings I had on the walls, made me feel that I had a true gift—an unfailing eye for art. As it turned out, I didn't, but he eventually taught me. He was in his late fifties but had the energy of a man in his early thirties, and his eager and avid sense of joy and good humor (if you dismissed the incessant puns) made him seem even younger than that. After five minutes with him, I could swear I had known him for years, and after ten minutes with him, I wished I *had* known him for years.

We talked for over an hour about everything except why he came there. He was too busy telling me what a genius I was and kept putting me in the same category as writers like Ben Hecht and Billy Wilder. I wasn't, of course, but I was too vain to stop him. Finally the reason for his visit. Would I be willing to write the sequel to *Funny Girl,* called *Funny Lady,* starring again, naturally, Barbra Streisand. It was an incredible opportunity—a fabulous offer to be writing for the most talented and exciting film star of the day. I surprised even myself when I said, "No," without hesitation. If Fanny Brice, and that's who Barbra Streisand was portraying, never existed, I would have taken the job. What I didn't want to do was research and/or be faithful to the true story of Fanny Brice's marriage to Billy Rose. It would confine me to the facts, leaving little to my imagination, especially since Mr. Stark was the producer and the son-in-law of Ms. Brice. As fine a filmmaker as he was, I didn't want to write with his fingers on my typewriter keys.

He accepted my answer graciously and didn't push it. I think I even earned his respect by turning down something that had all the ingredients of a surefire hit, although that would have depended on what I did with it. (Warren Beatty originally asked me to do the screenplay of *Heaven Can Wait,* which I turned down because I didn't want to do remakes. Elaine May took the job and wrote it brilliantly. After my daughter Nancy saw the picture and loved it, she said, "You should have done it. It was great.")

Ray Stark did not go home that day emptyhanded. He bought the film rights to my play *The Sunshine Boys.* I knew he would stay true to the tone and soul of the play, which was most important to me. A few months prior, I was playing tennis at a club when I received a phone call from agent Irving "Swifty" Lazar in Los Angeles. Lazar could trace you down if you were in a dungeon in Patagonia. Lazar had initially sold my first three plays, *Come Blow Your Horn, Barefoot in the Park* and *The Odd Couple,* all to Paramount Pictures. Irving now had another offer from Paramount to buy *The Sunshine Boys* as a vehicle for, and I gulped at this one, Bing Crosby and Bob Hope. I grew up listening to both of them on radio and had seen all their *Road* pictures as well as Hope's other wonderful comedies. But I told a stunned Irving Lazar that I was regretfully turning it down. The essence of my play was that these two aging ex-vaudevillians were Jewish, cranky and tired. Hope and Crosby were aging, but you would never know it then. They were still quick, topical and lighthearted and flippant, and they would sure be box office, but neither of them had ever been bar mitzvahed—not that religion was important to the characters, but their culture and background was.

I knew for certain that Paramount would want me to rewrite the parts to fit the considerable talents of Hope and Crosby. I wanted to do it the other way around. I wanted to find two actors, stars hopefully, who would fit the characteristics of The Sunshine Boys. I got that promise from Ray Stark. When he left my house later that day, he had my play, and I had a mentor, a tutor and a great friend for the next two decades. The next day, a huge vase of flowers arrived, so beautiful they could have been put in a frame and hung on the wall. From that day on, whether I went to Paris or a room in Mobile, Alabama, there would always be a gift waiting there from Ray Stark, whether we had a project going or not. He didn't buy me, but he sure did woo me. And Ray Stark was the best wooer in the business.

ST. LOUIS WOMAN
5

ONCE BACK in New York, my legs and spirits grew sturdier and I began to venture out into a more sociable world. Lunches with friends, going to the theater, out to a Mets game and, finally, to dinner parties. But always alone. Which automatically makes you the extra man, for whom, inevitably, the hostess would invite "an extra woman." There is always something implied by this arrangement—a hope that the extra man and the extra woman would somehow pair off into anything from polite conversation to marriage. I preferred it when the extra woman was already married and came to "fill in" while her husband was away on business. That took the pressure off both me and her, and put it all on our hostess's *crème brûlée*.

At one of these parties, the extra woman was someone I knew and liked, equally as much as I liked her husband. Until I found out they were now divorced, hence all the eyes staring at us from the first course on. She was charming, pretty and a good conversationalist, which was fortunate because no one wanted to interrupt us. We talked neither about my deceased wife nor her ex-husband, leaving us to choose from such varied topics as movies, books, plays and health, good or bad. When you meet someone who has the same back problem as you, you're set for the night. You find yourself saying, "Right. I know that feeling," over and over again. After a while I began to feel comfortable with her, although there was definitely no sense of romance in the air, from either of us. Still, I wanted to see her again, if only to go to a play or film; nothing further need be contemplated. Yet I felt guilty at the very thought of seeing or being seen with another woman so soon after Joan's death, no matter how slight my interest was in this woman. Most important, I did not want to offend Ellen or Nancy and have them think I was being thoughtless or callous to the memory of their mother. I knew a man who had lost his wife, and six months later he started to date some woman he met through a mutual friend. His sixteen-year-old daughter was furious with him. It may have partly been because she thought the woman was not right for him, and equally as important, that this woman was not the ideal stepmother for her. Or more painfully, she may have feared that if the father remarried, and possibly had more children, he might lose his need and love for her. The young girl won; the father broke off with the woman and ten years later he had still not moved on with his life.

I faced the prospect of "dating" with the same concerns. Nevertheless, I knew I had to start sometime.

I THOUGHT it important that Ellen and Nancy knew that I was occasionally dating, but made it clear that there was no romance pending. Their reaction was noncommittal, but certainly not negative. As a matter of fact, as they pored through movie and fashion magazines, they would sometimes hold up a picture of some beauty and say, "Do you think she's pretty, Dad?" One was a picture of Ali MacGraw, mostly because she resembled Joan so closely.

Finally, I decided to go to the next step. I asked the woman if she would have dinner with me and my daughters at home, the reasoning being that if the girls actually saw me in the company of another woman, it would break the ice for whatever might come later. This wasn't exactly playing fair with the woman in question, since she might think "taking her to meet the family" portended a relationship soon in the offing, but from my own observations, she gave no hint that that was what she was looking for. Nancy and Ellen, on the other hand, could not have been more enthusiastic. They felt they were playing out some important role in an exotic romance. They spent most of the afternoon trying on and changing dresses until the appropriate ones were selected. I could hear them buzzing and laughing in their rooms above me, trying out made-up English accents as if this was going to be a dinner party as written by Jane Austen.

At seven-thirty that night, my guest arrived. We had a drink together before the girls made their choreographed entrance down the stairs. They exchanged polite greetings, and from that moment on, for the rest of the evening, those were the only words they uttered. The silence was so deafening from their side of the table that I could hear the faucet dripping in my bathroom two floors above. What happened to laughing and buzzing in their rooms in the afternoon? What happened to six changes of dresses before they picked the right one? I suppose it's like public speaking: once you're introduced, you would rather be somewhere else. My guest, the former sparkling conversationalist, found fewer and fewer words forming on her lips. Aside from an occasional "Mmm" when asked if the chicken was all right, the remainder of the night was a monologue conducted by myself. The dinner took two and a half days, at least by my calculation, and when I finally exhausted all my stories, which usually got roars of laughter from the girls instead of the faint Mona Lisa smiles I was getting now, my speech was reduced to single sentences, then single words, and eventually guttural sounds that had no intelligible meaning. It was as though we were all sitting in a well-decorated Christian Science Reading Room.

I took my guest home in a cab, where we listened to the windshield wipers clearing off the light drizzle. When I said good night to her at the door of her apartment, we both knew that if we ever met at another "extra man/extra woman" dinner party, we would exchange a quick, "Hi. How are you? You're looking swell," and move quickly toward the nearest *hors d'oeuvre.* When I returned home, I found the girls upstairs waiting for me. Since their television wasn't on, I knew they wanted to talk. I didn't even ask if they liked her or not.

"Are you going to marry her?" Nancy questioned ruefully.

"Is she going to be our stepmother?" Ellen asked in desperation.

"No," I assured them, "of course not. She's just a nice woman and I think she felt a lot of pressure. Why were you both staring at her? Why couldn't you say anything?"

"She never swallowed her food," said Nancy.

"What are you talking about? She ate her entire dinner."

"She may have eaten it, but she didn't swallow it."

Ellen added her observation. "Wrong perfume."

"Really? I didn't notice. Is that why you didn't like her?"

"I didn't say I didn't like her. But it was definitely the wrong perfume."

I decided not to push this one any further. I gave them both a kiss good night and went down to my room. As I lay in bed with my eyes still open at two in the morning, I thought, if I were ever to meet another woman who even remotely appealed to me, she would have to pass muster with the toughest board of admissions this side of the Massachusetts Institute of Technology.

Rehearsals for *The Good Doctor* began around October 5 at the Ambassador, one of the oldest theaters in New York and one of the least desirable because of its dingy location. It was used more often for rehearsals than for actual productions of plays. The stage door was located down a long, dark alleyway that made a sharp turn left to another dark alleyway. Actors generally left in pairs at the end of the day for safety's sake.

When I arrived, the cast were already assembled. I saw Marsha Mason in a conversation with Christopher Plummer and waited for her to turn away before I could catch her eye and say hello. When she did, she looked as warm and pretty as when I had seen her a few months prior at her audition. This time, however, she seemed more subdued, more tentative, which I attributed to a case of "first day rehearsal shakes." Everyone gets them, stars and playwrights included. Each time we begin a new play, we are all about to enter a world where no man or woman has ever walked before. Strangely, I did not have the shakes that day. It certainly wasn't because of overconfidence or complacency on my part, but for another more profound reason. There was still a part of me that was going through a restoring process, of getting used to talking easily to actors again. This, plus the keen awareness that at the end of the first day, I would not, as I always did before, be able to rush home and tell Joan how the reading went and filling her in on all the details.

When the actors finally gathered around the table, their freshly rewritten scripts before them, I did something that was rare for me. I sat on a stool, not *at* the table, where I always preferred to be, next to the director, but this time a few feet behind it, distancing myself from the actors and perhaps even the play itself. I was a faintly disconnected observer, hoping once again in my life to be invisible. The actors started to read the play in a soft, low key, since no one wanted to commit themselves to a performance just yet. Marsha sat on the opposite side of the table, facing me but not looking at me. Her eyes remained glued to the pages, and she made little notes on a pad. I noticed she was left-handed. I always thought there was something quirky about left-handed people and also something more graceful. Perhaps it was because they were using a different side of the brain than I was. I liked watching this difference in baseball players, and now, I discovered, I liked it in actresses.

If Marsha had been subdued and tentative in her greeting, she was nothing short of enchanting as she read the first scene. She was in heavy competition with that veteran cast, but I couldn't take my attention away from her. When I laugh at what an actor says, it is almost never at what I wrote, but rather the way the actor has injected life into the lines. Marsha was not only giving the words life, she was dressing them, feeding them and sending them off to school with a kiss and a warm lunch.

I noticed she had one hand in the air at all times as she read, the left hand, of course, with a pencil clenched in her fingers, the point protruding out about an inch. It didn't seem as though it was tension that made her hold the pencil aloft, but more as if she had a baton in her hand, conducting her own performance. The orchestra followed devotedly. She began to hear my laughter and she looked up at me, both surprised and pleased to know that I visibly and audibly approved of what she was doing. She started to look up more and more, especially when she was *not* reading. I think she was measuring me as to what this fairly well known playwright with the brooding countenance really was about.

At the end of the first act, director Antoon called for a break and I walked around to Marsha's side of the table, stood behind her and put my hand on her shoulder and said, "I love what you're doing." Her hand automatically went up and touched the back of my hand and said, "Thank you." When we finished reading the second act, the stage manager announced it was lunch. Some of the actors paired off, and not even Manny Azenberg asked what I was doing for lunch. He knew I was heading alone to the nearest deli, with script, pad and pen in hand, ready to pounce on the cuts, notes and revisions, while I juggled a turkey sandwich on rye with my free hand. As I walked up that dreary alleyway, I found Marsha walking beside me.

"You going to lunch alone?" she asked.

"Yes. I always do on the first day. I've got work to do. What about you?"

"Oh. I'm meeting a friend."

It suddenly occurred to me that a friend could be someone she was going with, living with or even married to. I knew nothing about her personal life.

Then she said rather carefully, "I didn't know about your wife until today. No one told me. I'm truly sorry."

I thanked her for her consideration. Then she smiled and said, "See you later. You are coming back, aren't you?"

"Me? Oh, yeah. This is when I do my real work. Rehearsals are for you; for me it's the rewriting." She smiled again and then practically bounced down the street knowing she got off to a flying start at the morning's reading.

At five minutes to two, having finished my revisions but not my turkey sandwich, I headed back to the theater. But first I had to maneuver my way through that dark, ominous alley. Halfway there, I heard footsteps behind me, walking at first, then running, coming closer and closer. I expected either a gun in my ribs or a knife at my throat. What happened was more terrifying: I heard a scream that sounded like "YAHHHH," then a body, a human body, hurled itself onto my back. I pulled away instantly, ready to defend my life or willingly hand over my wallet, but not my revisions, when I saw who this attacker was. It was Marsha, standing there smiling. No, not smiling. Beaming.

"Sorry. Didn't mean to scare you."

"*Scare* me? How could you not scare me? Why did you do that?"

The smile remained, then with a shrug, she said, "I don't know. Just felt like it."

"Do you always do that?"

"Nope. First time. How was your lunch?"

And suddenly we were walking together as though nothing had happened. She said it so innocently, that I felt it was *my* fault for not enjoying it more. After all, it's not every day that an extremely pretty girl jumps on your back in a dark alley. I felt as if I had been given a shot of adrenaline. For the first time in months, here was someone not treating me with kid gloves. Someone not cautious about invading the dark world in which I had been living since Joan had died. Someone not afraid to push the clouds away and let some sun shine on my dour face. Her jump on my back said to me, "Smile, Neil. Life is back. Welcome to the world."

During the afternoon's read through, our eyes made contact quite a few times.

I FELT a strong need to keep Nancy and Ellen closer to me, more involved with not just my life but my working life as well. For the very first time ever, I invited them to come to the rehearsal of one of my plays. They came as soon as school let out the following day, and sat in the fifth row, entranced, mesmerized and stony silent as they watched the making of a play. When they wanted to laugh, they covered their mouths with their hands, afraid to intrude upon the serious effort that was going on up on the stage. When the director called a ten-minute break, I briefly introduced them to all the actors, who could not have been nicer. Once back in their seats, I asked them what they thought of what they had seen so far.

"It's keen," said Nancy. "I never knew they worked so hard."

"It's like doing a play in school," Ellen added, "except that the director is more patient than our teacher."

"Which part did you like best?" I inquired, meaning which scene in the play. They had a different interpretation.

"The girl with the red hair," Nancy quickly offered.

"Marsha Mason?"

"Don't you think she's pretty?" asked Ellen.

"Pretty? Yes. Very pretty."

"Is she married?" asked Nancy.

"Married? I don't know."

"Why don't you ask her?" Ellen quickly added.

"I don't see any wedding ring on her," chimed in Nancy.

"Is that all you've been watching?" I said. "Anyway, why do you want to know?"

"We like her," Ellen announced. "Don't you?"

"Yes. I do. She's a wonderful actress."

"No. We mean like as a person. Don't you think she's neat as a person?" Nancy was being relentless for a ten-year-old.

Ellen got this impish look on her face. "Why don't you ask her out to dinner? I bet *she'd* have plenty to say."

"Hey, girls. I didn't invite you here to promote my social life."

"Just to dinner," Nancy implored. "What's one dinner?"

To placate them I said, "Fine. Swell. I'll ask her to dinner sometime."

"Not sometime," Ellen kept at it. "What about tonight? You're not doing anything."

"I am. I'm rewriting. Why are you two pushing so much?"

"You don't have to rewrite tonight," said Nancy, not letting up. "The play sounds good to us."

At this point in the inquisition, A. J. Antoon dismissed Marsha for the day while time was spent rehearsing someone else's scene. Marsha started putting on her coat, bidding good night to the other actors, then squinted out front through the lights, hand over her eyes and called out, "Good night, Neil. See you tomorrow. Nice meeting you, girls." She headed for the door.

"Now! Now!" urged Ellen. "Before she goes home."

"Hurry, Dad. You can still stop her," pleaded Nancy.

"It's too late," I said. "She's out the door."

"You can run after her down the street, can't you?" suggested Ellen.

"Hey, girls. Enough. Don't do this to me . . . come on. It's late. I'll take you home. Do you have much homework for tonight?"

"She's really neat, Dad. You should have asked her," Nancy said in one final attempt.

"Put your coats on. We're going. And enough about Marsha Mason, okay?"

"Sorry, Dad," said Nancy.

"Sorry," said Ellen.

It was quiet in the cab going home. I was staring out the window, wondering what the scene at the theater was all about. The girls murmured to each other, whispering and still plotting between themselves. Just as the cab pulled up to our house, Ellen got in her last entreaty of the day.

"You could call her tonight and ask her for tomorrow."

"I said no! . . . Geez! . . . all right. I'll see. Let me think about it. But don't ask me anymore, okay?"

"We won't," agreed Nancy. "I swear."

"Maybe, just once more at dinner," Ellen said with a devilish smile. Then they both turned and gave me an exaggerated expression of begging and pleading, contorting their faces, trying for just the right comic tone to wear me down.

I glared at them, but they couldn't possibly miss the look of amusement in my eyes.

AT EIGHT O'CLOCK that night, I closed the door of my office; the girls were busy with homework on the floor above. I looked at the cast sheet that gave the addresses, phone numbers and agents for everyone connected with the production. I saw that Marsha Mason lived in the West 70s in Manhattan. I circled her phone number, then quickly dialed—and just as quickly hung up just after the first ring. What the hell was I doing? I knew if I called her, it wouldn't be because of the girls' constant hammering away at me. It would be because I liked watching her on stage and being around her during the breaks. Because I was taken with her incredible audacity when she jumped screamingly on my back in a dark alleyway. It would be because I wanted to. But wanted to what? It was too soon after Joan's death to contemplate any sort of relationship with someone new. I don't think the word "relationship" even came to mind. It was an attraction, to be sure, and if I could get past the first phone call, I would take the next step, if any were required, one careful foot at a time. Dialing the phone was my first problem. "Oh, what the hell," I said to myself nervously. The girls were right. It would just be for one measly dinner. I dialed her number and hoped she would be in.

"Hello?"

There was that voice of hers, with a trace of that endearing laugh even in a simple word like "hello." Now I was stuck for a first sentence. I was reduced to feeling seventeen again.

"Hello?" she asked for the second time.

Now I was reduced to fifteen.

"Marsha?"

"Yes."

"Hi. It's Neil."

"Neil? Hello."

"Is this a bad time for you?"

"No. It's fine. Is everything all right?" There was actually a trace of nervousness in her voice, as if she were worried that something was going wrong with the play.

"No. Everything is fine . . . I just wanted to thank you for being so nice to the girls today. They were really taken with you."

"They were? Oh, I'm so glad. They're really sweet."

"Thank you . . . so, er . . . they asked me if I, er . . . well, actually *I'm* asking if you'd like to, er . . . Wait a minute. This is dumb. Can I ask you something personal?"

"Yes."

"Are you married? Are you engaged? Or with someone?"

"No."

"No" sounded too simple an answer, as if there were something not included in the word. I'd better ask.

"No what?"

"No. I'm not any of those things. I'm divorced and living with a girl-friend of mine on the West Side."

"West 72nd?"

"Yes."

"I saw that looking for your number on the cast sheet." (On many oc-casions I have written scintillating and bright dialogue, but unfortunately, this wasn't one of those times.) "So, look . . . would you like to have dinner with me and the girls one night? When you're free. When you're not busy?"

"Oh . . . Well, er . . ."

Suddenly she didn't sound sure. I hardly knew her. Why did I let the girls do this to me?

"Okay. I'd love to. That's nice of you to ask. For when?"

"Oh, I don't know. This week. Next week. Tomorrow. You busy tomorrow?"

"Well, I have something to do later on, but if you mean an early dinner, that's fine."

"Early is good for me too. You like Japanese? The girls love Japanese."

"Same here."

"Great. See you at rehearsal. Good night."

I hung up and walked slowly and quietly up the stairs and opened the door to the tiny little den that Ellen and Nancy shared.

"Okay. It's done. I called her. Early dinner in a Japanese restaurant with Marsha Mason tomorrow night. She's not married. She's not engaged. I'm very tired. Don't stay up late. Good night."

I closed the door and as I started back down the stairs I heard two young girls screaming jubilantly.

DINNER was at Hime's of Japan restaurant on the East Side. I asked A. J. Antoon to let Marsha off a little early that night. I didn't tell him why. As she went out the stage door, I waited a few seconds and then followed. I didn't say good night to A.J. or the cast for fear of eyebrows being raised. Actually, I rarely say good night when I leave rehearsals. I don't want to interrupt the flow of the scene as it is being rehearsed, so usually I simply give a nod to the director and go, glad to be the writer who can leave whenever he wants. Marsha had an errand to tend to before meeting us and I was relieved. I was not quite up to sharing a cab with her and having a one-on-one conversation, since I had not been alone with someone I was attracted to, who was not my wife, in twenty years.

Things went considerably better at the restaurant than they had at the dinner at home, when my guest had found herself frozen out. This night the girls actually spoke. Full sentences and complete thoughts. Marsha was not only eating her dinner, she was also swallowing it. There was no indication that she was wearing the wrong perfume. There was laughter at our table and the two young members of the board of admissions were totally enchanted with the "girl with the laughing face," as I had one character describe her years later in *The Goodbye Girl*. Regretfully, she left early to fulfill her other engagement, and Nancy, Ellen and I walked home.

"She's nice," said Ellen cautiously.

"Very nice," Nancy added, looking for a hopeful sign from me.

"Yes," was all I could agree to. My mind was in a muddle, as if trying to walk up a down escalator. How can I have positive thoughts about this charming young woman while I knew that later that night I would be sitting on the floor of my room, candles lit, still trying to brand Joan's features permanently into my psyche? I had no idea if Marsha had any interest in me, so why was I, or the girls for that matter, even thinking of anything beyond a Japanese meal? And I still had a play to deal with.

"No rush," I said to myself. "All in good time." "What will be will be." "Time takes care of everything." I heard my head pouring out aphorisms by the dozens, even some that didn't apply, like, "Water seeks its own level," and "Feed a cold, starve a fever." If I kept at this, I would soon be throwing in, "A stitch in time saves nine," and "What's good for the goose is good for the gander." I find no solace or wisdom in simple homilies that were written and conceived before the Revolutionary War.

DURING the next weeks, the play and the rehearsals took second place to my attentive chats with Marsha, who at every break came down into the orchestra and sat beside me. We talked about everything except the job at hand. Those meetings led to more dinners, but now with just the two of us. The dinners led to my inviting Marsha up to the house on Blue Heron Lake, accompanied by two ten-year-old chaperones—Nancy and her best friend, Nicole Fosse, daughter of Bob, the noted director-choreographer.

Two weeks later, waiting for the elevator just outside Marsha's apartment, where I had just met her roommate, some close friends and her ex-husband, I kissed Marsha good night. The elevator door opened and I decided not to step in. Instead, I said partly in jest, partly in earnest and certainly a part in sheer madness, "So I guess we ought to get married, heh?"

She looked at me, not knowing which of the three parts this totally unexpected suggestion came from. A look of shock, bewilderment and joy appeared all at once on her startled face.

"Are you serious?" she asked.

To tell the truth, I didn't know what I was. If she had said, "Oh . . . Well, Neil, this comes as a bit of a surprise. I mean, it's only been two weeks. We hardly know each other. I think it would be rushing things, don't you?" I would have answered, "Of course, you're right. Just something that popped out, I guess." Then I would have quickly gotten on the elevator and into a cab wondering whatever possessed me to be so audacious and foolhardy. Since she didn't say that, my answer to her "Are you serious?" was, "Yes. I guess so." And that was it. I can't remember if she beamed or cried or screamed or threw her arms around me or if she even accepted my proposal. She probably did one or all of the above, but the only thing I remembered, even now, was that we were back in her apartment where she announced happily to all present that I had just proposed marriage to her. Everyone was appropriately giddy with excitement and even her ex-husband offered his congratulations. "What took you so long?" he said. Not a word from anyone about "in only two weeks?" I didn't even wonder why she was so friendly with her ex-husband but if I'd just proposed to a girl after knowing her for fourteen days, I wouldn't have noticed if she had two Arabian stallions in the room.

As I drove back across Central Park alone, I thought to myself, "Did that really happen? Did I actually say that? And what will I tell the girls?"

ON THE RUN
6

THE GIRLS were not the problem. They were more than overjoyed, and even supported the idea of Marsha moving in with us immediately. "Even before we're married?" I asked, as if the roles were reversed and it was me, the worried father, asking Ellen what she was doing rushing into a marriage to someone she scarcely knew.

If I try to reason out why the girls were so in favor of this quickly conceived union, inasmuch as they both loved their mother dearly, it occurred to me that they wanted to be a complete family again, one in which Dad could be happy and life could continue as it once was. They were too young to consider the ramifications and impact on our lives that a total stranger, no matter how winning, might have. Nor did they ever stop to ask if this new person could possibly fill the void that left us all bereft a few short months ago. I do not mean to imply that it was solely because of their urging that I contemplated taking this step, one that I actually already had put into motion. Clearly, I was moving very quickly and the question was why? I knew then, but I don't know now—not that I question its wisdom. I knew that I was going to be confronted with a barrage of raised eyebrows, but at the moment I could only think about four people and their happiness: me, Marsha, Ellen and Nancy. Explanations to friends and family would have to be dealt with later.

Years later Marsha characterized me as being "a very needy" person. I won't contest that even though the implication of her remark seemed to have an air of criticism to it. I've often thought of Marsha as being an *"un-needy"* person, without criticism implied. She could live alone on a farm fifty miles from nowhere, while I needed to hear the footsteps of friends and family. I needed humanity at my beck and call. Is one better or worse than the other? On the other hand, I do spend the greater part of my everyday life *completely* alone, spending more hours sitting over a typewriter in a room where the phone seldom rings and visitors rarely ever appear than I do with my family. The fact is, none of these considerations needed to be dealt with when I asked Marsha to marry me. Nothing was thought out. It was done purely on instinct, a belief that this would turn out well. The consequences could certainly be that it would all blow up in my face—*all* our faces—yet no one was saying "Stop!" What was going on in Marsha's head about all this, I never really knew and still don't to this day.

Two days after the proposal, I stood waiting at Park Avenue and 80th Street, outside Dr. Bornstein's office, looking for Marsha, who was to meet me in order to take the required blood tests. Dr. Jack Bornstein was the doctor who took care of Joan during her fight with cancer. It had to be early in the morning since we still had rehearsals that day. It was while I waited that I asked myself the questions again: "Why am I doing this? What's the hurry? Does this make sense at all?"

Before I could find a reasonable answer, I heard, "Hi," and saw the beaming smile on Marsha's face before me. "Hi," I answered in a noncommittal manner. Her look of dismay at my lack of enthusiasm was not so much one of disappointment, but more concern for my welfare.

"Are you all right?" she asked in utter sincerity.

"Yes. Fine . . . I don't know . . . Why are we doing this? This is crazy, isn't it? . . . Look, I need time to think about this, okay?"

She nodded and said warmly, "Of course. I understand. Whatever you want."

"It's not that I don't want to."

"I know. I'm scared too."

"So do you mind if we put it off for a while? To give us both time to get to know each other better?"

"I think that's a wonderful idea."

"Thank you," I said and pulled her toward me and hugged her.

She pulled her face back, looked into my eyes and said, "It's all right, Neil. Really."

Then I looked around to see where we were. What time was it? When did we have to be at rehearsal? Where was a cab? And suddenly air came back into my lungs and I breathed easily once again, then said, without looking at her, "Well, as long as we're here, we might as well take the blood test. Don't you think?"

"Sure. If you want."

"Yeah. Why not? We'd have to do it sometime anyway."

As we started for the doctor's office a few steps away, I stopped and said, "I forgot. This is for you."

I gave her a small box which contained an engagement ring that I had bought as soon as Tiffany's opened that morning.

"Can I help you?" said the saleswoman as I perused the rings under the glass. "What kind of ring are you looking for?"

"Something for a very short engagement," I answered, not noticing the bemused look on her face.

Now Marsha was opening the box, looking at the ring and then embracing me. We then entered Jack Bornstein's office to take blood tests, two very nervous and frightened people.

A few days later we were married in the Criminal Courts Building, the same place that Joan and I had been married nineteen years earlier. It was a different judge this time and instead of our parents as witnesses, we had Ellen and Nancy, giving me all the comfort and encouragement I needed at that moment. An hour later, Ellen and Nancy were back in school and Marsha and I were back at rehearsals at the Ambassador Theater. Before we started work, however, Manny Azenberg popped some bottles of champagne, filled the paper cups for all the cast, then held his up in a toast. "To the happy couple. May the play run longer than the engagement."

I ALWAYS HAD a soft spot in my heart for New Haven, Connecticut, because I had tried out so many of my early plays at the Shubert Theater there. I liked walking around the Yale campus during the day while my mind worked busily trying to shore up the small and large holes that constantly appear in a play during a pre-Broadway tryout. New Haven was not, however, the best place to have a honeymoon—not while we only had two and a half days to pull the scenery, lighting, costumes and the play itself together before its first public viewing. Instead of basking in the sun on some romantic Caribbean island, we were both working harder and longer hours and had far less time for each other than we did in New York. I was now spending hours in the hotel rewriting and Marsha was at the theater rehearsing my rewrites. Marsha was still appearing as five different characters, and to add to her workload, there was a new one that I wrote especially for her that was not pure Chekhov. Because she was so gifted, I wanted to write a scene that was hers and hers alone, something that I hoped would make her shine even brighter than any Tiffany ring that she wore on her finger. The scene was called "The Audition." In it she appeared as a poor country girl, an aspiring actress who walked all the way to Moscow from her home in Odessa, to audition for Chekhov himself. In the dead of winter.

We never see Chekhov but only hear his voice (Christopher Plummer); he was presumably sitting in the darkened theater auditioning young hopefuls. She has very little experience and Chekhov is about to thank her and quickly send her off to whence she came, when he is suddenly taken by her innocent humor, her dedication to her art and mostly by her passion for his work. He finally relents. "Oh, very well. What is it you want to read?"

"I'd like to read from *The Three Sisters,* sir."

"Really? And which sister will you be?"

"All of them, sir."

"*All* of them? Are you going to read the entire play?"

"If you wish, sir."

He is amused and doesn't take her seriously. Nevertheless, he allows her to go on. Marsha played the last scene of the play, doing all three sisters, giving each sister in turn their full weight and individuality, creating a distinct personality for each of them. When she is finished, she says humbly and quietly, "Thank you, sir," and starts to leave the stage even before she has heard his reaction.

Chekhov is so moved, so completely taken by her performance, that he can't pull himself together quickly enough to speak. She is gone when he finally calls out, "Will somebody stop that girl before she walks all the way back to Odessa."

As I watched the scene myself at that last dress rehearsal at the Shubert Theater, I felt as I imagined Chekhov himself would have felt. Everyone in the theater was still, as if we all needed a breath before we could move on to the next scene. I realized what a tremendous talent Marsha was, and thanked Phyliss Wender silently for sending her to me.

THEN CAME the other side of the coin. I soon realized that we could only be husband and wife when the workday was over or possibly during a quick meal together. But even then the talk was about the play and not about plans for the future—the kinds of things that most honeymooners would be caught up with while sipping margaritas under a star-filled tropical sky. Our director, A. J. Antoon, was consumed with his own stars in the heaven, these literally being part of the scenery in one particular scene. He spent so much time with the production values that he was now giving less time and attention to his actors. Marsha felt unprepared and under-rehearsed and complained to Antoon, who promised he would get to it as soon as he finished his scenery problems. I had never before taken sides in differences of opinion between a director and his actors. I felt if I came to Marsha's aid, it would appear that it was because I was her husband, and that others might resent it. Marsha was quite able to take care of herself in situations like this, and eventually Manny Azenberg intervened and told A.J. to stop being "lost in the stars" and get back to the live ones in our play. I was unsettled by this incident only because I felt helpless and because I worried if this was always an ongoing dilemma when spouses work together in the theater.

AS WE APPROACHED opening night in New York, it occurred to me that no one among my family or friends had met Marsha as yet. Most probably they never laid eyes on her before unless they saw the bank commercial or *Blume in Love*. The pressure on Marsha must have been enormous. Not only was she to be reviewed by the tough New York critics, but she was also going to get reviewed by everyone I knew except Ellen and Nancy, who had already given her their own Tony Award. In her first appearance in the play, I saw heads moving together and program pages turning as she walked on stage. She was playing a very naive and nervous young wife to a petty civil servant going to the theater, where her husband humiliates himself to an important member of the government. In character and in costume, Marsha looked plain and unworldly. Audiences sometimes cannot distinguish between actors and their parts. In her next scene, she played another poor girl, a servant and governess to a wealthy aristocratic family. The young governess was overwhelmed by her mistress, and could barely find her voice when she was unfairly mistreated by the family. Despite the fact that Marsha played both parts flawlessly, I still wondered what my friends thought of this unknown actress who so captivated me in such a short time and had also won the overwhelming approval of my daughters. When at last Marsha appeared as a beautiful and elegant woman in "The Seduction," you could hear the quiet mumble of voices from one aisle to the other. She was radiant in this scene and it was clear to see that this woman was an enormously skillful actress. When she finally appeared in "The Audition," Chekhov was not the only one who was enthralled. At the opening night party afterward, I proudly introduced Marsha to all my family and friends. I thought she did as well with them as she did in the play. I never once saw Marsha have trouble winning over people and attracting them with her luminous presence. And when she laughed, you couldn't resist her.

We went home that night and both breathed a tremendous sigh of relief at having gotten through a night that caused us so much apprehension. Perhaps now we could get on with our marriage. But first we had to get to know each other.

SUNNY BOYS

1

THE GOOD DOCTOR got my usual set of mixed reviews, but for the actors they were fine-plus. The audiences, although entertained, didn't know why I was making an alliance with Chekhov. Neither did Chekhov, I imagine. Manny and I never expected this play to be a huge hit, but rather something to occupy me in the aftermath of Joan's passing. Since plays then did not cost a million six hundred thousand dollars to mount on Broadway, as they do today, it was not too expensive an indulgence. But I found that writing in a new form and with new expression helped to get me out of a style that I did not want to go on repeating in play after play. And meeting Marsha was worth whatever effort had been expended in putting on the play. Sometimes it takes years to reap the rewards, and today *The Good Doctor* lives on in theaters, colleges and schools all over the world.

Marsha's and my courtship had been a whirlwind. Then we were married. Now the play had opened, and Marsha would be appearing in it for the next six months. But what about after that? It never occurred to me to think how she was going to deal with a seven-year contract with 20th Century Fox. Or how *I* would deal with it.

As her nights and two afternoons a week were now occupied, I left for California to deal with preliminary casting for the film of *The Sunshine Boys.* They were in a sense already settled. We had picked a truly odd couple, but I thought an inspired one in Jack Benny and Red Skelton. Since the play was about two former vaudevillians, Jack was perfectly at home, since vaudeville was where he got his start. I had first seen Red Skelton in his early MGM films and thought he was hilarious—a pratfall comic who also had the ability to move you. To promote his films, he would often tour movie theaters that also presented live shows, fronted by a big band like Glenn Miller's or Benny Goodman's. The first time I saw Red Skelton live was at the Capitol Theater in New York, where he did twenty minutes of his "drunken liquor spokesman" and a few other classics, and finished his routine by pretending to miss the wings and falling off the stage, a plunge of at least ten feet. He got up with a smile and dusted himself off before leaving more than a little wobbly. He did this every performance. Such a routine would have broken the bones in every part of the body of a normal man. Red Skelton either knew how to fall or walked around his entire life with a full set of cracked tibias.

Since neither Mr. Benny nor Mr. Skelton was any longer in his prime, MGM insisted on their doing a screen test to evaluate their chemistry to-gether. I was not there for the screen test, but they ran it for me when I ar-rived in Los Angeles. The image that Jack Benny had etched in our minds in a glorious forty- or fifty-year career was indelible, and it was hard for me to fully accept him as playing someone other than himself. Yet when I saw him in the screen test, I found him enormously funny and a perfect foil for the bombastic outrages of his betrayed former partner as played by Skelton. It was just a test and not a full-out rehearsed performance, but there was little doubt in my mind that we had put a perfect match together.

It was soon apparent, however, that all would not go well. Red Skel-ton objected to some of the language he had to say on screen, such as call-ing his retired ex-partner "a crazy bastard." A mild expletive even in the films of 1975, and certainly nothing to compare to the amusing off-camera, all-out cussing that Skelton did during the rehearsals of his TV show. He also felt uneasy that Jack Benny was getting bigger laughs from the grips standing by during the rehearsals of the test. As far as I heard, that wasn't true; they were equally appreciated. But it was not to be. Skelton left, turning down the part, and everything was on hold until we found an-other Sunshine Boy.

To the great dismay of everyone in the industry, Jack Benny suddenly took ill. He was diagnosed with stomach cancer and died soon after. I believe he was eighty years old, but no one would ever accept that he was anything other than the beloved perennial thirty-nine-year-old tightwad that many of us were lucky enough to grow up with.

The search for the new Sunshine Boys began, and I heard that shortly before his death, Jack Benny suggested to his longtime agent, Irving Fein, that he hoped his closest friend in the world, George Burns, would be offered the part. George's great popularity was sharply diminished after the death of his co-star and wife, Gracie Allen. Lately he had been making occasional TV appearances and working the Las Vegas circuit. MGM thought we needed a bigger name. The search went on and I flew back home to New York.

AS I ARRIVED at Kennedy Airport, I was happy at the prospect of seeing Marsha and realized how much I missed her, despite the fact I'd been gone for only a few days. It never entered my mind that when I walked in the door about eight P.M., Marsha would be in the theater until eleven o'clock. Six nights a week, plus Wednesday and Saturday matinees. There would be no three-day weekends in Pound Ridge, no flying off to the Caribbean for a week of sun, sleeping late and long walks on the beach. There wouldn't be even a walk on Third Avenue at night, a movie, a dinner with friends. From a completely selfish point of view, I would rather have had Marsha at home with me than in the theater doing my play. After nineteen years of all our nights together, I realized my life with Joan had spoiled me. On the other hand, Marsha had spent almost all her adult life being in a theater every night, and for her, the adjustment was that now there was a husband and two stepdaughters waiting for her when she was done. These were things to be worked out.

Marsha and I started having lunches together, something I rarely did with Joan, and I changed my writing schedule somewhat to accommodate the shift. I started later in the afternoon, and continued to work at night, something I was unused to. But while I worked, I remained anxious for the sound of Marsha's voice coming up the stairs announcing, "Hi, everybody. I'm home."

But was it a home for her? Since Joan's death, I had not changed one piece of furniture, had not redecorated a single room, and, worst of all, kept the four-poster bed that Joan and I loved so much. Everything was on my terms, yet Marsha made hardly a sound of complaint. Of course, even if we did want to change things, Marsha would not have had much time during her busy schedule to do it. But the truth was, I was not yet inclined to give up anything that I had in my prior life. It's my feeling now that at the time Marsha thought that when the moment was right, she'd be able to make a home that was ours, and not just mine.

So it was on to the next play for me, but even that, in some sense, was written to deal with my feeling about Joan's death, albeit in an abstract way.

THE GOD PLAY
8

I THOUGHT *God's Favorite* was a funny play, but possibly the darkest one I had written up until then. I wanted answers from God, as we all do in times of great loss, but I knew I was not about to get a letter in the mail from the Almighty explaining why He had to make this decision about Joan (which was too bad, since I also wondered what kind of stationery He used and would He capitalize His name whenever He mentioned it). Spinoza in his writings clearly states (although it takes four readings before the word "clearly" can apply) that with all the planets, the galaxies, the universe and the trillions of other masses floating around out there, God does not have time to answer questions made by individual request. Still, I hoped there would be something in my mailbox.

"Dear Mr. Simon," I imagined it would begin, but then reconsidered. Who was I to command the respect of God to be called Mr. Simon? You can already see the tone and direction I would take in writing this play.

"Dear Neil?" No way. Just plain "You," perhaps. Or, if I had already bothered Him with this small question, His irritation would produce, "You dot among insignificant dots on a planet I've long given up hope for." (God was allowed to end his sentences with a preposition.) I decided He would just write a one-line sentence, dignified, powerful, deity-like and clearly not leaving it open to further correspondence.

"And thus shall it be; and thus shall it always be."

A little cryptic for me and not exactly what I was hoping for. I decided to look for my own answers in Scripture, which was not easy to find in my house since I never owned one. Bibles do not come with houses as they do in hotels. I went scurrying over to Doubleday on Fifth Avenue and asked the clerk behind the counter, "Where are the Bibles, please?" It even occurred to me they may not have one since bookstores do not generally keep old books on the shelf. They have hotter-selling products to move. Possibly he'd have to order one from the warehouse. I was in luck, however, and they indeed had Bibles in stock. "Old Testament? New Testament? King James?" the clerk asked, speaking like the computer they all use these days to hunt down exactly what it is you're looking for. "Er, gee, I don't know. Just a regular Bible. Something that has the Book of Job story," I said, as the priest standing next to me reading *Best Country Inns in New England* chuckled to himself. I felt my line was going to be quoted in a small back room after Mass that night. I purchased my Bible and was surprised when the clerk slid it into a small open-ended bag like any other book. It was this kind of disrespect that probably made God angry with the likes of us. When I hit the street, I carried the Good Book with the pages up and the binding balanced correctly in my palm. I thought this would be worth a couple of points up in heaven.

Back in my den I closed the door and immediately plunged into the Book of Job. The story of God testing the faith of a simple, common man was fascinating. Job had an unwavering belief that God was All-Powerful, All-Merciful and All-Forgiving. He stood up to a great assortment of diseases, plagues, disasters and unbearable afflictions, yet Job never relented in his belief in the Almighty. I finally found out where "he has the patience of Job" came from. Amazing how many writers plagiarize Shakespeare and the Bible since there would be no lawsuits pending. Unfortunately, I did not have the patience of Job. Nor did I have his unshakable belief. I am neither an agnostic nor an atheist. I am, as a matter of fact, a Jew, and although Jews are devoted in their belief in God, they are not above asking pesky questions sometimes. They generally find the answers they're looking for, and when they can't find them, they accept the word of the great rabbis. If the great rabbis do not have the answer, they figure the question was not all that important in the first place.

In regard to my own feelings about God, the one thing I was quite positive about was that He had a sense of humor. If He had every other trait that man has attributed to Him, why would God be without the one quality holy men and critics do not consider lofty enough to meet the standards of their own idealistic vision? In the Bible, God is not funny once, that is, unless you read between the lines, and in most Bibles, there's not much space between the lines. My version of the story of Job would not be sacrilegious, nor would it be profane or held to ridicule. My goal was to translate its message into today's world, so that the viewers would grasp the power and the majesty in the story, yet, because it's a parable, they'd see the jokes as well. My basic question would be the same as that asked by Job's family: Why did he endure the suffering and still not give up his faith? My answer, however, would just be funnier.

I recognized the danger that audiences watching the play might cringe at such irreverence, doubly irritating after paying top dollar for good seats. Still, I hoped, in our enlightened world, intelligent people would be able to accept *all* interpretations of biblical stories. If our own Constitution allows us such freedom of speech, why wouldn't a munificent being such as God do the same?

The first character I changed was the messenger who brought Job the bad news. If he was an angel, he was unlike any angel we'd met before. My messenger was named Sidney Lipton and he lived in a small apartment in Queens. He carried an umbrella and wore rubbers on his feet when it rained . . . or even if rain was just predicted. He was as susceptible to colds as all of us, and received no perks just because he worked for the Highest Judge in all the universe. To him, his is simply a nine-to-five job, and his dream in life is to retire soon and live in a condo in Florida within walking distance of the beach. He comes to warn Job (or Joe as he's called in the play) of impending disasters. And disasters they are, coming one after the other, like twisters in Kansas. Joe's house burns to the ground, then his factory burns to the ground. He is now penniless and is visited "with boils, itching, dysentery, blisters, fever and the heartbreak of psoriasis." Still he believes in the goodness of God. The messenger pleads with Joe to give up this folly and take a tiny, minuscule ad in the *New York Times* classified section, so small you'd need a magnifying glass to see it. The ad would say simply, "I, Joe Benjamin, renounce God."

JOE

Never! I will never renounce. I will endure.

MESSENGER

If I told you who renounced God today,
you would be shocked. Do you want to
know who?

JOE

I don't care who.

MESSENGER

Detroit. The entire city of Detroit
renounced . . . including three hundred
tourists just passing through.

JOE

I am what God made me.

MESSENGER

Oh, stop talking like you're Moses. Moses
was a big star. He was a headliner. You are
nobody. I told God I was coming to see you
tonight and He said to me, "Who?"

And so on. The play starred Vincent Gardenia as Joe and the brilliantly funny Charles Nelson Reilly as Sidney Lipton, God's messenger. It was directed by Michael Bennett, the future director of *A Chorus Line* and *Dreamgirls*. I had met him when he was the young choreographer of the musical *Promises, Promises,* which I wrote with Burt Bacharach and Hal

David. Michael had an enormous talent, and occasionally an enormous ego. For the most part he earned the right to be proud of what he'd accomplished in a few short years in the theater.

I will pause here for a moment to tell you a recurring nightmare I have had in all the years I've been writing plays. It may, in fact, be the same nightmare other playwrights have had. I never asked them. This is it.

I am in London or Los Angeles, New York or any other major city where I am about to have a new play open. In the dream, this play is the best one I'd written to date, the one I was most proud of. I attended rehearsals almost daily until the last week before we were to open. Then something keeps me from getting to the rehearsals. No matter how much I try, I can't get there. But I feel comfortable that my play is in the good hands of my director. I finally show up just as the house lights are dimming on the opening night and the curtain goes up. The first scene goes extremely well. I relax. This is going to be everything I hoped for. Then suddenly the leading actor starts to sing. Out of nowhere. There is no song in my play—why is he singing? Then the leading lady sings too. And then a chorus of twenty wearing garish costumes come out and dance in a number that would seem odd in *any* show. George C. Scott is doing a tap dance. Al Pacino is playing a saxophone. Robert Redford is singing like Ezio Pinza in *South Pacific*. I can't breathe. I'm suffocating. I turn to the director, scream at him and grab him by the lapels shouting, "What have you done to my play? You've turned it into a musical" . . . and the surprised director looks at me, nods and says, "I know. Don't you like it?" End of nightmare.

Now the beginning of a real-life nightmare. In the second week of rehearsals of *God's Favorite*, I was suddenly called to serve on jury duty. No matter how many excuses I made to the judge, no matter how many strings I pulled from some power lawyers I knew, the judge would not let me off. On the fourth day he relented and sent me home about noon. I rushed in a cab up to the Eugene O'Neill Theater and as I got out of the cab, I heard the sound of drumming coming from somewhere in proximity to the theater. I wondered how long that noise would go on and if it would hinder the actors during their rehearsals. I opened the stage door and entered the theater. The drumming was coming from inside, from our stage. As I came around to the orchestra, I looked up at the stage. There was the cast, clapping their hands in rhythm, some pounding the floor with their feet. Instead of what I had written—that Joe Benjamin was praising the name of the Lord as his family and servants would murmur their "Amens" to each statement—it was now an all-out revival meeting, the actors choreographed, moving like dancers, swaying their heads and hips. I thought I was hallucinating. I went over to Michael Bennett, having to scream to be heard above the din of the actors-chorus doing what seemed to me to be something like the finale in *Show Boat*.

"Stop them!" I screamed. "Stop them!" They stopped. I shouted to Michael, "What are you doing? You've turned my play into a musical."

He looked at me, surprised, then he nodded and said, "I know. Don't you like it?" No discussion followed. Michael simply went back to the text.

I decided to find a doctor who would give me a sleeping pill which would prohibit me from ever having dreams again.

At the end of Act I of *God's Favorite,* the curtain goes down as Joe Benjamin's stately home is about to go up in smoke. As the curtain is raised on the second act, all we see are charred, smoky ruins. Gone are the library's splendid wood panels, gone are the first-edition leather-bound volumes. Gone are the antique furnishings, tapestries and paintings. They are nothing now but cinders and ashes.

The Benjamins' maid walks on in an apron and carrying a dustpan, takes one look at all this rubble and says, "Well, I'll tell you one thing. I ain't cleanin' up *this* mess." I thought it was funny. Gallows humor, I admit, but funny. The audience did not. They were too stunned. They gasped at the sight of it. They took it absolutely literally, that at every performance, we built this huge, expensive set, burned it down during the intermission, and came up with charred ruins in the second act. Eight times a week. That was the second mistake I made. The first mistake was even deadlier.

I never expected the play to be a huge hit. I did not envision lines around the block with ushers giving cups of hot coffee to those who braved the frigid weather to get tickets to this, the hottest show in town. What I *did* expect was a play that most of the audience and many of the critics would enjoy. I hoped we'd have a decent run and that the backers would make a small profit on their investment and that I would have brought closure to my questions of God, Joan and death. What I did *not* expect was what eventually happened.

I repeated a blunder that cost me dearly. When we did *The Gingerbread Lady,* I permitted a journalist from *Life* magazine to accompany us on the journey from the first day of rehearsal to opening night in New York. The intrusiveness of this writer disquieted us all. To put on a play is hard enough. To do it under a public microscope, diverting our attention from the work at hand and, instead, whispering in the darkened corners of a theater lest your remarks show up in a national magazine, is theatrical suicide. Why then did I permit myself to say yes when an offer came from the most popular television show on the air, *60 Minutes,* inviting us to allow them to cover our play during the trials, tribulations or occasional joys that occur during an out-of-town tryout? The reporter was to be Mike Wallace himself, once an actor on Broadway and now the program's number one cover man. The sales pitch made by CBS and our own publicity man was all about numbers. Millions would be watching us on some Sunday night in the future. Fifteen to twenty million possibly. More people than would see *any* play, no matter how successful, if you ran on Broadway for ten years. I listened to that old bromide, "You can't buy publicity like that." It was also insane to accept it as a gift. We were going to expose ourselves even before the show was ready to be seen in New York. The list of shows that turned themselves around from failure in a tryout to a hit six weeks later is a long one. But you need the time. A honeymoon is not a marriage and we were dumb enough to not only invite the public to our honeymoon, but we were also putting a cameraman lying between a man and his wife in the marriage bed and saying, "Don't mind me. Act as if I weren't here at all."

At our very first preview performance at the Shubert Theater in New Haven, Mike Wallace and his *60 Minutes* crew took their positions in the lobby, waiting to catch the first-night audience as they filed out, and to capture their opinions on film. As I watched the show from the back of the house, I realized this wasn't a preview at all. This wasn't the night I begin to take my notes on what to cut, what to rewrite, what to restructure, a time that I usually enjoy. Removing the deadwood and replenishing the script with new and fresher ideas, watching the play rise from its semidormant state to a blossoming flower, is for me what the fun of this process is all about. I realized suddenly that I had to forgo all that, because for all intents and purposes, this evening's performance was tantamount to an opening on Broadway.

Mike Wallace and his two cameramen were poised outside, ready to document what should not really be seen or judged by anyone except the eleven hundred people in the audience that night. They were all part of the break-in process. You try the show out, you weigh the problems, you fix it and hope for the best. What was on the stage that night was a play that you would describe as "needing work." I rarely did an opening out of town that *didn't* need work. As I documented in *Rewrites,* the first preview of *The Odd Couple* in Delaware drew notices that were anything but exuberant. We had a third act that didn't work at all. Seven weeks and fifty pages of rewrites later, we had a smash.

The audience filed out of the Shubert Theater, and Mike Wallace was there, microphone in hand. The first couple out was the first couple interviewed.

"What did you folks think of the play?"

"It was strange. Not the usual Neil Simon."

"Give a quick review. Good or bad?"

"Well, it was okay. Not great."

The second couple snared by Mr. Wallace looked at the camera nervously.

"Tell me about the play."

"We laughed some. They still have a lot of work to do."

And on and on. Some were out-and-out positive responses, others completely negative. Most felt it was in the "not really ready yet" category. I knew we had some trouble, but what I needed was to work on it in the seclusion of a hotel room, with a typewriter and plenty of paper. Instead, I knew these negative responses were soon going to be viewed by millions of people. Tens of millions.

The verdict on the play was fatal and I was the coroner for permitting *60 Minutes* to see and report that we were bleeding. Despite the fact that we eventually got a rave review from Walter Kerr in the *New York Times,* we ran for just two months on Broadway, the shortest run I had with all of the thirty shows I've written to date. Today, if our press representative comes to me a few weeks prior to our going into rehearsal and says, "Neil, we've got a great publicity opportunity—I just got a very exciting call from—"

"No," I say, before he ever finishes the sentence. "And don't ever ask me again."

MARSHA'S DECISION
9

MARSHA HAD FINISHED her six months in *The Good Doctor* and 20th Century Fox now wanted her to fulfill her seven-year deal. It would mean her going to Hollywood or wherever they might be filming. I couldn't leave New York without Ellen and Nancy. Marsha postponed her decision as long as she could. The film she had made prior to our going into rehearsal with *The Good Doctor* was about to be released. The girls and I went with her to the first preview screening in New York.

"Cinderella Liberty" was not a girl, as most people thought, but a term used in the Navy for a short leave of duty, the requirement being you had to be back by midnight. In *Cinderella Liberty* James Caan played the sailor on leave who drops in at a pool parlor in downtown Seattle. We hear the sound of cue balls banging off each other, slamming into the pockets in rapid fire while a crowd of beer-drinking sailors cheer some unseen, phenomenal pool player. When Jimmy Caan steps through the shouting sailors and Marines, we see the focus of their rapt attention. The picture of Marsha Mason with a cue stick in her hands, bending down over the green table, the overhanging light above her casting shadows on the table and highlighting her eyes and pouty, voluptuous lips, with a look of smirking disdain at her adversary as she clips another ball into the corner pocket, was one of the greatest introductory shots of an actress I've ever seen on film. The hint of sexuality which she kept under wraps in that Manufacturers

Hanover Bank commercial now came at us like a fiery red-hot bomb exploding on the screen. True, it was her second film, the first being *Blume in Love,* but this was a starring role. All I could think of as I saw her chalking up her cue stick, then knocking balls down with almost demonic confidence, was, "My God! In her first ten seconds on screen, there's not a doubt in my mind that Marsha's a star. She couldn't miss."

I was enormously pleased. Pleased for her because I knew she was going to make a huge impact on the film colony, and pleased for us as a professional couple. What would it be like if I thought that Marsha were only a competent film actress, and that if we worked on pictures together in the future, would I be doing it out of some sense of obligation? That question need never be asked now that I saw the power of her performance in this film. In fact, the reverse was true: I'd be lucky to have her star in something I wrote. I also knew there would soon be many long separations as her career took off, and since we were only married about eight months, still trying to mesh our lives together, I wondered how we would deal with this, the girls included. It also became apparent that Marsha had a lousy contract. When you're hungry for that first starring role, you unwittingly sell your body and soul for a pittance, or you allow your agent to make that decision for you. Even if *Cinderella Liberty* was a smash hit, Fox would not have paid her more than thirty thousand dollars for her next film, which was only about five thousand more than they just gave her. As it happened, she very smartly turned down the next script they sent her because it wasn't any good.

THE PICTURE, when released, was a moderate success, but Marsha's reviews were almost unanimously great. There was talk of her getting an Academy Award nomination. She, however, refused to even acknowledge the possibility. I don't think she believed it even when the phone call came from California telling her that she was nominated in the Best Actress category, in this, her second film. Our phone started ringing off the hook and Marsha was besieged with requests for newspaper interviews. "Who was this girl?" "Where did she come from?" "What's her next project?"

We sat in the kitchen one morning as she awaited her first big press interview, with the *New York Times*. She was drinking coffee, having trouble keeping her hand and the cup from shaking. She turned to me. "You've been through this before. What do I say to them?"

"Nothing. They'll ask you questions, you answer them."

"I mean, it's the *New York Times*. What if I make a fool of myself?"

"You won't. Trust me."

"Why am I so nervous?"

"Because you're empowering them with too much. Just be yourself. And don't try to please them. If they have something you want, and you let them know it, you'll never get it. Then they have you. Not just the press but anyone in this business."

"I have to remember that," she said, jotting down my elementary words of wisdom on a piece of paper, the pencil in her left hand, her head cocked to the side, as if taking notes in a college class. The interview went just fine. As I had found out a year earlier, she was hard to resist.

Marsha, myself and the two girls all flew out to California to attend the Academy Awards. I was nominated once before for the script of *The Odd Couple,* but did not attend the festivities, since I was in rehearsal with my next play. I was always in rehearsal with my next play. This trip, then, was the first for all of us. The shopping trip that ensued the following week for the three right dresses is something a man neither has to deal with nor truly understands. He puts on his four-year-old tux and he's ready. The girls had no trouble in finding the right dress for the other one ("Oh, you look great in that. Marsha, doesn't she look great in that?" which produces the inevitable answer, "If I have to wear this, I'm not going."), but finding the right one for themselves was like trying to cross the Rubicon. No one dared take the first step. The girls roamed around Bloomingdale's by themselves, searching for the perfect dress for Marsha. They came back brimming with excitement, holding something in red with little things that glittered.

"You're kidding," said Marsha. "I'd look like a prostitute."

"No," begged the girls. "You'll look hot. Don't you want to look hot?"

"I looked hot in the movie. In life I want to look lukewarm."

With all three looking absolutely fetching, we arrived early at the Dorothy Chandler Pavilion, mostly so the girls could ogle all their favorite movie stars, some of them wearing red dresses with little things that glittered. From our aisle, you could hear the excited murmurs of two young girls who were fulfilling their childhood dreams.

"Oh, my God. Jane Fonda. She is GORgeous."

"Ellen, Paul Newman's staring right at you, I swear."

"Dad! Dad! It's Al Pacino. Do you know him?"

"No."

"Well, make friends with him so we can meet him."

The interesting phenomenon for me was that we were all at this gala event, our hearts pounding in expectation of who would win, and for the first time it wasn't about me. For once I was rooting for someone else, and who better to cheer for than your own wife? Stars, directors and studio execs were crossing to Marsha, eager to shake her hand and to tell her how wonderful she was in that film.

The competition in her category was tough, and Marsha, being a newcomer, knew she was a long shot. She was up against Barbra Streisand in *The Way We Were*, Ellen Burstyn for *The Exorcist*, Joanne Woodward for *Summer Wishes, Winter Dreams* and Glenda Jackson for *A Touch of Class*. My guess was either Barbra Streisand or Ellen Burstyn, because they were in the two blockbuster hits of the year, and in those days that's how the conservative bloc of voters in the Academy would go. I was wrong, it went to Glenda Jackson for her performance in a nice, light comedy. Go figure. A few years later when I wrote *California Suite*, the British actress played by Maggie Smith was, in some sense, fashioned after Glenda Jackson. She says to her husband while dressing to go to the awards, "I've done twelve Shakespeares, eight Shaws, six Ibsens and five Pinters, and I get nominated for a nauseating little comedy." *A Touch of Class* was far from nauseating, but I think they gave the brilliant Glenda Jackson the award because she surprised everyone in showing that she could also do comedy. Marsha was too pragmatic to be disappointed. The attention and respect paid to her at the awards was more than she ever expected. We flew home the next morning and Marsha's spirits were as high as the plane we were flying in.

Since a long time passes between the making of a film and the time it's actually released, the way most Hollywood stars keep their faces before the public is to start another film before the previous one hits the theaters.

Marsha could not because of her commitment to the play and because we were still making an effort to get our marriage off the ground, which took work, considering the limited time we were spending with each other. Offers were now coming in to her, although none of the roles was as promising as that of *Cinderella Liberty*.

Then Marsha made a decision—a momentous decision, not based on the film offers or any contractual conflicts with the studio. She told me she would not take on another film until she felt that we had secured our marriage; that way, any separations would not endanger what we were just starting to build with each other, including her desire to be there for Ellen and Nancy in this critical time of their lives. I breathed a sigh of relief, not even realizing what an incredible gesture she ultimately would be making. Between *Cinderella Liberty* and the release of her next film, three years went by. Three years in the life of any film actress is time you can never get back, and considering that Marsha was past thirty when she made this commitment, the significance of what she gave up was inconceivable to most people. No matter what painful circumstances transpired between us many years later, I could never forget nor have my feelings diminished toward Marsha because of the sacrifice she made in giving up those years. For that alone she has my love and respect forever. It was wake-up time for me in terms of what I could give to her and to our marriage.

I knew I had to make it up to her in the only possible way I knew how, by writing a film for her considerable talents. That opportunity soon presented itself at the unlikeliest time, in the most unlikely place.

WE TOOK a belated honeymoon and flew to Italy. It was truly our first time alone and I brought no spiral notebook with me, thus avoiding the temptation of starting a new play instead of a relatively new marriage. Since we went to many of the major cities in Italy, as I had with Joan nearly twenty years before, it was hard to avoid sensing the shadow of Joan following me about. Despite the constant reminders of that first marriage and of the love and happiness that went with it, it was now Marsha's face that I was seeing each morning when I awoke, Marsha's face that was the last thing I saw each night. My imaginary clandestine meetings with Joan had now disappeared. I found my feelings toward Marsha were now deepening, even more than when I first met her. It was a sensation that I feared because just as I had lost Joan, so this one might not last either. Yet it was irresistible and I began to give myself over to it completely. I was falling in love with Marsha. This sensation, almost a year after the wedding, may sound strange, but what I initially committed to was a marriage, a partnership, and as strong as my first feelings for her were, it was also a way out of despair and hopefully into a place where I could breathe again. We were tentative with each other that first year. Now walking hand in hand with Marsha through the curved streets of Florence, I had this incredible feeling which seemed new, not familiar. New because this was Marsha and not someone else, and I was suddenly and completely in love. In *Blume in Love,* Marsha lost the leading man to his wife. In *Cinderella Liberty,* she runs away from her lover, James Caan, and even her own son, both of whom set out to find her again although no happy ending was guaranteed. Here in Florence I wanted her to get the guy. And I wanted desperately for the guy to be me.

FRIENDS had given us a list of Florence's better restaurants, any of which we could ride to, but we decided to walk—in a city as beautiful as Florence, a taxi ride being almost sacrilegious. We talked as we walked, and soon found that we were lost in those curved streets which seem to lead to no place very hospitable. Because we were cold and hungry, we wandered into a small, unpretentious restaurant, one that obviously generally fed local families, not tourists. We were shown the only empty table there, and we heard not a single English word from anyone, nor did we see a menu. Instead, we watched these incredible dishes pass by, and we just pointed out the most appetizing ones to the waiter. A sightless, nonspeaking person would not go wrong ordering anything in this restaurant. All that was really needed was a sense of smell.

We never got to the list of restaurants our friends had given us. We went back to the same place every one of the four nights we spent in Florence. In fact, so anxious were we to get there, we kept arriving too early and had to wait outside until they opened for business. We did not, however, find the restaurant easily, and each night we depended on getting lost and just wandering into it by chance. Indeed, those are the only directions I could give you as to finding this secret haven. Just get lost—you'll find it. Sometimes usually after vino, we weren't quite sure that this restaurant really existed except in our own minds. We were two chilled, happy lovers, ordering the exact same dishes each night for fear of breaking the magic spell. One glass of wine led to another and we began to feel free enough with each other to talk about the future, and about our future together, because we were both now confident enough to believe we actually would have one. We started to talk about working with each other, of me writing a film for Marsha to star in. "*Co*-star in," she added. "I don't want the responsibility of being up there alone."

There was no thought as to career or profit or even success in this joint venture we talked about. Our discussion was mostly about the joy of spending our days together on a project that was of our making, and that joy wouldn't end at the finish of each day's work. It would continue until our heads hit the pillows next to each other as sleep finally overtook us. "It's got to be a love story," Marsha said between bites of bread sticks and pasta. "A funny love story," I said, scribbling notes on the bill instead of a spiral notebook.

"Like one of those old Spencer Tracy–Katharine Hepburn movies," she said as my napkin wiped a speck of sauce from the side of her lip. I would have preferred doing it with my own lip.

"Old-fashioned but contemporary," I added. "Kind of corny but smart. These should be really bright people," I mumbled, my mouth full of osso buco.

"Jimmy Stewart and Margaret Sullavan," Marsha said with a giggle as she rubbed her shoeless toes on my cold ankles.

"Let's never go home," I said to her, now rubbing my warmed ankles on her hot toes.

"Okay," she said, smiling. "I'll get the check and you go back home and get Ellen and Nancy."

We wandered out on to the curved streets, back to the hotel, and having had two bottles of wine, I'm not positive the hotel was ours. When you're in Florence and in love, details aren't really important.

LADY ANNE
AND THE SUNSHINE BOYS
10

IT WAS TIME for me to make the film of *The Sunshine Boys* and Marsha went back to the stage in New York, accepting the role of Lady Anne to Michael Moriarty's Richard III at Lincoln Center. The pressure to return to Fox Studios to fulfill her seven-year contract was alleviated by her buying herself out of her commitment. It was costly, but the other studios were clamoring for her to come work for them.

Richard III was to have a limited run and it turned out to be more limited than Marsha anticipated. I was and am a fan of Michael Moriarty and find him to be an enormously intelligent and sensitive actor. I do not believe his Richard was conceived by Michael but rather was the choice of the director, whose name fortunately escapes me. I sat in my seat opening night, aware that Marsha had been uncomfortable all during the rehearsal period. The house lights dimmed and slowly Richard III appeared, hunched over slightly, showing a trace of his deformed hand. He spoke in a voice that was higher than I anticipated and seemed somewhat effeminate. It wasn't obviously so, but there was a trace. Moriarty spoke his first line, "Now is the winter of our discontent," and before he finished "discontent," I said to myself, "Wrong! This production is doomed." True, I hadn't given either him or the director much time before I made this rash judgment, but as the evening wore on, you could sense others in the audience coming to the same conclusion. Marsha's Lady Anne was quite good, but it was apparent that she was trying to fight through a director's concept of the role that was giving her much trouble. The newspapers at least had the courtesy of letting them finish the performance before stating their negative opinion. Unable to come to terms with the director, Marsha left the production of her own accord and sooner than she had signed on for. Little did I realize that Lady Anne and an effeminate Richard III would soon be playing a major role in that film Marsha and I had dreamed of as we sat in that wonderful little restaurant in Florence.

Most of *The Sunshine Boys* was shot on location in New York and New Jersey, and I had to spend only a few weeks in Los Angeles while they shot the interior scenes on a soundstage. Red Skelton was replaced by Walter Matthau and I couldn't have been more relieved. In all the films I've done, no one served my material better than Walter. Although he was twenty years too young for the part, he agreed to shave almost all of his rich thick head of hair, and some superior makeup made it easy to believe he was in his mid-seventies. None of that truly works, of course, unless the actor himself makes the change from within. Walter looked older when we made the picture than he does today, when he is past his mid-seventies. Director Herbert Ross and I went on auditioning other actors for the part of Al, his longtime vaudeville partner. The name George Burns came up again and this time Dan Melnick, head of the studio at the time, left the decision up to Ross and myself. George Burns, then seventy-nine years old, walked into Herb's Beverly Hills living room with his agent, Irving Fein, sat down, chewed on a cigar and started to read for us. After only three lines, I looked at Ross and tried to convey by the smile on my face that it was pointless to even go on reading—the man was perfect. Herbert knew it was as well as I did, but gave George the courtesy of at least allowing him to read a few more pages. He was signed the next day.

George Burns had the reputation as being the only man able to make Jack Benny laugh convulsively, and in only a matter of seconds. He never did it with jokes. He clearly had a wonderful acerbic comic mind and his age notwithstanding, he was as quick as anyone forty years his junior. The third part to be cast was the important role of Walter's nephew slash agent, a young man in his thirties who was Walter's/Willie's only surviving relative and more or less his caretaker. Although he cared very much for his irascible uncle, he was the constant victim of Willie's insensitive and cruel jokes.

BEN

I brought you six different kinds of soup. All low-sodium, no fat . . . are you listening?

WILLIE

I'm listening. You got six lousy-tasting soups.

BEN

You think that's funny? I don't think that's funny, Uncle Willie.

WILLIE

If you had a sense of humor, you'd think it was funny.

BEN

I have a terrific sense of humor.

WILLIE

Like your father. He laughed once in 1932.

BEN

If you're waiting for a laugh, you're not going to get one from me.

WILLIE

Who could live that long. Get me a job instead . . . you're a good boy, Ben, but you're a lousy agent.

BEN

I'M A GOOD AGENT! Don't say that to
me, Uncle Willie. I'm a God damn good
agent.

WILLIE

What are you screaming for? What is it,
such a wonderful thing to be a good agent?

One of the best young actors at the time was Harvey Keitel. Some
twenty odd years later he still is a fine actor. He gave an excellent reading
for the nephew Ben, and was hired the next day. Rehearsals began a few
weeks later. Most films never rehearse—since there is so much action and
so little dialogue, what would you rehearse? However, since my films were
eighty-five percent dialogue, we rehearsed it like a play, although only for
five days. It didn't really occur to me as I was writing the play of *The Sunshine Boys* that after doing a vaudeville act together for forty-five years,
Willie and Al spoke to each other in the same rhythms off stage as on, not
by telling jokes, but just the way they communicated with each other.

WILLIE

You want tea?

AL

If you got.

WILLIE

I got tea . . . you want a cracker?

AL

What kind?

WILLIE

All kinds. Chocolate, coconut, graham,
whatever you want.

AL

You got a plain cracker?

WILLIE

Sure, I got a plain.

AL

Then I'll have plain.

WILLIE

They're in the kitchen. In the cabinet.

There were no pauses. The words shot out of their mouths in rapid-fire precision. A pause was filled in with a nod or a shrug or a knock on the chair. There was very little air between their speeches. Since Harvey Keitel read for us without the benefit of Walter and George doing the scenes with him, we realized we had a problem the first day. Harvey was—if not literally, then in essence—a method actor. His speech was realistic. What he said was always basically true and honest, but his speech rhythms were varied, according to the emotion, sometimes rapid, sometimes halting, thinking things out. What he was doing was creating a character, but unfortunately the delivery of his dialogue did not mesh with the staccato beats of Willie and Al. Why should it? He had not been a vaudeville partner of theirs for the past forty-five years. But stylistically it didn't work; it was at odds with the music that was orchestrated on the page. It needed to mesh more. One could reason that having grown up with his Uncle Willie, he would just fall into the pattern of Willie's speech, sometimes just to make conversation between them easier.

Herbert took me aside and said he was worried. As good an actor as Harvey was, we realized we may have made a mistake. Herbert gave it two more days, then called me aside again and said that we'd have to find a new actor before we got too close to the shooting date. Herbert went with Harvey into his office and told him, regretfully, that we'd have to let him go. No actor likes to be fired, and although he would still receive his full salary, Harvey fought to stay on, convinced that he'd be able to give Herbert what he wanted. Herbert Ross was originally a choreographer, a very good one, and he had a choreographer's temperament. He was stern, professional, dogmatic, and when a decision had to be made, he wasted no time in making it. Harvey Keitel was gone from the film that day, although fortunately he went on to prove himself a fine film actor and has given us one great performance after another over the years. Herbert was stern, but he was not coldhearted, and he knew it was his place to tell George and Walter of the change, knowing that both actors had quickly grown fond of the young man. George was the most sympathetic.

"Oh, no," he said. "He was a nice kid. I liked him."

"We all did," said Herbert. "But I think it's best for the picture that we make this change."

"What if I came in early and worked with him on his lines?" offered George.

"That's very sweet, George, but you have enough to do."

"I could work with him at night. He could come over to my house, have dinner with me," George said.

"You're very thoughtful, George, but Neil and I have to find a replacement today."

Having explored all the reasonable avenues, George made a last effort to see that Harvey didn't leave completely empty-handed. "Well, then, ask him if he'd like to fuck my sister, Trixie." My mouth fell open, first in shock, then in laughter. At seventy-nine, George knew that life goes on, and there was no harm in saying so and getting a laugh at the same time. It wasn't said at Harvey's expense. It was the philosophy of a man who had been performing comedy longer than most of us had been alive. We didn't even know if he *had* a sister Trixie, and if he did, she must be about eighty-one. Plus, by using the name Trixie, he painted an image in our minds that was hilarious. In some respects, George had the youngest and fastest mind among us.

TO REPLACE Harvey Keitel, we hired Richard Benjamin, whom I had worked with before in the national companies of *Barefoot in the Park* and *The Odd*

Couple. Richard fell into the speech pattern of the two men as though he were born to it.

Our troubles weren't over though. Another problem surfaced when Herbert said to me, "What am I going to do about George's hairpiece?"

"What do you mean?" I asked.

"He's worn it every day to rehearsals. He wears it to lunch. He never takes it off. I've never seen him bald. But in the scene where he's at home in New Jersey with his daughter and grandchild, the character wouldn't wear it. How do I get him to take it off?"

It was at moments like this that I was glad I wasn't a director. Two days later, Herbert was now rehearsing with the camera, lining up the shots to be filmed later that day. In the most matter-of-fact way, Herbert said, from a safe point behind the eyepiece on the lens: "George? Could you do me a favor? Take your hairpiece off a second?"

"Sure," said George, and took it off, tossing the piece into a saucer on the table. "Okay?"

"Thanks," said Herbert. "Looks swell."

"Nobody drink from that saucer," said George.

I sensed at that moment that Jack Benny was laughing himself silly somewhere in the confines of Los Angeles's Hillside Cemetery.

I WAS unusually quiet at dinner in the little Italian restaurant on Third Avenue that Marsha and I frequented on the nights we wanted to be alone. The place was, I'm sorry to say, nothing compared to our small discovery in Florence, but the food was adequate. When I was pensive, she either assumed I was lost somewhere in the contemplation of a new play or just brooding, as I was prone to do. She was quite surprised when I finally spoke.

"I think it's time to move . . . Out of 62nd Street . . . What do you think?"

If this was the day she'd been waiting a long time for, I didn't expect to catch her quite so speechless. She looked at me for a moment, waiting to see if I was going to say anything else. I didn't; it was her turn.

"Really? Leave the house?"

I nodded. "Yes. Put it on the market. Sell it."

"Wouldn't the girls mind?" she asked carefully.

"It's not about the girls. I'll talk to them, of course, but I think they'll be happy wherever we're happy."

"I think that would be wonderful," she said. "Did you have any particular neighborhood in mind?"

"Yes . . . not in New York."

She stared at me, not really comprehending what I was saying.

"You would leave New York?"

I nodded. "The city has too many memories for me. They're getting in the way. We have to move on. I think we should be closer to where you could start making films again . . . California, I guess."

She sipped her wine. A healthy sip.

"You mean Los Angeles?"

"I don't know. L.A. scares me. I'd be so out of touch with the theater there. I need a city. A real city. A place where you could walk the streets, browse in bookstores. What about San Francisco? You worked there for a few years. You seemed to like it."

I could see the excitement building inside of her, but she was being careful not to jump at my suggestion lest it frighten me off.

"Well, yes. I love San Francisco. And there *is* a lot of good theater there. Great shops, restaurants, lots of interesting people. I don't think we should do anything though until we look it over. All of us. To be sure."

On the girls' next school break, we all flew out to San Francisco. The girls surprised me with their own exuberance at the prospect of moving. A new adventure in their lives—they were all for it.

We spent three wonderful days there. Marsha took us up to meet the actors at the American Conservatory Theater where she had worked. They were all ready to go to New York and help us pack. Everything felt so fresh, so new—and ultimately, so frightening. On the plane back to New York, I had changed my mind. As beautiful as the city by the bay was, it seemed foreign to me. Marsha had all her friends there, but I didn't know a soul. Not one. And you just didn't go out and walk the city streets there. You had to climb those hills before you found a place that was walkable. The views were great, but I knew I'd feel lonely there. My thoughts turned in a direction I never imagined I would contemplate in my lifetime: Los Angeles—Joan had hated it there, and I never liked it much. I didn't understand it. On the other hand, the work was right there for Marsha. She could do a picture and still come home every night. I had dozens upon dozens of friends there, the entire writing staff of *Your Show of Shows,* for starters—Sid Caesar and Mel Brooks and Carl Reiner and Larry Gelbart. Larry was as bright as anyone I knew and he loved it there. Then again, he grew up in L.A. But my brother, Danny, was there also; we had been separated for years, and I missed him. And Roy Geiber, the original model for Oscar in *The Odd Couple,* he was there. I could write plays just as well in California as anywhere else.

I realized, of course, that a lot of these thoughts were pure rationalizations. Los Angeles was Hollywood, and Hollywood was television and movies, not Broadway. Not by a long shot. But if, as in the past, I was able to write plays in Spain and in London and in Switzerland, surely I could write in Los Angeles, which in a sense was just as foreign to me as the cities I just mentioned. Marsha and I decided to visit there the next chance we had and investigate the possibilities.

That night I began to worry about it. I began to worry that in the end I would reject the idea, and worse, decide to stay in the same house on 62nd Street. I tried valiantly to quiet the little voice that was murmuring to me from the back of my head: "You're selling out. It's not you. You belong in New York. You'll never write a good play out there. Remember what Fred Allen said about California? 'It's a great place to live if you're an orange.' "

I turned the volume down on my thoughts as Marsha looked at me before we turned out the lights. "Are you sure about Los Angeles?" she asked.

"Yes. I'm sure." Then, as the lights went off, I said, "I'm pretty sure," leaving myself a much needed escape clause.

MARSHA DECIDED to fly to Los Angeles a few days ahead of me to scout houses on her own, mostly to avoid my having to look at dozens and dozens of homes and risk the chance that I would suffer a major attack of ennui and start asking, "Why are we leaving 62nd Street?" We talked out the kind of house we wanted, the price range, accessibility to places I could browse in and walk about and a school for Nancy, since Ellen would soon be graduating from high school and looking for a college.

When Marsha called two days later, I expected to hear her gushing with enthusiasm. Instead, I heard hesitancy, and, as good an actress as she was, she couldn't avoid the hint of what seemed to me to be a bit of a letdown.

"You okay?" I asked.

"Yes. Yes, fine," she said, sounding anything but fine.

"How'd it go? How many places have you seen? How many have you liked?"

"Well, I saw about ten. No. Nine."

"That's all? Not dozens and dozens?"

"There were very few worth seeing in our price range. Maybe three or four. It's much more expensive out here than in New York. They charge you for the sun."

"What about the ones you liked?"

"There were two, actually. But they needed work."

"How much work?"

"Almost everything."

"If it needed everything, what did you like about it?"

"Not much, really. I don't know. I'm in way over my head with this stuff. Except for this year, I've been living in two-room apartments all my life. I'm also worried you're not going to like it here. You'd better come out and look with me. I don't want the responsibility."

I flew out the next morning, and as we neared Los Angeles, I looked down and saw a desert, then the mountains, then the miles and miles of small houses bunched together and freeways circling and entwining each other endlessly like a massive nest of anacondas with millions of flies on their backs. I'd seen this sight for years now, but never through the eyes of someone who might actually be living there. It was not exactly as stimulating as the skyline of New York, whether seen in the morning or at night, or even from a steamer coming up through New York harbor as you passed the Lady with the Torch. I pondered going to the pilot and saying, "I'm really not feeling well. Could you possibly turn around, go back to New York and I'll repay the airline for the fuel a little bit each week until we're even."

Marsha looked more relaxed when I met her at the hotel, knowing that I would be lifting a large burden from her suddenly stiff shoulders. The real estate agent, who reminded me a little of Norma Desmond in *Sunset Boulevard,* with dyed black hair and makeup that looked like it was permanently scorched around her eyes, packed us into her shiny new white Cadillac. I immediately started looking around the car for a dead monkey.

"As I told Mrs. Simon," she said, enunciating as clearly as a former speech teacher who made the transition from the silents to the talkies, "I don't think there's anything you'd like in your price range. But I think I should show you what I *have* in your price range and you can judge for yourself." She kept saying "price range" as if I had a skin disease and she had no desire to get too close. Los Angeles is actually a lot prettier from the ground than from the sky above, and the orange circle of smog, which is visible at twenty thousand feet, is invisible when you inhale it into your lungs.

We drove through the Beverly Hills area and there were some very pretty houses, but the only ones that looked indigenous to the area were the Spanish-tiled ones. Most of the others looked as if they were flown in from abroad and had to show their passports before they were lowered into their two lots of land. I like my architecture old and authentic and I'd have to wait about eighty years before any of these homes became fairly old and slightly authentic. They were also out of my price range because this is where Lucille Ball lived and Gene Kelly and Alfred Hitchcock. I think Norma Desmond drove us out of our way so we could see what *she* thought we should be buying, before she made a left turn into our price range. The white Cadillac climbed up one of the canyons that stretch out above Beverly Hills and Los Angeles (they are two different cities, you know) and we were soon approaching the dirt road neighborhood.

Driving off the canyon road, we stopped at a house that looked a little better than a newly painted "tear down." The new paint did not conceal the flimsy interior, which didn't look like it could withstand a strong wind, let alone an earthquake. It did, surprisingly, have a tennis court. The court was not adjacent to the house, it was *part* of the house. As you stepped out the back door, you were *on* the court and you had to climb over the net to get out of the house. There were no sidelines to the court, unless you wanted to count the kitchen, and right on the back baseline was an iron meshed fence, giving you no room to go back for a shot. You'd have to go *outside* the fence to swing at the ball. The court was also covered with enough dead leaves to conceal a squadron of B-29 bombers, left there, no doubt, to prevent you from seeing what the last earth tremor did to the surface of the court. This house cost twice what my little town house on 62nd Street cost—the one near Bloomingdale's and twelve movie houses and great bookstores and incredible restaurants.

When we went directly back into the car, the agent said to me, "Don't you want to see the inside?"

"Why?" I asked. "I thought we *were* inside."

Two hours and ten houses later, the gloom had turned to a pall. On the few occasions that Marsha lifted her gaze from the floor of the car and her fading future, it was evident how downhearted she was. I turned to the agent and said, "Okay, let's try upscale."

Upscale houses, at least the ones she represented, all looked a little like Tara before the Civil War took its toll. Once inside, there was usually a very large vestibule with two rounded staircases coming down each side, where any minute you expected a smiling Loretta Young to descend, floating in a fluffy chiffon gown and saying, "Welcome to this week's show." These plaster and brick birthday cakes seemed less like homes than some expensive attempt to show the rest of Hollywood that they too could afford to have their bagels and Nova Scotia salmon flown in on weekends from New York, since at that time in L.A., a good deli, like a good man, was hard to find. Inside these houses hung some of the best paintings in the world, which seemed to be saying to me, "You can't judge a Matisse by its cover."

After three such houses, which fortunately for me were unaffordable, I asked the agent, "Do you have any houses where regular people live? Something that doesn't look like a fragment of a movie set, ready to be moved into storage space to make room for the next scene?"

Miss Real Estate didn't take kindly to my derisive humor, since it was clear she didn't have an inkling that it even *was* humor, which, I assume, came rarely into her life.

"I only have one last place to show you. I'm not sure you'll like it. It just came on the market. The sellers are very difficult people. It's not available to see until five o'clock, but I can drop you at your hotel and pick you up about four-thirty. It's above your price range but maybe not as high as what I've been showing you. Are you interested or shall we just forget about it?" Before I could say, "Why don't we just forget—" Marsha looked at me and said, "We might as well. We have nothing else to do at five." My feeling then was that we'd have nothing else to do out here till I died, but I nodded and said, "Sure. Why not?"

"Unless you'd like to live out at the beach. It's quite beautiful there." Ahh. Now the beach sounded promising. Since I had spent some childhood summers at Far Rockaway Beach and occasionally Brighton Beach, here was a suggestion that touched on my very roots. We took the hour-long drive out and the hour-long drive back and we were still at zero. Beaches were only for the summer, I reasoned from a mind-set that was entrenched in the past.

We had pretty much given up hope that the last house she was going to show us would be what we wanted, especially since the sellers were difficult people. As if the real estate lady wasn't.

"Should we reconsider San Francisco?" Marsha asked.

"Maybe we should just rent a house here for a year," I counteroffered, "before we decided how much I really hate this place."

At four-thirty on the dot, Norma Desmond showed up in a different outfit—a yellow tailored suit, the kind you see in Neiman's windows and are bought only by little old color-blind ladies in Texas. I guess she thought that if the house didn't cheer us up, her MGM musical costume would brighten the atmosphere. We had no expectations whatsoever as the car drove us down Sunset Boulevard, then through the gates of Bel Air. Bel Air was an anomaly in Los Angeles. It had less glitter and more taste than, say, Beverly Hills. You felt a certain serenity as you moved along the quiet and uncrowded roads. Many of the houses were not visible from the street, hidden as they were behind tall hedges or clustered trees. I looked at Marsha with my eyebrows surprisingly raised and she was obviously impressed as well, although she silently mouthed the words to me in the back seat, "Way too expensive." Norma Desmond, who apparently could hear a prospective buyer's thoughts, said, "Well, you can *try* negotiating, if you want."

What made me a little nervous was that the roads kept winding, turning and twisting, going ever upward. I knew I could never find this place again with a Sherpa guide and ten members of the Explorers Club. Norma finally turned in to a driveway and suddenly we were facing a gate. A bell had to be rung and answered before the gate opened and the price of the house went up about thirty percent. The driveway turned up a hill, and then we saw it. There was a large, flowing ficus tree, its branches spreading far and wide, and behind it—was Connecticut. Magically, we had just left Los Angeles, Beverly Hills and California behind us, and we were back East. Not an L.A. version of back East. Not a movie studio mockup. This was the real thing. A single-level house, painted white with dark green shutters. There was nothing showy, nothing ostentatious about this house. No manicured lawns, just a simple white-pebbled driveway. It was so definitively Connecticut that I was sure it was the only house in Los Angeles that had snow fall on it during the winter months. I braced myself for disappointment because this house had to be five times what I expected to pay. That figure became six times once we entered through the front door. The place was empty, devoid of furniture, not a stick, which only added to its charm. So often a house loses its advantage by the overdone or pretentious interior decorating imposed on it by someone who didn't realize what they really had. We wandered from room to spacious room, each one more spacious than you'd ever see in a large New York apartment. The views were not spectacular in the conventional sense. It was not the kind of house that wherever you looked, you saw the shining, glittering lights of Hollywood below. What you saw here were trees and more trees and, in the distance, other houses nestled quietly into the hills. The house had been built around 1930 and had lost none of that era's sense of understatement. Marsha's eyes and mouth had opened wide, each to about the same size, and they stayed open the entire time she viewed the house.

"Well, obviously I can't afford this," I said to Miss Desmond, "but how much is it?" She told me. It was a lot, but only about twice what I expected to pay and far less than the Hollywood museums I had seen earlier that day. I think because the house *was* so understated it was not as popular to more flashy-seeking minds. The money suddenly seemed less important to me, inasmuch as we were getting Connecticut with southern Italy thrown in.

"It's not negotiable," Norma said. "I've tried. They turned down ten offers. They won't come down a nickel. You pay their price or that's it. Walk around again. Look outside. I'll wait for you in the car." With that she left.

Marsha was obviously overwhelmed, but she remained cautious. "Oh, God," she said. "It's so big. I'd never be able to clean this." She wasn't joking. That's what a lifetime in two rooms will do to you.

I opened the front door and asked Miss Desmond to return. I thought that "it's not negotiable" was agent talk.

"We like it. Obviously we like it. It's beautiful. But I'm not used to figures like this." Having lost a great deal of money in previous bad investments, I was now trying to be careful about financial matters. I made a lesser offer on the house and asked the agent to put it before the owners. She shrugged skeptically and drove us back to the hotel. Marsha and I sat there without saying a word, transfixed on the picture of that utterly charming house you would never imagine existed in Hollywoodland. In the morning came the answer I pretty much expected. No deal. Not only no deal, but the owner said that for each week I didn't buy the house, the price would go up five thousand dollars. That's five thousand a week. I laughed at the insanity of it.

"Is that five thousand dollar increase limited to just a few weeks," I asked, "or does it go on for the rest of my life?"

"That's his offer, Mr. Simon. I told you they were difficult."

"No. Climbing Mount Everest is difficult. Buying this house is impossible."

We drove back to the hotel and I immediately called Ray Stark, who lived ten minutes away, outside Bel Air. I asked him to come look at the house with me the next morning.

"Do you really like the house?" he asked while we were still on the phone.

"Yes. It's beautiful. But I can't make a deal with this man. The house comes with a taxi meter that charges you while you're waiting." I told Ray what the price was.

Ray said, "If you like it, I don't have to see it. Here's what I'll do. I'll buy the house from him today myself. Then I'll sell it to you for the same price. I will also give you a note saying that whenever you wish to get rid of this house, I will give you back exactly what you paid for it. You can't lose a nickel."

"Why would you do that, Ray?" I asked.

"Because you and I will be working together for a very long time. And you won't write well if you're unhappy. Do we have a deal?"

It never came to that, but Ray's offer pushed me to make my own. I bought the house the next morning. It was ours. Well, it was ours until two more conditions arose. In the large bathroom off the bedroom, there was a mural painted on the wall. And it was a pretty ugly mural at that.

"The mural doesn't go with the house," Norma Desmond told me. "If you want it, you have to buy it. It's seventy-five hundred dollars."

"You don't understand," I said to Norma. "It's paint on a wall. What are they going to do, suck it off with sponges and take it with them on a blotter?"

"I don't know," she said. "Do you want to buy it or not?"

I was now wondering if even as smart a businessman as Ray Stark could pull off this deal.

"No. I pass on the mural. Now how much are the trees and the pebbled driveway?" Somehow the owners backed off their demand and I signed the papers before the week was over, just barely saving myself an extra five thousand dollars. But they weren't through. They then asked if I wanted to buy the complicated security system they had built in.

"No," I answered. "Tell them to rip it out of the walls. Instead I will put scarecrows all around the house." Well, they didn't pull the security system out, but I had to rebuild it anyway. They were so manic about their security, that when you put the system on when you went to bed at night, every window and every door in the house had to be closed. This meant that if you wanted to go to the bathroom during the night, you'd have to turn off the system, turn it back on when you were in the bathroom, turn it off when you were through in the bathroom and back on again when you went back to sleep. I understand that when these people moved to Nevada, they had the moving vans with their furniture drive very slowly because they would be in their car right behind the vans, making sure no one would steal anything from them. I believe they are now living inside a bank vault somewhere out West.

The next afternoon, we were given the keys to the place, and Marsha and I walked around the empty house. It was the very first house she could call hers, or at least, ours. We stood there, looking at our future together. Tears suddenly came to her eyes but they didn't seem to be about happiness.

"What's wrong?" I asked.

"I don't know," she said. "Do we deserve this?"

"Probably not," I answered, putting my arms around her. "But let's enjoy it anyway."

We went outside and looked at the trees.

"Uh oh," I said.

"What is it?"

"They forgot to charge us for the birds."

THE END OF NEW YORK
11

WE WOULDN'T make the move for another seven months so that Ellen and Nancy could finish their school terms. In the meantime, Marsha arranged to have two friends, young L.A. decorators on the rise, help to furnish and redo walls, floors and ceilings, which hadn't been repaired or painted by the two former owners since the understated 1930s. If we shipped out all the furniture we had from the small rooms on 62nd Street, it wouldn't have filled a third of the new house in California. We decided, with Marsha's blessing, to take all the best and prettiest pieces with us when we made the move to L.A. The four-poster bed that had been mine and Joan's would go into storage, simply because it was too difficult for me to give up completely. I also stored some other pieces that I thought Nancy and Ellen might want for their own homes some future day. A new bed was built for us in California and this, in a sense, was the official beginning of a new life for me and Marsha.

She was soon offered a film by Fox called *Audrey Rose,* a thriller dealing with reincarnation and co-starring Anthony Hopkins—before Anthony Hopkins became *the* Anthony Hopkins, one of the world's best actors. It was to be filmed in L.A., where Marsha could also oversee the redoing of our house and be back in plenty of time before we had to make the inevitable move. I use inevitable because it describes the fears that still clung to me concerning this transplantation of my soul, body and mind. I worried that after three months there, I would be completely unhappy, and

THE PLAY GOES ON

even worse, that I couldn't find the house driving up from Sunset Boulevard. I pictured myself calling from some stranger's home on the other side of Bel Air, pleading with Marsha to come and get me.

As for my own work, I started thinking about two projects. One was the romantic comedy film that was born in a Florence restaurant, the other was a new play I wanted to follow the disappointing *God's Favorite*. I made notes on the film to be called *Bogart Slept Here,* meaning the Chateau Marmont Hotel in the Hollywood Hills, where so many neophyte actors stayed before they became major film stars. The basic idea of the story was that Marsha, an ex-dancer, was married to a very promising but struggling off-Broadway actor who gets discovered in a small play and is whisked out to Hollywood, where he reluctantly moves with his family. He feels very out of place there (autobiography often sneaks in when you least expect it), and they have trouble adjusting, especially after his first film makes him an international star (picture Dustin Hoffman in his debut performance in *The Graduate),* and it creates chaos in their marriage. The story was coming out a little darker than I had imagined, but I envisioned the character of the wife as a very good role for Marsha.

When thinking of the new play, I was reminded of an item from a California paper sent to me by a friend. It said that playwright Neil Simon was moving to L.A., and questioned if that meant he would start to tear apart California's mode of living as he had New York's in his previous *Prisoner of Second Avenue.* Obviously that was impossible, because a man who can't find his house in Bel Air doesn't know enough about California mores to write about them. But it did occur to me to do a play about people in California who do not *live* there. In other words, it would be about people staying at a hotel—the Beverly Hills Hotel, in fact, because to the rest of the world it was L.A.'s most famous hostelry. Since I had successfully done *Plaza Suite* a few years back, why not *California Suite?*

Before any words were put to paper, Marsha and I were summoned by director-choreographer Michael Bennett to see his new show, then previewing at Joe Papp's Public Theater, called *A Chorus Line.* Michael conceived, choreographed and directed the show based on interviews he had conducted with dancers about their dreams, hopes, fears, aspirations and their personal background. He and his book writers, James Kirkwood and Nicholas Dante, then made a coherent script out of that material, and Marvin Hamlisch and Edward Kleban wrote a most wonderful score. The musical was to run close to fifteen years on Broadway and still continues to be seen today in any country that has a theater. Marsha and I were thrilled and awed by the incredible show that was so brilliantly mounted on the stage that night. At the end of the performance, Michael waited for us in the lobby, then pulled us aside and asked our opinion.

"It's a smash, Michael. You have nothing to worry about," I said exuberantly, genuinely enthused about his achievement.

"But what didn't you like?" he pushed. "Was there anything you would change?" Marsha loved the show as much as I did, but she made one important suggestion about the character development of Cassie, the lead dancer in the show. Michael loved what she said and agreed to put it into the show, which he did. He then turned to me and said, "It's not right yet. It needs more humor."

"It might, it might not, Michael," I added. "It doesn't make any difference. It's a winner just the way it is."

But he persisted with his concerns, and asked me if I could go out for a drink with him and his assistant, Bob Avian.

"When?" I asked.

"Now," he answered. "Please. It's important to me. I really need to talk to you."

Marsha urged me to go with him, and she returned home as it looked like this was going to be a long drink.

In a booth in a small, dark Greenwich Village restaurant, Michael proceeded to reiterate his fears about the show's lack of humor.

"It needs what you can give it," he said to me. "It wouldn't take you long. A few hours' work, that's all."

Everyone presumed because I was prolific that I could knock out dialogue on the spot. It never happens that way. It only starts to flow when you know the characters well, when you have a keen grasp of the story. I had only seen one performance of A Chorus Line. But Michael was in a hurry; they were nearing the end of their previews and had to open within a week. The timing, however, was the least of my concerns.

"Michael, I can't write anything without the permission of the authors. Jim Kirkwood and Nick Dante would have to agree to my coming on."

"They accept," he said quickly. "It's not a problem."

"It is to me, Michael. I'm a member of the Dramatists Guild. It's against their rules. You have to speak to them and assure me that they've agreed."

"All right," he said. "I'll talk to them. But I promise it's no problem. The only thing is, we won't be able to give you billing."

"That's fine with me," I said. I didn't ask if I would be paid for this and frankly I hadn't expected it. I again followed the old, unwritten law of the theater that states that writers go to help other writers when they're in trouble, although Michael didn't seem to be in any trouble. I soon found out, however, that that unwritten law had not been in use since the grand old playwrights like Moss Hart and Marc Connelly and George S. Kaufman had ceased working in the theater. Someone should have told me.

The next morning I received the script of *A Chorus Line* by messenger, followed by a phone call from Michael.

"It's okay with Jim and Nick. They just wouldn't want it to get around. But they would welcome your help," said Michael quickly, obviously anxious for me to get to the typewriter. I would have preferred to have heard it from Jim and Nick personally, but if they knew changes were being made in the script, and it was obvious they were, they surely would have complained to the Dramatists Guild if they were against it. Since I had not heard to the contrary from the Guild, I started to write.

I read the script through twice that morning and then picked my spots to add or change lines. Five, ten, twenty of them, maybe more, were interspersed throughout the script. I gave most of them to the character played by Kelly Bishop because Kelly could deliver a funny line better than anyone in the show. That night I sent my additions off by messenger to Michael, not knowing if he would use just a few or all of the lines I had written.

I was not witness to what happened the next day, but a friend in the cast told me that Michael sat in a chair with the pages containing my new lines sticking out from under him just enough for him to see them. He gathered the cast in front of him and said he'd been thinking of some new things for them to put in their scripts. I suppose Nick and Jim agreed that it was all right for the cast to think that Michael had rewritten them, but not for me to be given credit for the additions. Michael would look down at my pages (giving the impression that he was thinking of them on the spot), then up at an actor and say, "Honey, instead of your old line, say this." Then he gave her my line. They laughed. They laughed at the second new line, and then at the third. Someone said, "Michael, when did you get so funny?" He said, "I've just been thinking about it, that's all." I have no idea, as I said, how much actually went in, and when I went to see the show weeks later, I *never* knew what of it I wrote. I never remember what I write, even in my own plays unless someone tells me what play it's from. It's possible that Michael never told Jim Kirkwood and Nicholas Dante about the lines I wrote. Perhaps they did know. I don't recall ever meeting them later or hearing from them, or from the Dramatists Guild. I received no money from the production, but if I had insisted on even a small royalty, with a show that ran for fifteen years, I probably would have made close to half a million dollars. Another bad business judgment on my part? I don't know. I didn't do it for the money.

For years no one on Broadway ever mentioned it, and then suddenly it became part of the lore of the industry. Everyone knew I had worked on the show. Michael did send me a gift: a pair of pillowcases. Why pillowcases, you may ask, as *I* have for twenty-five years? Maybe he meant to say, "Thank you for keeping this under your pillow."

But Michael wasn't witty enough to use that double meaning. Smart, yes, but not witty. On the other hand, I was witty, but maybe not smart enough to ask to get paid for my work. The true answer, I suppose, was that helping make the show just a little better (although I still didn't think it needed to be better) was gratification enough for me. I don't think Marsha and I ever slept on those pillowcases, but if I had taken the money, Marsha and I would have slept very well in a deluxe suite in the Ritz Hotel in Paris.

IN THINKING of *California Suite,* four separate one-acters, all taking place in the same hotel suite, what I looked for first was the centerpiece. Not the funniest one, necessarily, but the most provocative, the most compelling one, so that I knew I was starting with something rock solid to build on.

I knew a number of couples in the theater and in films who had, what you might call, a marriage of convenience: the husband was bisexual, the wife heterosexual. I knew them well enough to be good friends but not intimately enough to understand exactly how their marriage worked. I suppose I wrote the way my instincts dictated. They were definitely devoted to each other, a traditional loving couple in all respects except one. She knew he had a separate life—his other lover or perhaps lovers—and she either condoned it or made a compromise with herself, realizing that if she demanded he be faithful, she would lose him. In many respects it was a poignant, if not a truly sad situation, while in other respects it was a courageous and difficult endeavor. Most of us would not tolerate such an arrangement, but those who do never let on that it's anything but bliss.

In my play, Diana Nichols, a British actress, has come to Los Angeles to attend the Academy Awards, for which she is nominated as Best Actress. She is accompanied by her husband, Sidney Nichols, an erstwhile antique dealer, a former actor and a bisexual. This one-act play was divided into two scenes. The first scene was their preparation before leaving for the awards—her complaining about how she looks and her worry that the expensive gown that producer Joe Levine bought her makes her look like Richard III because of the hump on her back that she suddenly has acquired since putting on the dress.

"Isn't that your usual hump?" Sidney says chidingly. "Or perhaps you forgot to take out the tissue paper." His quick biting humor matches hers, and although they can be cruel to each other, they adore each other's jokes. Where else would they find anyone so entertaining?

"Why didn't I dress simply?" says Diana. "Why didn't I just wear my plain black pants suit?"

"Because *I'm* wearing it," says Sidney, preening in his nifty tux. Even in their banter, their sexual differences or similarities come into play without rancor. In the second scene, they come back from the awards in the wee hours; both are fairly drunk. It's clear that Diana has not only lost the award, but she spotted Sidney paying a good deal of attention to a young, handsome actor at the Gala Ball after the proceedings. It leads to a knock-down, drag-out fight between the two when Diana realizes that she cannot bear losing the award and possibly her husband to a "young gorgeous twit," both on the same night. Sensing they are going too far this time, possibly taking that one step over the line that could destroy their marriage, they reconcile in bed, and in the darkness, Diana crawls close to Sidney, hoping for the physical affection that she gets all too infrequently.

DIANA

It's my fault, Sidney, for being a hopeless
romantic. I keep believing all those movies
I've made . . . And you do make love so
sweetly.

SIDNEY

Would it help any if I made some empty
promises?

DIANA

It never has . . . What's wrong with me,
Sidney? We've been fighting this for years.
Why haven't I left you for a hairier
person?

SIDNEY

Because we like each other. And we are a
refuge for our disappointments out there.
(She lies back)
Tired?

DIANA

Losing Oscars always does that to me.

SIDNEY

I'll get up first thing and order you eggs
Benedict.

DIANA

You do take care of me, Sidney, I'll say that.
And good help is hard to find these days.

SIDNEY

You scratch my back, I'll scratch yours.

DIANA

It's been an evening of ups and downs,
hasn't it?

SIDNEY

Mmm.

DIANA

Care to continue the motion?

SIDNEY

Tacky. You're getting tacky, angel.

DIANA

I love you, Sidney.
(He leans over and kisses her tenderly)
Don't close your eyes, Sidney.

SIDNEY

I always close my eyes.

DIANA

Not tonight . . . Look at *me* tonight . . . Let
it be *me* tonight.
        (The lights dim. Curtain)

When the play successfully opened at the Ahmanson Theater in Los Angeles, actress Lee Grant, with whom I had worked before, came to me just as the curtain went down. She looked at me in amazement.

"Where did this come from? What part of you knew who these people were?" she asked.

"I simply didn't think of him as gay," I answered. I paraphrased Tolstoy. "Any marriage in trouble is the same as all marriages in trouble."

THE SUNSHINE BOYS film came out in the latter part of 1974 and the reviews were ecstatic. The Academy Award nominations came out and we received three: Walter Matthau as Best Actor, George Burns as Best Supporting Actor (although it was far from a supporting role, but I think MGM submitted him in that category so as not to have him compete with Walter), and I received one for Best Screenplay Adapted from Another Medium, which was my own play. I was disappointed that director Herbert Ross was not nominated because I thought he did a masterful job. His big day was to come two years later.

Marsha, Nancy, Ellen and I flew out to attend the awards and to take a look at how work on our house was proceeding. Marsha and I had been married almost a year and a half at that point, and things could not have been better. In the cool, crisp winter air, the sky was practically cloud-free, although it occurred to me that the former owners might have taken them in the van back to Nevada as well. We also used this opportunity to look for a school for Nancy, and were fortunate enough to enroll her at the Westlake School for Girls. It was one of the better private schools in Los Angeles with a great reputation and the added advantage of being literally seven minutes away from our new house.

On the night of the awards, with so many things to do concerning the new house, the school and preparing to shoot *Audrey Rose,* Marsha never found time to eat a proper meal before we left for the Dorothy Chandler Pavilion. She ordered up a hamburger and a milk shake, which she soon regretted. During the ceremonies, she started to get sharp stomach pains and not even George Burns's popular win as Best Supporting Actor could assuage her discomfort, which got more severe that night back at the hotel. She finally fell asleep, however, and felt a little better in the morning, even opting to go on to San Francisco with me for a two-day vacation while the girls flew back to New York. In San Francisco she began to feel sick again, and a hurried visit to the doctor confirmed that she had a gall bladder that needed to be removed very soon. Whatever was wrong with it before had not been helped by the hamburger and milk shake on the previous night, just the kind of fatty foods that send gall bladders into an uproar.

Against the doctor's urging, she declined to have the surgery in San Francisco and instead opted to fly back home that day. The doctor told her that flying with a gall bladder problem could be risky business, but she insisted on going anyway. I called ahead to Lenox Hill Hospital in New York and they arranged to see her as soon as she arrived. Within twenty-four hours she was in the operating room, while I walked the halls of Lenox Hill, where only three years ago I learned that Joan had a cancer that had metastasized and that she only had a year and a half to live.

Marsha was brought down from the operating room and all had gone well. I walked into her room, then suddenly stopped short. This was the very same room that Joan had spent her last few months in, the very same room in which she died. The doctor walked in to tell Marsha she was fine. I took one look at the surgeon and realized he was also the one who had found the tumor in Joan's breast and in her hip, the same one who took me out to an empty stair landing to tell me that Joan's life was going to be a short one. Every horror that I had gone through three years ago, and again a year and a half later when she died, rushed into my head as if time had never passed. I ran out of the room, out of the hospital and can't even remember where I ended up.

It was the coldest and most thoughtless thing I could have done to Marsha and the hurt I caused her had to be far greater than the effects of her operation. I could say that my actions were inexcusable, but I genuinely saw no other way to control the powerful emotions that had surged inside of me. When I returned to Marsha's room, her anger and pain were apparent. It took some time for her to get over my abandoning her, and I don't know that she ever fully forgave it. Joan had popped up once again, getting in the way of our marriage. Put yourself in Marsha's place, and imagine what it felt like to have your husband run out on you just as you're wheeled into your room after an operation. It was not my finest moment.

WHEN I TOLD my mother, who was then living in Manhattan on 57th Street off Third Avenue, that we were moving to Los Angeles, she looked at me and said in no uncertain terms, "Not without me, you're not." She was in her early seventies then and had lived in New York all her life. No longer working, she still loved walking to the grocer's, to the bank, to her dentist and to the movie house just around the corner where she mostly waited for my films to appear. I couldn't picture her leaving her beloved city but the same could be said about me. To facilitate matters, I had my brother, Danny, look for a place not far from him in Sherman Oaks, about a twenty-minute drive from where I'd be living. I moved her and all her furniture out about three months before Marsha and I did, and within six weeks after arriving there, she had found a grocery she could walk to, as well as a bank, a dentist and a movie theater, and had made friends with everyone in her small apartment house. The only thing that alarmed her there was that in the morning when she awakened, instead of seeing the traffic of 57th Street, she saw snow-capped mountains in the distance. It took Danny a few days to convince her it was not an oil painting on the wall in her neighbor's apartment.

JUNE 7, 1975: The huge van stood in front of the house on 62nd Street. The first thing that was loaded on was the brown Mercedes I had bought three years earlier to drive Joan and the girls back and forth between New York and the house in Pound Ridge. That house on Blue Heron Lake, where things looked brighter and more hopeful for Joan for a year and a half and then finally turned dark and distant, was now sold, and hopefully was cheering up another family's life. The house on 62nd Street was also sold, to a family from Philadelphia. They requested we leave the four-poster bed in the bedroom, and I decided to part with it. It was too big a memory of the past for me to carry any longer.

The furniture and our clothes were loaded on carefully, and we all stood on the steps of the house as the big van moved slowly away, starting its trek across the country. It was a solemn occasion for me, Nancy and Ellen, as if we were attending one more funeral. A limousine pulled up and we all got in with our new dog, Ponti, a small white Lhasa apso, who was a gift from my former producer Saint Subber, after our first dog, Chips, passed away peacefully a few years before. As the limo pulled away, I took one last look back, allowing myself, for just an instant, a worried thought: What if, one night, Joan came back to the house looking for us? Would she be frightened not to find me and her daughters there, without a clue of where we went?

On the flight west, Marsha seemed happy and exhilarated, as if the world she always dreamed about was finally opening itself up to her. Five and a half hours later, the jumbo jet set down on the tarmac at Los Angeles Airport, in the bright afternoon sun. As soon as the engines were cut off, we were instructed not to leave our seats and to keep our seat belts buckled. We would not be taxiing to the gate just yet. They announced on the intercom that at that very moment Los Angeles was experiencing an earthquake.

"I cannot believe this," said Marsha, admitting that this was one hell of a welcome to California.

BOGART TO GOODBYE
12

AS MARSHA was finishing *Audrey Rose,* I was completing the scripts of both *Bogart Slept Here* and *California Suite.* I worked in a room in our new house that was set up to be a replica of the room I worked in on 62nd Street. Dark wooden panels with cabinets ran along the lower part of the room. The fabric on the walls was more English than California, and I had my own desk that I had been writing on for years. The electric typewriter was at my right-hand side, and even when computers made their inroads, they got nowhere near my office. There was a pretty view from the large window, but I kept the shades down halfway in an effort to avoid anything that didn't feel familiar to me. The bookcases were filled with all my favorite books. I was very happy with these surroundings, and the writing part of my brain was neatly tricked into thinking that when I wanted to take a break, I could walk around the corner to Third Avenue and have a tuna salad sandwich in a friendly luncheonette.

I sent the first draft of *Bogart* to my good friend Mike Nichols, who was now one of the most celebrated film directors in the business, with his enormous hits *Who's Afraid of Virginia Woolf?, The Graduate* and *Catch-22.* He read the script, loved it and agreed to direct it, making this the first film we'd do together. He set up a deal with Warner Brothers and for the lead opposite Marsha, he signed Robert De Niro to play the off-Broadway actor whose very first film becomes an international success. Though still early in his career, I thought it was a coup to land De Niro. He was clearly on his way to becoming a major star and eventually the icon that he is today. We had to postpone rehearsals of the film for a few days while De Niro was finishing *Taxi Driver* for Martin Scorsese. Travis Bickle, his character in that movie, was one of the most dangerous and complex characters De Niro ever played, and the scene where he looks at himself in a full-length mirror, armed to the teeth with weapons and challenging some unseen enemy with the threat, "You talking to me? . . . Are you talking to *me?*" and then springing one of the guns out of his sleeve, taking dead aim at his own reflection, is now part of film history. It is shown on practically every film montage put together for the Academy Award shows.

De Niro finally finished *Taxi Driver* on a Friday in New York and three days later, on a Monday morning, he appeared on the set in California to start *Bogart Slept Here*. Although not nearly as big and strong as George C. Scott, to me De Niro was equally as intimidating. He didn't say very much, but what he said, you listened to. He spoke softly, nodded and shrugged a lot, and occasionally he gave you a quick smile that caused his eyes to squint. It was, however, difficult to know what he was thinking.

He looked tired on that first morning and with good reason. Having just finished one film, it's difficult for any actor to jump out of the skin of one character into the skin of another with only a weekend's rest, half of it spent on a plane. I knew instinctively that if De Niro were acting in a Scorsese film, he would have spent the last three months working in the darker shades of life usually found in Scorsese's work. How would he respond then, stepping into the light, gray areas that he would find in the more romantic-comedic areas of *Bogart Slept Here*?

De Niro was easy to deal with, however, and immediately started to immerse himself in the part. He began to think of how the character would dress, walk, carry himself, and who this man was inside, and he did all this much before he would think of how he related to the other characters in the film. He decided this young Broadway actor would wear one earring, so De Niro asked the propman to show him a few. The property man brought over a tray of earrings, followed by still another tray. He spent what seemed to be hours turning earrings over in his hand, holding them up to the light, trying them on one ear and looking at them in a mirror from every angle, as if this earring would tell us everything we wanted to know about this character. In my memory the entire day was spent with De Niro searching for the right earring. I saw that Mike was getting slightly impatient, but he was getting to know De Niro as well.

As I recall, there was very little rehearsal because I think Mike believed De Niro would be fresher before the cameras without it. I did not mind when De Niro sometimes strayed from my lines because what he paraphrased seemed just as good to me. I think Marsha was willing to go along with this sort of improvisational acting, but in the first few days of dailies, it was clear that any of the humor I had written was going to get lost. It's not that De Niro is not funny, but his humor comes mostly from his nuances, a bemused expression on his face or the way he would look at a character, smile and then look up at the ceiling.

The first scene they shot had De Niro's character coming home to tell his wife that he just got an offer to appear in his first film. Marsha's reaction was to be overjoyed, exuberant, wildly excited and happy for her talented husband's big break. De Niro, however, never told her the news as if he too was overjoyed with it. He seemed uncomfortable with happiness and good fortune. Instead, he told her the news matter-of-factly, introspectively, as though wondering if taking this job was the right thing to do. This reading, of course, made it difficult for Marsha to be overjoyed.

It was certainly not bad acting on De Niro's part because he's incapable of that. The moment did, in fact, seem very real, very honest, but if there was no joy in him, this first scene seemed confused. Why is a man who just got an offer he dreamed of all his life not excited about it? Mike said to me in confidence that he was worried. On the other hand, I was willing to compromise.

"Well, maybe it shouldn't be funny. Maybe it *should* be a more serious picture," I suggested.

Mike answered, "That's not what you wrote and it's not what I saw when I read this script. If there's no humor in the first half of the film, we're dead."

We went on this way for five days, and Marsha, try as she might to make her character and her scenes work, found it difficult to find solid footing for herself, since the picture seemed to be going in three or four different directions at one time, and none of them appeared to be right. After seven days of shooting, Mike asked two of Warner's top executives, John Calley and Frank Wells, to the screening room to view the results of the first week's filming. Calley and Wells were two of the smartest people I ever met in the film industry, and I certainly was willing to trust their opinion. Glum was their opinion, but these were two pretty cool guys. Instead of panicking, they treated the situation as a difficulty, but not as a life-and-death matter. It was a movie, and a movie, after all, is just a movie.

John smiled and said, "Well, we certainly have a problem, don't we?" No one admired Mike Nichols more than John Calley. "What do you want to do, Mike?" he said.

"Stop the picture," said Mike.

"Reshoot what we have?" asked Frank Wells calmly.

"Yes," said Mike. "But not with De Niro. He's a brilliant actor, but we've miscast it."

"Fire Robert De Niro?" John asked, knowing that this had never been done to De Niro before, nor apparently had there been any reason to before. Even when they asked my opinion, I considered it just a courtesy—my vote was not going to make any difference, and I really didn't know what my vote was.

The next day the picture was shut down and De Niro learned he was going to be replaced. He was, of course, livid, and luckily I was not in the room when he was told. It made headlines in *Variety* and in the major papers across the country, and no one could quite understand it. During the next few weeks Mike went about the business of trying to find a replacement for Robert De Niro, which in itself sounds like an oxymoron. No one was found. Eventually Mike took another film, De Niro went off to do something else that was no doubt brilliant, and Marsha and I were left with no movie and our dreams and hopes in Florence sadly dashed. The seven days on film was relegated to a small shelf in the Warner Brothers archives. I only met De Niro a few times in all the years that passed, but it was very hard to look him in the eye when I saw him again. If there's any consolation, a few years later I found two wonderful paintings in a gallery in New York, and I was so taken with them I bought them immediately and hung them in my home. The artist was Robert De Niro, Sr., Bobby's father.

Bogart Slept Here was not quite dead, however. There was always Ray Stark riding to the rescue. It was Ray's production company that was producing *Bogart*. He called and asked me to come to his office.

"Let's not give up on this," said Ray. "These two characters are wonderful and there's some really great writing in the script. We'll look and we'll find someone else." Someone else appeared a few days later. Richard Dreyfuss, fresh from *Jaws* and *Close Encounters,* expressed interest in doing the film. We decided to get together—Richard, Marsha and myself—and have them read the script aloud. As I listened to them, it was apparent they were wonderful together. Their chemistry was perfect. Marsha felt free to read the scenes the way she originally intended, and Richard's intelligence and quickness made it so easy to listen to. Although I realized they were right for each other, I thought the script was not right for them. It had to be funnier, more romantic, the way Marsha and I first imagined the picture would be. What I wanted to do was a prequel. In other words, instead of an off-Broadway actor, married with a child, why don't I start from the beginning? I'd start when they first meet. Not liking each other at first and then falling in love. I told them both to hang in while I rushed to the typewriter to write an entirely new script. As a tentative title, I put down *The Goodbye Girl.*

SETTLING IN
13

IN THE FIRST fourteen months in Los Angeles, I worked on three projects almost simultaneously: the script of the play *California Suite*, the new version of *The Goodbye Girl* movie, and another original screenplay that I had started while we were still living in New York, *Murder by Death*. I found that I now had more time to write each day than I did in New York, simply because I didn't have the stimulus and vitality of the city to otherwise occupy me. I missed the habit of walking along the New York streets, starting from my house on 62nd Street and taking a different route each day, something I did during the hour-and-a-half lunch break I took before tackling the afternoon rewrites of the pages I had completed that morning.

What I also missed were the chance meetings on the street in New York of a familiar face, very often four or five faces on the same day. With these people I'd exchange the small talk of life, the good news and the bad: the breakup of a twelve-year-old marriage you thought would last a lifetime; an affair between the most unlikely of people that made me aware of how easily shocked I could be; the sudden and serious illness of someone I hadn't seen in years and thought of calling that very day. Of course you can get all sorts of gossip in L.A. as well, but what's often discreet in New York is amazingly blatant in Los Angeles. Just walk into any Hollywood party and you will hear more than you want before you're handed a drink. By the time you start to juggle your first hot canapé, you've heard that the entire executive leadership of a major film company is about to be fired. I was always the last to hear these stories of thrones falling because I was never considered an insider in the film business—not then and not today. It was assumed I was mainly a playwright who only dabbled in films on occasion (the occasion happened about twenty-six times), and they always thought I was just visiting the Coast.

"Hi, Neil. What brings you out here?" was the standard greeting.

I never had a good answer for them because I never had one for myself. So I let the misconception linger that I was just visiting for all the years I lived here. I liked not losing my New York identity and my New York way of saying "wintuh" in February and "waituh" in restaurants. When I walked the streets of New York, cops in police cars would call out, "Hey, Neil. How you doin'?" with just enough of the sound of Little Italy or a hint of an Irish brogue passed on down through their family of patrolmen. It made New York seem like a small town to me. I knew where you could find a store on 62nd Street where they only sold buttons, or a luncheonette off 56th Street that had the best chocolate cake I ever tasted. In Los Angeles you would never just run into a friend on the street. The first year and a half I was there, walking the streets at ten in the morning in Beverly Hills for a dentist appointment, there was not a soul to be seen. I thought every day was either Sunday, the Fourth of July or one of the Jewish High Holidays.

CALIFORNIA SUITE opened on June 10, 1976, at the Ahmanson Theater in Los Angeles, almost a year to the day of our moving there. Or out *there* as I referred to it when I was away, or out *here* when I was talking to my Angelino friends who thought it was an unnecessary description of a place we were standing in. It's not that I wasn't happy in Los Angeles or that I didn't appreciate the virtues of a city whose temperature was wonderful to bearable for most of the year. What I was most afraid of was becoming *part* of it, the part I didn't understand, the part that was as foreign to me as Tibet. In many ways, I thought eleven months of sun was almost as bad as six months *without* it. I was not a palm tree. I was more of a small unidentifiable tree planted practically in the cement on the streets of New York, fighting for its life but always hanging in there. Still, I felt an ingrate because the critics and audiences who came to the Ahmanson accepted *California Suite* with open arms. It was rare in those days to have a play originate in Los Angeles. It was still considered the lucrative prize at the end of the tour of most big hits that came out of Broadway. L.A. audiences were used to seeing finished plays and musicals. I was wary of how they'd react to a play that was being viewed by the public for the first time, wondering why there seemed to be something incomplete about it.

What was incomplete was that normally one does a play for a year or so on Broadway before it appears in L.A. The kinks, therefore, already had been taken out, and the scenes rewritten before Los Angelinos got their first viewing. Thus, when you open first in L.A., the play is shown with our kinks still showing and our rewrites still waiting their turn. It's called "opening cold," and cold is the reception you can sometimes get with a play that is not quite ready. Miraculously, *California Suite* came together almost from the first rehearsal. What they saw in L.A., even in its raw state, was pretty close to what we opened with in New York. Despite my early fears, I originated my next seven plays at the Ahmanson. The critics became a little stingier with their passing grades, but all seven of those shows were hits in New York. The only drawback for some of us was that the Ahmanson Music Center was located a fair distance from Beverly Hills, where most of my friends lived. It was built much farther east, to harness the loyal audiences who lived in Pasadena and Glendale and made up a large bulk of the yearly subscription buyers. Thanks to them, when I opened a play there, I was always guaranteed a large audience. Their attendance could be counted on, while my own friends, those who worked in films or TV, showed up less frequently. "It's too far a drive," they would say. "We'll see it when it comes to New York." As I said, it's a strange place.

AS WE BEGAN to prepare for the production of *The Goodbye Girl,* now directed by Herbert Ross, it was clear that Richard Dreyfuss was going to be the driving force in the film. Richard was highly intelligent, a true actor and not a comedian, which only made him funnier, with a rich, clear voice that strangely had a New York accent despite the fact he was raised in

Southern California. He clipped off sentences as if each word were born afresh in his mind; there was virtually no hint his speech ever came out of a typewriter, especially mine. He is short, which made him empathetic, a little chubby at the time, which made him an unlikely leading romantic figure, and he had graying hair on his thirty-year-old head, and a scruffy beard which grew in any direction it chose to. He scratched it continuously throughout the shoot, making him look a little like Gabby Hayes, Roy Rogers's ancient, toothless sidekick in countless Westerns. He wore mostly recycled army clothes that appeared never to have been touched by a tailor. He also wore rimless eyeglasses which had trouble clinging to the bridge of his nose and had to be pushed back incessantly with his fingers. In short, he was a mess, and consequently turned out to be one of the sexiest leading men I ever wrote for, perhaps coming in a dead heat with Robert Redford.

Herbert Ross also decided not to glamorize Marsha. Playing Paula MacFadden, a thirty-three-year-old ex-dancer with a ten-year-old daughter, left holding an empty purse when she was jilted by her lover, Marsha was to appear flat broke—she and her wardrobe achieved it to perfection. Her clothes looked like they'd been purchased in a thrift shop. Herbert had her hair cut off close to the neckline. The less hair, the less need for expensive haircuts, thought the frugal Paula. With her fairly tight weathered jeans, Marsha looked like any other struggling mother you'd see coming home lugging two heavy shopping bags to her dull, small apartment in the declassé Upper West Side of New York. With all this going against her, I defied any healthy, heterosexual man from falling in love with her at first sight. If Richard was the driving force of the film, Marsha was the backbone. Marsha's intelligence matched Richard's and she was quite able to handle this fast-talking actor from Chicago. *The Goodbye Girl* had something going for it not often found in a funny, romantic comedy in the 1970s: sheer authenticity. There wasn't a trace of Hollywood up on the screen either in the design or in the performances.

There was one last role to be cast, that of Marsha's ten-year-old daughter, Lucy. Every agent submitted every aspiring actress from eight to twelve years old, plus sneaking in an occasional sixteen-year-old who was short and who had a high-pitched voice. There are at any given time more aspiring child actresses in Hollywood than there are cars on the freeways, and more often than not, it is the parents who are more aspiring than the child. "We have an audition at MGM today," a mother would tell anyone within earshot, never leaving out the "we," since Mama often dreamed that her own failed attempts at a film career would be fulfilled vicariously if baby got the part. Sometimes the father would come to the audition as well, making you wonder what he did for a living, and hoping that it wasn't being the child's business agent and self-appointed manager.

Betting on a ten-year-old to be the family's breadwinner is more than any preadolescent girl should have to bear. At the audition, many of the children gave you all the smiles and personality their fragile little frames could muster—or that our patience could bear—and their line readings sounded very much as if the words had been driven into their heads with spikes the night before. Some of these kids, of course, were talented, and some may even have been the ones—rather than their parents—who had the overwhelming desire to "get into movies."

But then there were the kids who didn't care if they missed the audition, and cared even less if they got the part. Invariably, they were looser, more relaxed; for them, going to an audition was simply a great way of getting out of school for that day. When one of them walked in, you couldn't help but sit up and pay attention. It was someone in this category who walked into Herbert Ross's office one morning, amazingly the first face on a huge pile of photographs and résumés on Herbert's desk. Her name was Quinn Cummings, she was ten years old, she was neither pretty nor unattractive, and she didn't seem to care which way we saw her. She was neither impolite nor blasé, but she also made no effort to charm us. There was, however, an intelligence in her eyes. And she laughed loudly when we said something funny, and squirmed a little when we talked down to her, as adults have a way of doing. When Herbert finally asked her if she was now ready to read for us, she said, "Sure" in a way that meant "if you've seen enough of me, that's okay too."

The reading was perfect. She was smart, slightly brash and loving toward her mother, but forthright in dealing with Mom's predilection for getting into trouble with men, mostly actors. In the script, when she learns that Paula's live-in, deadbeat lover has dumped them without a cent or a place to live, she says, "What a shitheel," and then flashes a lightning-quick look at her mother with an apology for overstepping her bounds. Herbert and I were entranced by her, since she was funny, quick and human. When Quinn left the office, I turned to Herbert and said, "That's her. That's Lucy."

Herbert nodded reluctantly, "I know, but you can't take the first one who walks in here."

"Why not?" I asked. "She's perfect."

"Because someone could walk in here who's better," he answered.

"That's not possible," I argued. "If she's perfect, how can someone be better than perfect?"

Directors usually prevail because it's in their personality and in their contracts, so we saw forty to fifty girls during the next four days. After the last one left his office, he turned to me and said, "I like the Quinn Cummings girl."

"No kidding?" I said wearily. We signed her the next day. Quinn turned out to be a highly intelligent, sweet young lady, and her mother, happily, was not a stereotypical stage mother, and was very careful of Quinn's well-being. Three weeks before shooting was to start, Quinn's father died. We felt her and her mother's loss would turn into our loss as well, but they talked it over and decided that Quinn would still do the film. Together with Richard and Marsha, I now had my first Odd Trio.

GRINDING IT OUT
14

IT NEVER OCCURRED to me at the time to count up the years passing and the pages written, but by 1976 I had written fifteen plays and ten films. I had done all that in fourteen years, with no sign of slowing down. Why so much, so fast, so relentlessly? I didn't ask myself the question then, but I do now, now when I've reached my thirtieth play and twenty-fifth or twenty-sixth film. As you can see, I don't really keep score with the films. I can place where I was and what was happening in my life during each play I wrote, but the making of a film is a different experience. Very often I left the film in the hands of the director and had minimal involvement afterward, but with the play, I was there almost every day, rewriting in the rehearsal room while the actors were busy going through a scene, wondering what I was scribbling so incessantly. A play was my lifeblood; a film was my craft.

Each new play was like the beginning of a new life for me. In each new production, I met two new sets of interesting people—the actors, and the characters they played. It was possible for me to like one and not the other. If I didn't like the actor, I would have to decide if I could live with him or her. Very often, the director, producer and myself would fire an actor. I was the only one who fired a character. I would watch rehearsals and suddenly think, that character is extraneous, he doesn't push the play forward. And I would cross him out of my script. Unfortunately the actor who played him had to leave as well, even though he may have played the character faultlessly. I knew the actor was terribly disappointed, but I never knew how the character felt. Sometimes I would envision him going around to producers' offices looking for a job.

"Hi. My name is Ned Morton. I'm twenty-eight years old, and as you can see from the way I'm dressed, the year I'm living in is about 1938 or '39. Even though I'm the black sheep in the family, I'm very funny and I have these terrific lines that that Neil Simon guy isn't using anymore. If you are doing a period play, I could fit in very nicely and I think there's a lot of really good actors out there who would love to play me." So much for abstractive meditations.

Any life other than playwrighting would have been hell for me. Working in another field, spending forty years with some company, would be a lifetime jail sentence. The writing of thirty plays in thirty-six years has been liberating. I had no boss. I had no hours. There was no one place of work I would have to travel to and from, no co-workers I would have to see year after year and at the annual Christmas party, all wondering when we'd be laid off or forced to retire. I have never found it to be a lonely profession despite the fact that I speak to no one for the better part of seven hours a day. I either have a pen in my hand or a thought in my head, and both completely fill all those hours spent looking into a notebook or staring out a window, all the while never noticing that there might be something of interest out there for me to see. If anything gets my attention at all, it's the weather. I love looking at rain, pelting across the windowpane, or at snow, swirling around in the wind or falling gently on the street below. In New York especially, I'd put down the notebook and pen or hold the thought in my head, cross to the window to watch the snow pile up on the streets. As I stated earlier, I wrote more in California because I was never compelled to look out the window to see the sun. Sunlight seems so inactive, and interests me only when it comes or goes. A heavy storm, though, blowing and bending the trees, always seems to be moving, causing problems and discomfort in people's lives. Nature's conflict is as interesting to me as the conflict I give to the characters in my plays, and sunny day after sunny day is sorely lacking in excitement.

That still doesn't answer the question of what was driving me to start a new play on the day after I finished writing the previous one. One possibility was that I thought my work was a greater representation of who I was than was the person I became when I *didn't* write. Whatever I may have had on my mind, I felt more secure putting it on paper and letting that character speak for me, than in expressing it to someone as myself. In the early 1980s, I was still some years away from developing a personality that I was comfortable with. I often felt like a boxer heading toward the ring, surrounded by his coterie of bodyguards and trainers. The more success you had, the less you needed to say; others said it for you. My work served as my bodyguards and trainers, and if I surrounded myself with enough plays, I felt safe, immune from scrutiny. I knew I had matured intellectually, but something was keeping me from playing out that role in my personal life. For one thing, I truly didn't know where the plays came from, where the ability to put these thoughts on the page, shaping them and forming them with clarity and intelligence started. Because of this insecurity, I felt I was not yet ready to sit down and handle a good conversation with Arthur Miller or Tom Stoppard without embarrassing myself. Maybe one more play would put me over the top, I thought; after one more hit, Arthur and Tom and I would become lunch buddies, with me dominating most of the conversation. Being alone in a room from nine to five was a wonderful way to keep me from being discovered as simply an average man who just happened to get lucky almost every time he picked up a pen and put it to paper. So often I thought that in choosing me the gods picked the wrong man to work in the same field as Shaw and Ibsen and Kaufman and Hart. They were giants; I was not. The irony is, I never felt inferior while in the act of writing. On the contrary, in my little room, and even while in the theater, I felt secure, strong and as capable as most of my peers. It was this living-in-the-world business that I was daunted by. I probably had at least as many commercial successes as either Truman Capote or Gore Vidal, yet I cowered at the thought of meeting them personally. But meet them I did. Gore Vidal called me Doc when he showed me and Joan around his beautiful house in Rome, and I felt fortunate that he was such a wonderful wit and conversationalist that he did almost all of the talking and I nodded and laughed in the appropriate places. I learned the art of becoming a good listener, which sometimes won me such accolades as, "He's so humble for a man so witty. So quiet that I couldn't help wonder what interesting thoughts were going on inside that head of his." I met Truman Capote on a number of occasions, and even if I *did* want to state my opinions, it would be late into the night before Truman would yield the floor. And then, in one of those really odd twists, I actually *wrote* for Truman Capote. He played a part in the film *Murder by Death,* and since this was a game played on my home court, it was Truman who was nervous and ill at ease. I quickly and effortlessly wrote him a new line for one he was having trouble with. He read it, looked up and said, "Perfect. Thank you, Neil. I feel much more comfortable with this."

As time passed, I felt myself easing into the public light, looking less to hide in the shadows. Do enough TV interviews; give a few talks at Columbia University, Harvard; deliver a forty-five-minute speech at Williams College (for my daughter Nancy's commencement, with an honorary doctorate thrown in for me); participate in a three-hour informal chat at the NYU Film School; make ten appearances on the Johnny Carson show—and if you're not talking by then, check your parents to see if you were born in a foreign country, because it's possible that English is not your language.

I knew I really had gotten over my jitters when I accepted the most unlikely invitation: as guest star on a Bob Hope special for NBC. Why me? He knew I wasn't a performer and I knew for certain this was not going to be an interview. I'd never seen a writer as a guest on the Hope show (unless, of course, she was twenty-one and the current Miss America), and even though I suspected I probably would be asked to do only a walk-on line or less, I couldn't imagine why I accepted the invitation in the first place. The head writer called me and told me not to worry—he'd send me a script in a few days. To my utter surprise and shock, I discovered that the entire show was devoted to Hope and his two guests, Lucille Ball and Neil Simon. Surely they made a mistake. They probably thought I was *Paul* Simon and was coming on to sing, "Me and Julio Down by the School-yard." Or perhaps they thought I was Neil *Diamond* coming out to sing, "You Don't Bring Me Flowers."

A chauffeured limo drove me out to the Burbank Studios while I looked over the script they had written for me. I never had cared much for actors who wanted to rewrite my lines, and now I found I didn't care much for writers who wanted to write what I should be saying. I wanted out of this desperately, so much so that I was prepared to give the driver all my money to drive me to Canada. I don't mean all my money I had *on* me. I mean *all my money*. Why did I say yes to this? I thought. I'm not an actor. I'm not a comic. And I had just recently learned to talk. Maybe they thought I was Neil *Armstrong* and they were going to do a sketch where Hope and Lucille Ball were astronauts. But it said Neil Simon on the script . . . and the script wasn't all that funny. Now I suddenly was being picky. I didn't want to be on the show, but if I had to, then I wanted to be a hit. Maybe NBC would say, "Hey, he's good. Let's give him his own show."

I thought again of Hope and Lucille Ball—didn't they care that a less-than-an-amateur was on the show with them? I guess not. They could take care of themselves. They were pros. They could ad-lib their way through anything. They had timing. They had experience. They were stars. I was a playwright. Maybe I could just go out on the stage, sit at a typewriter and write something. It wouldn't be funny, but it could work if we turned it into a documentary of some kind. Like a boring kind.

The limousine arrived at the studio, and against my better judgment, I got out. I was sent to the makeup room and sat in the chair. The makeup lady asked who I was.

"Neil Simon. I'm a guest on the show," I replied.

"What show?" she asked.

"The Bob Hope show?" I answered as a question because I didn't believe it any more than she did. She just shrugged and slapped powder on my face.

They finally put me in a dressing room, which was unnecessary since I was going to be wearing my own clothes. In the room was a large gift basket with my name on it, and inside was fruit, candies and a bottle of vodka, all heavily wrapped with clear plastic. I didn't have the strength to break the plastic and get at that much needed vodka. With time on my hands before I met Hope, I did the one thing in this life I knew how to do. I rewrote. I rewrote all my lines so that it at least sounded like me, not that anyone in the audience would know what I sounded like. A writer came in and said, "Hi, Neil, Bob's ready to see you in his dressing room." We walked down the hallway together. Dead Man Walking would sum up how I felt about taking that long walk. The writer asked how I liked the script. I told him I loved it, but had just made a few small changes if he didn't mind. He didn't mind. He said Hope always changed everything he wrote. The door opened and I entered Bob Hope's dressing room where every-thing in *his* gift basket was opened and used. He smiled and called me kid. He called everyone kid. He even called Lucille Ball kid.

He said, "This'll be a snap. The boys really came up with some funny stuff. Why don't we just go over it a few times? When we're out there, don't get nervous if I don't look at you much. I'm reading everything off the cue cards."

I took my life in my hands and said, "Bob, if it's all right with you, I rewrote my lines a little, but they still fit yours. You don't have to change a thing." He didn't bat an eye. We read the script but with my substituted lines. He nodded, smiled and said, "Great. No problem. If I ad-lib, just go along with me." And that's what happened on the show, if I remember cor-rectly. Actually I have no memory of doing the show and perhaps this whole thing was a dream that I told my analyst a few weeks later. But I do remember getting laughs. Big laughs. That was real. If you're in front of an audience and you get laughs, you never forget it the rest of your life. I was chauffeured home and on the way gave the driver all my money. I have never once watched the tape of the show. Some experiences are best left to not dwell on. NBC never called about my getting my own show. I thought my best move was to return to playwrighting. My only regret was that I forgot to take my gift basket home.

SO I COULD NOW TALK, but I still had not solved the mystery of where the plays come from; sometimes I had doubts that I wrote them at all. I know I didn't write *Lost in Yonkers*. It didn't come from me. I saw the play a num-ber of times and there's no chance that I'm the author. Yet I remember each day as I sat at my desk, the words and pages flowing from my pen, the emotions of the characters taking over all my senses, so I must assume that I was the one who wrote *Lost in Yonkers*. Recently, at a tribute in my honor, I watched as scenes from various plays I had written were performed.

When they got to *Lost in Yonkers,* I listened in awe at the power of the words, and silently I said to myself, "God, I wish I could write like that." No one said you had to be sane to be a playwright.

IF I HAD any regrets, it would be that I always wondered what it would have been like if I had been born ten or twelve years sooner, and been around to write films for the great stars in the Hollywood of the 1940s and 1950s: Humphrey Bogart, Cary Grant, Rosalind Russell, James Cagney, Jean Arthur, Henry Fonda and James Stewart. I never had that opportunity, but I was fortunate enough to meet James Stewart a few times, and I actually got to know Henry Fonda and Cary Grant. It wasn't hard to meet Henry Fonda, since his house was directly across the street from ours in Bel Air. He lived there with his wife, Shirlee, and Hank, as most people called him, often came over to our house to give Marsha pointers with our gardening. He had a green thumb and I thought maybe he had this avid desire to grow things because he and his family had been blown out of the dust bowl of Oklahoma in *The Grapes of Wrath.* Oddly enough, Henry and Shirlee lived directly across from us in New York as well, when a few years later Marsha and I bought an apartment on 57th Street and Park Avenue. I guess while my plants were growing in California, my roots were still in New York.

I met Cary Grant for the first time at a dinner party at the house of Robert Evans, who was then the head of production at Paramount. Bob Evans introduced us: "Cary, Neil Simon. Neil, Cary Grant."

Grant smiled his perfect smile, put out his hand, shook mine and said in that slight cockney accent, "Hello, Doc, how are you? Good to see you. Loved *The Odd Couple.* Maybe we'll do something one day," and then he was off to kiss Barbra Streisand on the cheek. I met him again, usually at other parties, but the best time of all was when I boarded a plane for London and discovered that Cary Grant was in the seat just behind me. Make that the *two* seats behind me, because whenever he flew to London, he reserved the last two seats in first class in order to stretch out and sleep during the night flight over. It was said that the secret to his constant good looks was his ability to sleep ten to twelve hours a day and/or night. If I did that, it would be the secret to my red puffy eyes and my inability to straighten my back from sleeping that long. He was on his way to Brighton (could have been Bristol) to visit his aging "Mum," as he called her. "Where's that screenplay, Doc?" he asked me, as if all he had on his mind the past year was the screenplay I was going to write for him. But who knows? If I had written it, he might have done it. We chatted for a while; then he said good night, stretched out (if you can do that on two seats) and slept like a baby until we were a half hour out of London. He woke up looking better than when he went to sleep. I said goodbye to him as we were about to land at Heathrow Airport.

"Nonsense," he said. "Come with me. I'll get you right through customs, won't have to wait a minute." An entourage of representatives of the airline were there to greet him, and sure enough he ushered me right through customs and introduced me by saying, "This is my dear friend, Doc Simon. He's writing a screenplay for me. Take good care of him." Then he was whisked away in a Bentley limo to see Mum in Brighton or Bristol. The chief of customs turned to me and said, "Right this way, Dr. Simon. Pleasure to meet you. Don't meet many in the medical profession who write films as well." I nodded in agreement because I knew it would get me through customs much quicker.

MURDER, HE WROTE
15

THE GOODBYE GIRL was cast and ready to go, but we had to wait until Herbert Ross finished shooting *The Turning Point,* a film he was making with Shirley MacLaine and Anne Bancroft. In the interim, Ray Stark and Columbia Pictures put *Murder by Death* into production. During that time, Marsha and I began to socialize, and eventually we met, through Ray Stark and his dinner parties, most of the people who ran Hollywood and many of the stars that dazzled us almost as much as Ray's incredible art and sculpture collection. If Maillol, Giacometti and Henry Moore statues stood coolly and silently in his magnificent garden, Warren Beatty, Barbra Streisand, a young Goldie Hawn and directors like Sydney Pollack and Billy Wilder made his dining table sparkle. Years before, when I wrote *Plaza Suite,* one of the one-act plays was about a Hollywood producer who bought Humphrey Bogart's home after his death. I had no one in mind when I wrote the piece, since I never knew where Bogart's home was and what happened to it. Little did I realize as I sat in Ray Stark's luxurious house that Bogart had lived here with his wife Lauren Bacall, and their children. It took on a new meaning to me since Bogart was, and is to this day, the actor I most admired—not necessarily for his skill as an actor, although he was one of the best, but because of his charismatic quality on the screen. In roles like Sam Spade in *The Maltese Falcon* or Rick Blaine in *Casablanca,* he had portrayed the quintessential loner. I admired that quality in someone, the man who couldn't be bought and who went his own way. If there was anyone else who had that quality in the years I was growing up, it would have been Joe DiMaggio and Ernest Hemingway, although Hemingway needed an entourage around him to help him stand out as a loner. One would also have to add Albert Camus to that illustrious group of brooders. Although I never thought I was charismatic, I fancied myself a loner, but only in terms of my work. As a boy, I affected that pose, fashioning myself after my heroes; later, as success came my way, it became less of a pose as the loner actually became more and more a part of my personality. Years later when I briefly signed with the Creative Artists Agency to represent me in films, I first met its now famous ex–corporate leader Mike Ovitz. As we were introduced, he put his hand out to me and said, "Oh, sure. The man who says no to everything." I treated that remark as a compliment.

After dinner at Ray's house, I wanted to see the room where Bogart died, the little dumbwaiter in which Bogart painfully curled himself up when he needed to be lowered to the floor below, during the last months of his life in his slow death from lung cancer. The house was now completely redone and redesigned, and was the in place to be invited by Ray and his lovely wife, Fran, who reigned over these soirees. Following dinner, there was *always* a new film to be seen in the living room, even when a guest like President Reagan was present, while Secret Service men in helicopters hovered noisily above us (needless to say, the sound drowned out the dialogue of the film we were watching). A very large Picasso hung on the rear wall, and the painting was raised electrically to make room for the projectionist to show that night's film. Writer Arthur Laurents used a Picasso painting in the same position and for the same purpose in his film *The Way We Were*. In that film, the FBI planted a bug on the back of the canvas in an effort to smoke out any would-be Communists, and as the painting rose, the bug ripped a hole from top to bottom of the Picasso. A Communist was the last thing anyone would call Ray Stark.

If Ray sensed boredom with the film among the fourteen or so guests, he would simply press a button and say "Next," and the film disappeared from the screen, even if we were only fifteen or twenty minutes in. In its place would appear an entirely new film. If that film didn't win favor with those who remained, you'd hear a few whispered good nights and thank-yous as famed guests tiptoed out to their cars. Marsha and I almost always stayed because we did not consider ourselves important enough to be blasé.

Ray Stark was one of the few people in Hollywood I almost never said no to, not because of the enormous power he held in the community, but because I learned a little of everything from him. We had a symbiotic relationship, we made each other laugh, he taught me how to find the fun in life when I somehow let my moods sink low, and despite the fearsome clout he had in that town, I always saw more boy in him than man-eater. I called him for advice on everything and he had the name of a doctor for every ailment, not to mention a lawyer, a plumber, a personal trainer, a restaurant, an acupuncturist, a museum, a chiropractor and even a dog breeder.

He had about five large Labrador retrievers roaming freely through his house except during meals and Marsha and I fell in love with his dogs. Ray immediately arranged for us to buy a puppy from the breeder in Idaho. Marsha, Nancy, Ellen and I drove out to the airport one night and waited for this mid-sized cage to be removed from the plane. Out came the most beautiful whitish yellow Labrador puppy I'd ever seen. We called him Duffy and he lived out his entire life with us. Ray not only made Los Angeles bearable for me, but he taught me how to find the joys of life in places I never thought of looking. Ray had everything he could possibly want in the world but he always said to me that he envied me because I was creative and he wasn't. But creation needs to be nurtured by those who hold the creation and the creator in esteem, because I'm an authority on how quickly confidence, with no one to bolster it, can disappear on a daily basis.

MURDER BY DEATH was a spoof on every all-star murder mystery in an English mansion that I had seen and loved as a boy, the best one being the film of Agatha Christie's *And Then There Were None*. My story was simple and motivated by my own frustration of never being able to guess the murderer when I read a mystery novel. Figuring out who did it was much easier when the story was done as a film because inevitably the director would give away something or the actors tipped their hand by acting much too innocently. The authors of books were much more cunning and at times even cheated by withholding information you needed to be able to solve the crime until five pages from the end. "I DIDN'T KNOW THAT," I would yell after three hundred and twelve pages, and I'd fling the paperback against the wall.

My story was about a multimillionaire eccentric amateur detective who sets out to put the five greatest detectives in the world to shame. He invites them all for a weekend, with their wives or guest of choice, to his gloomy mansion in some even gloomier forest. The detectives in my movie were all famous because they were all fictional: Sam Spade, Nick and Nora Charles of *The Thin Man* series, Charlie Chan and his Number One Son, Hercule Poirot and Miss Marple, both Agatha Christie creations. Besides dinner, their host had arranged for an actual murder to take place, and in addition to dessert, there was to be a prize of one million dollars tax free to the sleuth who solved the crime.

On the first day of rehearsal, the actors filed in slowly at ten A.M. and I kept blinking my eyes in wonderment at the incredible cast Ray had assembled for me: Alec Guinness, David Niven, Maggie Smith, Peter Sellers, Peter Falk, Eileen Brennan, Nancy Walker, James Coco and Elsa Lanchester. Alec Guinness was to play a blind butler, and he came from England fully prepared with his own props, having already worked out his walk, his feeling the ground with his cane and making his pupils all but disappear. The comedy I wrote was broad and I feared Sir Alec might want to soften it. But he fell in quickly and he seemed to love doing the scenes although I rarely saw him smile. Perhaps he felt secure because of the next picture he was to make directly after ours—something called *Star Wars,* he said. He was quite marvelous in one scene where he is on the upper landing, leading Dick and Dora Charles (David Niven and Maggie Smith) to their rooms. Alec had the first line.

BENSON

Not many people come to the manor these
days. It's nice to hear guests again.

DORA

Oh, thank you, er . . .

BENSON

Benson, mum.

DORA

Thank you, Benson.

BENSON

No. That's Bensonmum. Jamessir
Bensonmum.

DICK

Jamessir?

BENSON

Yes, sir.

DICK

Jamessir Bensonmum?

BENSON

Yes, sir.

DICK

How odd.

BENSON

My father's name, sir.

DICK

What was your father's name?

BENSON

How-ard. Howard Bensonmum.

DICK
Jamessir, are you saying your father's name
was How-ard Bensonmum . . . ?

DORA
Leave it be, Dickie. I've had enough.

The only mistake Ray Stark made was casting Truman Capote as the slightly deranged host of the manor. He certainly didn't do it for Truman's acting ability, since it was nonexistent. Ray made no bones about wanting Truman in the picture for the sheer publicity value that Truman Capote attracted everywhere. I was more pragmatic. If I owned the New York Yankees, I wouldn't want Tom Cruise for my second baseman no matter how many tickets his fans bought; therefore, although I didn't own Columbia Pictures, I wouldn't want Truman Capote—who couldn't blink his eyes on cue—in a pivotal role in the film.

Actually, the man Ray and I both first wanted but couldn't get was Orson Welles. We had given it a good try, though. Weeks before the film was to start, my phone rang at home. I picked it up. On the other end I heard one of the most famous voices in the world.

"Is this Neil? Orson Welles here."

"Orson Welles?" I said in a voice that cracked just about the way it did when I reached puberty. I thought it was a gag but there was no mistaking this voice.

"I read your script, Neil. Absolutely loved it. I'd give anything to play the role but unfortunately I'm committed to do some classic for no money in Italy, which is why they treat me like a king over there."

I was astonished that he was actually calling to apologize for not being able to do my film.

"Oh, Orson," I said, pretending to be worthy of his call. "I understand completely. How wonderful of you to phone yourself. I'm honored."

"Who is playing the role anyway?" asked Mr. Welles.

"Truman Capote."

It was quiet for a moment. I thought he hung up.

"Excuse me. It's difficult drinking wine and thinking about Truman Capote acting at the same time. He's actually going to play Charlie Chan?"

"No, no," I said. "Peter Sellers is playing Chan. Truman is the host of the party."

"Oh, well, that makes sense but not much. It was the Chan role I wanted to play. Peter will be simply marvelous doing that. Truman will make a fool of himself but he does that splendidly anyway so he may just turn out fine. I wish you luck, Neil. Maybe we'll do something together one day. Goodbye."

He hung up just as Marsha walked into the room.

"I just spoke to Orson Welles. He called me. Orson Welles."

"Really?" said the impressed Marsha. "What did he want?"

"To tell me he couldn't do *Murder by Death*. But that he'd like to do something else with me one day. So far I've got Orson Welles and Cary Grant who want to do something else some day."

With those two actors I had a five million dollar check in my hand—one that I knew I could never cash. "Some day" is NO day, but I was still feeling like the most important writer in Hollywood, even though I suspected Orson Welles turned down the role to Ray Stark and Ray in turn asked Orson to call me because "Neil is your biggest fan." Ray had his way of making me feel important, and he never did it in small measures.

ALEC GUINNESS is a regal man. To me he was almost unapproachable, not because of any coolness on his part, but simply because of his bearing, his poise, his presence and the enormous respect I have for him as an actor. While Peter Sellers would clown on the set, while David Niven had wit, style, humor and a propensity to giggle on the set, telling us that he was only outgiggled by Sir Laurence Olivier, while Maggie Smith could be as droll as Noël Coward without ever using his dialogue, Alec Guinness seemed to be quietly introspective, and if he did say something amusing, you had to be on your toes to catch it. It sounded more like information than humor. We did chat between scenes, but not often, and when I asked him about the *Star Wars* script that was always protruding from the pocket of his canvas chair, he would say succinctly, "Futuristic, actually. Rather clever. We'll see."

Peter Sellers, on the other hand, usually had me in hysterics, especially when he continued to play Charlie Chan off camera either as gay, Jewish or as the Queen. One day he was late to shoot his next scene. He was soon found in his trailer reading *Variety*. When summoned by the assistant director, Peter said, "Tell them Mr. Sellers won't be filming today," and went back to his reading while reclining on a banquette.

Robert Moore, the director, who had already done two of my plays, *Promises, Promises* and *The Gingerbread Lady,* made his way quickly to Peter's trailer. "Peter, I hear you're not filming today," he said calmly.

"Ah, good. Then you got the news," said Peter, turning the pages of his paper.

"May I ask why not?" Robert asked diplomatically.

"It's this fucking article they've written about me in this paper. It's filled with fucking lies and I will not be on the set until they retract it."

Robert grabbed the paper, read it quickly just to show Peter he was interested, then said, "You're right, Peter. They should retract that. And I'll ask the publicity people to get on it right now. The thing is, even if they retract it, it couldn't be in the paper until tomorrow."

"When it's in the paper, I'll be on the set," said Peter, who was in costume and full makeup.

"What if we called them and they said on the phone they'd retract it?" Bob offered, grasping at straws.

"Well, they'd have to phone all the readers of this tripe and I'd have to listen in on all the phone calls," said Peter as if he were making sense.

"Right," said Bob, who left the trailer at this point, deciding to leave this problem to Ray Stark. He went back to the set to shoot the next scene without Peter.

Ray was outraged when he got the news, but he knew that screaming at Peter Sellers would get him nowhere. Instead he went to Peter's trailer and they had a quiet talk, the contents of which none of us ever heard. An hour later Peter was on the set, ready to shoot. Later that day, Ray sent a mock-up of *Variety,* and on the front page in large letters it said, *"Variety*

Retracts Its Fucking Mistake." Peter appreciated the joke, or, as is entirely possible, thought that *Variety* actually put out an early edition to satisfy the disgruntled actor.

Whenever Peter Falk was missing from the set, everyone knew that he could be found walking around the lot learning his lines. "I can't learn my lines without walking," said Peter.

One morning Ray sent a treadmill to the set with a ribbon saying, "Here. Now we know where you're walking."

ONE NIGHT, about two weeks into the filming, I received a phone call at home that was so shocking, I didn't quite know how to handle it. It was from Alec Guinness, with whom I still hadn't had more than three brief conversations.

"Hope I'm not interrupting anything, Neil. If you're busy, I could call back," he said almost timidly. I had never seen or heard this side of him, and having him call me at home surely meant something important was up.

"No, no," I said. "I'm not doing a thing. Is anything wrong?"

"Wrong? Oh, dear, no. Things are going quite well, aren't they?"

"Yes," I said quickly. "I'm really happy. I think you're really amazing in the film, Alec."

"Oh, you're very kind. Good fun. Nice change of pace for me," he said, although I knew he hadn't gotten to his point as yet. "I was just thinking . . . ," he added, but then trailed off into nowhere.

"Is it the script, Alec? Because if there's anything you don't like, I'd be more than glad to rewrite it."

"The script? Oh, dear, no. Very happy with the script . . . No, no, it's er . . . well, to tell the truth, I'm all alone out here, you know."

"No, I didn't." He suddenly sounded lonely. Was that it? Did he want to socialize, have dinner with me? Since we hardly spoke before, why me? Why not his fellow Englishmen? Peter, David, Maggie? Still I pursued it. "Would you like to have dinner one night, Alec? I know my wife, Marsha, would love to meet you."

"Dinner? Oh, yes, dinner would be fine. I'd love to meet Martha. Very nice of you to ask . . . but you see, my wife doesn't get in until next week.

And as I said, I'm quite alone here . . . By myself, I mean . . . You do understand, I hope."

"Oh, yes. Yes, of course." I still didn't know what he was getting at and why it was taking so long.

He continued, practically stammering.

"The thing is, I er . . . I feel very awkward asking this."

"No, please. Tell me what I can do for you, Alec."

He blurted it out. "Would you know where I could get a tart?"

A tart? Did he mean a small dessert? The English eat tarts, don't they? And then I realized—he was asking for a woman. A tart. A hooker. A prostitute. Alec Guinness calling me asking for a hooker—I couldn't believe it. And why me, of all people? And where would I find one? Drive downtown to Santa Monica Boulevard, pull my car over to the curb and ask some six-foot-two woman in a blond wig if she'd like to spend an hour with Alec Guinness? I realized I had not answered him yet, so I started my mouth moving again.

"A tart?" I asked. "A woman, you mean . . . Well, gee. Gosh, I don't know . . . The thing is, I really haven't been living out here all that long . . . It's not exactly what I would know how to do best, Alec, you know?"

"No tart, heh?" he said rather disappointedly. "She could be an older woman, I really wouldn't mind . . ." and with that I heard a break in his voice. At first I thought he was crying, but then I realized he was giggling.

"Are you really serious?" I finally asked.

"No. I'm Peter," he answered, now fully hysterical. It was Peter Sellers doing an absolutely perfect imitation of Alec Guinness, down to the slightest inflection.

"PETER," I screamed. "You bastard . . . Why me?"

He then told me that he first did it to Ray Stark. Ray laughed so hard, he told Peter to call David Niven, Peter Falk, me and for all I know, Maggie Smith as well, but Maggie would have spotted the imitation in a second. I don't know if Alec Guinness ever heard of the prank and I was grateful to see his charming wife turn up on the set the next day. Then one day in the commissary, we were all eating lunch together and I noticed on the menu that among the desserts they listed were tarts. I was afraid to look into anyone's eyes as I put my head down and skipped dessert for that day.

THE DREAM YEAR
16

MURDER BY DEATH was a moderate success for Columbia, making a nice profit and providing a memorable experience for me. In today's world, however, the studios are not looking for moderate successes. Since so few hits come out of the studios today, they need at least one, hopefully two mega-hits that will bring in enough bucks to balance their losses on the failures and give them something to crow about in the trade papers and to the conglomerates who own the studios. The big surprise is what happened to *The Goodbye Girl.* It had only one real star, Richard Dreyfuss; one rising star, Marsha Mason; and one cute ten-year-old, Quinn Cummings, with a slight love story directed extremely well by Herbert Ross and a rather nice script by me, if I have to say so myself. Having said that, no one expected any miracles from this film and it probably wouldn't have been made were it not for Ray Stark's faith in it. Since Warner Brothers owned the underlying rights to *Bogart Slept Here,* which then became *The Goodbye Girl,* Warners had the option of staying or dropping out of the project. Since the head of Warner Brothers at the time had little faith in my script, he wanted MGM to buy him out. Others at Warners figured, however, in for a penny, in for a pound, and so decided to split the costs and profits (if any) with MGM, then run by Daniel Melnick.

The making of the film gave rise to very few problems thanks to the wonderful chemistry between Richard and Marsha, and best of all, I got to see Marsha every day on the set. A lot of free ones, you could say. We all collaborated on the film, much as if it were a play (the stars, director and writer all came from the theater), all with the blessing of Ray Stark. During the shooting, if I felt a line or even a word was needed, I'd just call it out. When Elliot (Richard) confronts Paula (Marsha) about keeping herself and her daughter out of his way in his newly acquired apartment which he has agreed to share with his two new tenants, he warns her that he likes to walk around the house at night without pajamas, which he doesn't own in the first place. I called out to Richard, "buffo!" Richard, without blinking an eye, said the speech again and threw in "buffo" at the end of the sentence, putting, as we say, a button on it. Marsha and Richard were a perfect match and you could practically see the sparks between them lighting up the screen.

On the day I was to see the first cut of the movie, I was being interviewed by a bright young journalist who kept talking to me all the way from my office to the screening room. As he turned to say goodbye, I decided I wanted another opinion and asked him to come in and view the picture with me, with the proviso that he would not write a word about the film, which was still in its early state. He agreed, surprised and delighted with the invitation. I could have had my head removed for doing that. I'm not always very objective the first time I see a project and although I liked what I saw on the screen, it seemed so effortless to me that I wasn't sure if an audience would think it was enough. "It seems pretty good to me," I said to the writer as the lights went up. "What did you think?"

"Pretty good?" he repeated, questioning my indecision. "It's absolutely wonderful. I don't think you realize what you've got here. I'm talking major hit."

I felt I was being buttered up for another favor.

Marsha and I did a long press tour and I loved sharing the stage of a TV show with her. We bantered well together, we knew each other's timing, enjoyed each other's stories, and if I surprised her with a funny line, there was not a better laugher in the world. Magazines started to write about us as one of Hollywood's happiest couples. I thought we were too. *People* magazine ran a Valentine's Day issue in which they listed the ten most romantic couples of all time, from Napoleon and Josephine and on.

Marsha and I were on the list. High on the list, I might add. Things were going so smoothly for us that the only thing that could dim our spirits was if the picture didn't make it. It opened all around the country the week before Christmas.

The reviews everywhere were mostly wonderful. They raved about all three actors. It would have been a good time to go out and celebrate except for one thing. It didn't do much business. Many of the theater owners talked about moving it out after one week and replacing it with a film with more star power than we had. Columbia and Ray Stark campaigned hard, both in newspaper ads and with the theater owners, pointing to the great reviews. The theater owners pointed to the empty seats. Sometimes you just need to allow a little time for the word of mouth to spread before a movie catches on. That's all we had, was a little time. As it turned out, that's all we needed. Business started to pick up and the theater owners gave us another week. And then the picture exploded. At the beginning of the second week, lines started to form at the box office . . . and then down the street . . . and then down the street and around the block. It was so popular that even on *Saturday Night Live,* John Belushi and Gilda Radner, playing Richard and Marsha respectively, did a takeoff on one of the scenes when Richard starts to pull off one by one Marsha's panties hanging on the shower rod in what was now "his" bathroom. We had a gigantic hit. In 1977, we grossed around fifty million dollars. Translate that to today's dollars and it would be close to a hundred and fifty million. There was suddenly talk about Academy nominations. Marsha and I were jubilant, stunned and extremely happy that the not-yet-born movie we talked about in a small restaurant in Florence turned out to be everything we hoped for and more. We even thought about going back to Florence, finding the restaurant again, ordering the same dishes, just to see if it produced another film.

Amidst all the excitement, Marsha and I drove into Westwood, a small community just below UCLA and where we lived, to see a movie. Afterward we went to Hamburger Hamlet for a bite to eat. It was the first time in a while that we had a chance to be alone and relax. Suddenly we saw a group of people milling around. Then they multiplied.

"What's that about?" Marsha asked.

I didn't have the slightest idea. I looked up again and now there were twice as many people, so many that you couldn't see outside the windows in the elongated restaurant. I got up and went to the door to find out what was happening. Then I stepped out to look. I came back, sat down next to Marsha, playing it very cool, and said offhandedly, "It's nothing. Just a line waiting to get into *The Goodbye Girl*. It goes completely around the block until the end of the line meets the beginning of the line. They're selling tickets for shows back to back." I finally smiled because you can't carry on being cool indefinitely.

Marsha's face turned white. She suddenly didn't look well, and I couldn't imagine what was happening. I paid the check and got up to go. Marsha couldn't move.

"What's wrong?" I asked.

"I can't do it," she said.

"Can't do what?" I asked.

"Go through that line. I can't cross that line. I'm scared."

"Of what?"

"I don't know. I'm just terrified."

"Nothing will happen," I tried to assure her. "I'll put my arm around you and we'll just go through."

She held my hand as we went and I could feel her trembling. Nothing happened as we cut through the line and crossed the street, nor did I think anything *would* happen. The thing Marsha had wanted most as an actress was now happening to her. The three years she gave up for us was starting to pay her back in a bigger way than we ever dreamed, and yet she was momentarily terrified. It wasn't the last time I saw this happen to her, and whenever we had to mingle with a crowd of people, she had to get out of it as quickly as she could. Not being an analyst, I could only conjecture what was going on inside her head. Since she spent the better part of her adult life as a working actress and loving it, was stardom more than she could handle so quickly? In time, she dealt with it and the terrors seemed to disappear. Another thing that occurred to me was what she said when she moved through the large empty rooms in the house in Bel Air just prior to our buying it.

"Do we deserve this?" she said that day.

With that question comes the accompanying fear of losing it all, and thinking, "I knew it wouldn't last." Nothing does. Enjoying what's given to you, for some people, is an acquired taste.

WHEN OSCAR TIME rolled around, we hit the jackpot in nominations. Best Picture; Best Actor, Richard; Best Actress, Marsha (her second nomination in her first four films); Best Supporting Actress, Quinn Cummings; Best Screenplay, c'est moi. Herbert Ross really scored when the other film he directed that year, *The Turning Point,* also received the Best Picture nomination. I can't recall when one director had two Best Picture nominations in the same year. Our chief competition was Woody Allen's *Annie Hall,* his most commercial picture to date. It ultimately won for Best Picture, Best Actress—Diane Keaton, and Woody for Best Screenplay. We did pull off one major win, however, when Richard Dreyfuss became the youngest actor ever to win as Best Actor.

WITH ALL THIS going on, my two daughters, Ellen and Nancy, were growing up. Nancy was doing well at the Westlake School nearby and Ellen was off to Pomona College. The house seemed quiet without Ellen, whose bubbling personality was sorely missed. It was the first time in their lives that the girls were living apart. It must have been a difficult time for them, without their mother, without each other, transplanted to an environment not of their choosing. It was now just the three of us, but Marsha and Nancy grew closer now that they were spending more time with each other. Nancy's bedroom was five times the size of her tiny room back on 62nd Street, but it was also three thousand miles away from the streets and stores, her grandmother and friends she left behind. Both girls made it clear that when they were finished with their schooling, they would be moving back to New York. I projected the loss and the isolation I would feel being alone in that distant house, especially when Marsha would be off working. Because of this, it was inevitable that my thoughts would go back to Joan and perhaps that's what Marsha meant when I mentioned earlier that Marsha thought I was "needy." If she wasn't there, then I summoned up the "company" of Joan in my thoughts. I don't think this sat well with Marsha, and to tell the truth, I could see why she felt that way. I had a habit of mentioning Joan's name in conversations and when I talked of places I had visited and loved, they were obviously places that I had been to with Joan. The happiest couple in Los Angeles was showing signs of slowly surfacing trouble. The only place in the house that I kept pictures of Joan were on the walls of my office, where I spent so much time. That didn't seem to be a problem with Marsha, mostly because I chose to think it wasn't. When I embedded Joan's face deeply into my brain after she died, the aura of that imprint floated about the house, making something that was not visible into a vision that could be felt rather than seen by both Marsha and by me.

Writing, I think, is not always an act of creation. Sometimes I think it's like a poison that inhabits your being, and the only way to get rid of it is to have the pen press deeply and quickly on the empty pages, releasing your darkest secrets and your most shameful thoughts, which may be minor discretions to most, but to you are something you have to expel in order to free yourself. If you are successful, along the way it gets tempered so that your audience can see themselves in your misdemeanors, and not be so horrific that it will prohibit them from sharing your common experiences. Those writers who go to the deepest and darkest of agonies are the ones who have lived there as well: O'Neill, Chekhov, Tolstoy, Beckett. The rest of us are not so brave, or perhaps not so damaged and broken, so we do not soar. For us, to look at our own lives and to expose as much as you can allow yourself to, is to bring relief and understanding to what pains you. I wish I could go deeper, further, but then again I think I do. I make the effort if not the entire journey, but the effort exhausts me as much as the farthest journey I could take.

For all these reasons, I decided to tackle a play that would test me like no other until then.

THE DARK CHAPTER
17

BEFORE I COULD write the play *Chapter Two*—which I knew was going to be a fictionalized account that began with the way Marsha and I met, wooed and married quickly, and continued to the point that major cracks began to appear in our marriage—I felt I had to go to Marsha to get her consent to do the play. If this was too personal to go public with, despite the fact that I would try to give the characters their own personalities separate from ours, I would still have to adhere to her wishes. When I finally asked her, she said, "It's fine with me because what you'd be telling is *your* story, not mine. You'd write about what was going on in your head and could only presume what was happening to me. If I want to tell *my* story, maybe I'll put it in my own book one day." I was enormously grateful for her consent and encouragement, and although I knew I'd made no promises to her, I would have to treat the story as truthfully as I could. I already knew that in most respects the problems that occurred between us were mostly of my doing, and it was Marsha who hung in stoically until she made it clear to me that she could endure just so much before taking a very strong stand with me.

The first two acts of the play were romantic and amusing. George, the sometimes successful novelist, who sells his British style spy novels under a pseudonym that buys him a modest town house in New York, doesn't do quite as well with his more personal and serious books written under his own name. He has just returned from Europe and a dismal vacation he had undertaken alone to try to put some distance between his new life and the loss six months ago of his beloved wife. His older brother, Leo, meets him at the airport only to find George more depressed than when he left. In an attempt to move him into a new life, Leo presses George to meet a woman, any woman, just to get his mind away from the recent dark past that clings so tenaciously to him. After a catastrophic blind date that Leo arranges for George with a bombshell named Bambi ("Her name told me everything," says George the following morning), who had a platinum streak through the center of her jet black hair and wore a dress that made her look like the cover of a rock album, George decides to fend for himself, and eventually he meets the warm and likable Jenny, an actress. Since Marsha *was* an actress and my brother, Danny, *had* arranged a date for me with a Bambi-like girl, I wasn't straying as much from the truth as I had thought I would. Art not only copies life, it steals from it.

Through the rest of the act, the whirlwind romance builds to a crescendo and it's not long before George proposes marriage to Jenny. It took place not in the hallway outside her apartment as had happened with Marsha and myself, but in the play as in life, Marsha did have an ex-husband. And Danny, like Leo, tried to stop my rush into a marriage that I might not have been prepared to deal with, coming so soon after my wife's death. (Or perhaps *any* marriage, since Danny's, like Leo's, fell apart in his own life.) But the marriage takes place and George and Jenny fly off to a honeymoon in the Bahamas.

The first traces of problems arise when, on their honeymoon, George becomes moody, even sullen. It was as if his dead wife had accidentally checked into the adjoining room. When they go back to New York, Jenny starts her new life in the house and bedroom where George spent the happiest years of his life with someone else. It is a tremendous burden to Jenny, but still she tries to fight to save the marriage before it unravels completely.

In a sense, my own situation with Marsha was worse than it was for George and Jenny, because now we were living in a house three thousand miles away, with the ghost of the past in a cemetery in Pound Ridge, New York. I don't mean for it to sound as if this summoning up of a ghost was an everyday occurrence, as if it was so pervasive that we had no marriage at all. The truth is, we had a wonderful marriage, and I believe we loved each other enormously. It wasn't Joan I was missing. There were no memories lying about in the Bel Air house, no furniture, no rooms, no views that constantly brought the specter of Joan in front of me almost everywhere I turned. It was something else. Perhaps it was the newness of this house, these trees and hills, this place called Los Angeles that seemed foreign to me that caused me to lose my bearing. It almost bothered me that Marsha was comfortable here, so happy with her life while I was living in *her* world, *her* house, breathing *her* air. It was Marsha who had to make the adjustment when she first moved into Joan's house on 62nd Street. Now it was *my* turn to make the adjustment in an environment that seemed almost hostile to my way of life. Marsha gave up almost three years of her life to cement the marriage, and here I was complaining about the adjustment *I* now had to make, and we were here far less than three years. Marsha put up with my dissatisfaction as long as she could, then suddenly one day an explosion came.

After some stinging words from me, in which I threatened to leave, to get out, Marsha came to me with a torrent of words that flowed out with such anger, but such truth, that she never missed a beat, never tripped over a single syllable or consonant. Each thought was fully formed, each one following the other as if she had learned it, practiced it, rehearsed it—but I knew it was spontaneous, that it was coming from the bottom of her heart and soul, her one last chance to save something good. She always knew I was the better one with words, whether on paper or in a bedroom brawl; I was the wittier one, the quicker one. But on that day, during that speech, I sat silently, looking at her, amazed at her breathtaking demonstration of someone saying something that she knows to be so right, so honest, so truthful, that she has tossed away the possibilities of the consequences and fired away. Two things happened to me at the same time. One I was grateful for; the other I was almost ashamed of. I was grateful for her bravery, her intelligence and her love. I was ashamed because I knew that what she said was so powerful, I was going to put it in the play. It was so organic it needed to be in the play, needed to be said so that my couple could save their marriage. George had to learn from the speech, just as Neil learned from it as he listened.

There was no way I could remember exactly what she said, of course, but I paraphrased it, remembering the essential thoughts. If it sounds well written, it's not. It was a gift of words and feelings that I did not invent. I would like you to hear now what essentially Marsha said to me. In the play it happens just after George announces that he is leaving, for how long he can't say, but his bags are packed and staring up at Jenny from the floor. He expects silence, pouting, acceptance, but she surprises him. She strikes back.

JENNY

You know what you want better than me,
George . . . I don't know what you expect
to find out there except a larger audience
for your two shows a day of suffering . . . I
know I'm not as smart as you. Maybe I
can't analyze and theorize and speculate on
why we behave as we do and react as we do
and suffer guilt and love and hate . . . You
read all those books, not me. But there's one
thing I do know. I know how I feel. I know
I can stand here watching you try to destroy
everything I've ever wanted in my life,
wanting to smash your face with my fists
because you won't even make the slightest
effort to opt for happiness—and still I know
that I love you. That's always so clear to me.
It's the one place I get all my strength from
. . . You mean so much to me that I'm
willing to take all your abuse and insults
and insensitivity—because that's what you
need to do to prove I'm not going to leave
you. I can't promise I'm not going to die,
George, that's asking too much. But if you
want to test me, go ahead and test me. You
want to leave me, leave! But I'm not the
one who's going to walk away. I don't know
if I can take it forever, but I can take it for

tonight and I can take it next week. Next
month I may be a little shaky . . . But I'll
tell you something, George. No matter
what you say about me, I feel so good about
myself . . . better than I felt when I ran
from Cleveland and was frightened to death
of New York. Better than I felt when Gus
was coming home at two o'clock in the
morning just to change his clothes. Better
than I felt when I thought there was no one
in the world out there for me and better
than I felt the night before we got married
and thought that I wasn't good enough for
you . . . Well, I AM *WONDERFUL!!* I'm
nuts about me. And if you're stupid enough
to throw someone sensational like me aside,
then you don't deserve as good as you got.
I am sick and tired of running from places
and people . . . And don't tell me what I
want because *I'll* tell you what I want.
I want a home and I want a family and I
want a career. And I want a dog and a cat
and I want three goldfish. There's no harm
in wanting it, George, because there's not a
chance in hell we're going to get it all
anyway. But if you don't want it, you've got
even less chance than that . . . You want me,
then you fight for me, because I'm fighting
like hell for you. I think we're both worth
it. I will admit, however, that I do have one
major, monumental fault . . . Sometimes I
don't know when to stop talking. For that
I'm sorry, George, and I apologize. I am
now through . . .

I sat stunned and quiet in our bedroom, as she sank into a chair, breathless, exhausted, not knowing what my reaction would be, and almost not caring. I remember my reaction exactly. I looked at her, in awe of her candor. "You're right," I said. "You are absolutely right."

She looked at me in surprise, and a slight smile crossed her face. "Really?" she said, almost like a young girl whose teacher just said in class, "Marsha, I'm giving you an A-plus for intelligence, honesty and for teaching us what love is about." If I remember correctly, Marsha burst into tears of gratitude, knowing that she had broken through my sometimes obstinate nature. She might also have thought to herself, "I'm glad I got through, but why does he always make it so hard?"

Marsha decided not to do the role of Jenny on the stage but *did* decide to play it in the film, since she felt that so much time had passed before the picture was made, she could separate herself from Jenny and simply think of the role as a character she'd like to play.

Through her effort, not mine, she also got her third Academy Award nomination. But the speech she delivered that day in our house in California was not spoken by someone looking to win an award. She said it as a woman, a grown, mature woman who finally had found the strength to take charge of her own life. When she said it as the character Jenny, audiences in film theaters often applauded her when she finished, grateful that she was a spokeswoman for wives who might have had the same trouble in their own marriages.

Our lives together got considerably better after that, and I would have been a fool and a dolt not to learn from her wisdom delivered on that late afternoon in California.

THE WRITER WRITES
AND HAVING WRIT, WRITES MORE
18

CHAPTER TWO was a resounding success when it opened on Broadway, garnering five Tony nominations. After that, one would have thought I'd put my pen down for a while, rest and contemplate my future. But my future refused to wait. It was today. Not even later today, it was now, right now, this minute. I had to keep on writing, continuously, compulsively, relentlessly, and I had so many projects started in different notebooks that I had to search through the pile that was mounting on my desk each morning to see what I wanted to work on that day. The ideas flowed, not like a stream, but from atop a huge waterfall, cascading down the mountain and crashing one upon the other, flooding my brain and washing away the possibility of discovering some other outlet for my energies, leaving no room for investigations of a more subtle, potentially richer life. I played tennis with the same demonic drive, four days a week instead of two or three, and still finding time to get back to my office and put out my three to four pages a day. I often went to lunch alone, taking my pad with me and actually writing between bites.

What amazed me was that this prodigious amount of work that was pouring out of me didn't seem to amaze anyone else. Others accept what comes out as the norm for you, and my friends apparently assumed that I had some trick or device to make my brain function more rapidly than most people's. The work came out regularly, and although it probably seemed to many that I was doing it feverishly, that was not the case. I worked long and hard on each project, rewriting five times as much as I was writing, and unlike a Noël Coward, who is said on occasion to have written a play in four days during a steamer trip to Jamaica, it still took me six months to a year to complete a play. I suppose what made it noteworthy in my case was that there was never a year skipped, never a season without a new play or film and sometimes both. If the picture you get in your mind is that I was a Dr. Jekyll working through the night into the dawn to achieve the fulfillment of his scientific dreams, you may erase the image. I still worked normal hours and I was chasing neither awards nor money, nor was I looking to lighten the plight and suffering of the human race. I was having fun, and I loved hearing audiences laugh, partly because I could share something with them that would otherwise never have transpired between us. The other joy was that like a teenage boy reaching his physical maturity, I felt I could now jump ten feet in the air, hang there and drop the ball through the hoop. My energy was boundless. I felt special and unique, but in no way superior. I had a gift, albeit a simple one—but then fortunately I was not the one who God chose to lead His people out of Egypt. I might have gotten them to laugh a lot, but they wouldn't have lasted forty minutes in the desert going in my direction, much less forty years.

And still the plays and films kept parading out on the field and I was the Pied Piper leading my little band of comedies and musicals to theaters everywhere. There was *The Cheap Detective* in 1978, a film sequel in the style of *Murder by Death*. I blended the stories of *The Maltese Falcon* with *Casablanca*, getting my chance to at last work vicariously on two Humphrey Bogart classics, unfortunately without Bogart.

Then there was a new musical in 1979, *They're Playing Our Song*. It was originally to be a musical version of my earlier play *The Gingerbread Lady*, with a score by Marvin Hamlisch and Carole Bayer Sager. In real life at the time, Marvin and Carole were not only collaborators but were living together as well. Each morning Marvin would arrive at my house to begin work, but Carole rarely showed up before twelve. I truly liked Carole because she was an extremely talented lyricist with a wonderful sense of humor and irony, and as Marvin and I waited patiently for her to show up, instead of discussing the project at hand, Marvin was complaining about how difficult it was to work closely with the woman you're also romantically involved with. Carole was also writing songs on her own and had just come out with two albums on which she performed her own work. She had a small voice, not even all that melodic, but she had a wonderful style and she did her own songs better than anyone. This seemed to be another problem for Marvin. I don't want to cast aspersions on his ego, but it looked like he was afraid to be outshone by his collaborator, since he was a pretty big name in the music industry then. Carole said he wanted her to stop making albums.

I didn't take part in these confrontations and had no idea how deeply they went in the bosom of their rented house in Los Angeles, but one thing suddenly occurred to me. That the idea of a male and female composing team, fighting, scratching, loving and writing might just make a better musical than *The Gingerbread Lady*. The one thing you look for in a musical is the reason why people actually sing songs, a piece of advice that Stephen Sondheim had given me years earlier when I suggested he and I do a musical version of *The Front Page*. Stephen is a brilliant man, as anyone can tell you, and a unique voice among his generation in the musical theater. *The Front Page* is a great play, said Stephen, but why do they sing? I looked him right in the eye and said, "I haven't the slightest idea—except that you write such incredible songs." "Not without good reason," said Stephen wisely, and instead of writing with him, I decided to just enjoy listening to everything he wrote without me getting in his way.

Marvin and Carole, no doubt flattered to be the inspiration of the characters of a new musical, agreed to work on my idea. I did make a point not to ask them too many direct and private questions about their life. I was not out to write a biography but a simple, romantic comedy with characters that I invented rather than the ones who really existed. What also intrigued me was the idea to make it a very small musical. Two characters, to be exact, with an offstage character named Leon, who was the former husband of Carole's character but is never seen in the show. The shadowy ghost in Carole's former life is a much greater threat to the relationship of the two lover-composers, and his insistence on calling their house night and day or asking her to help bail him out of trouble, caused by his dependency on her, is a continuing problem.

We cast the show perfectly with the delightful Lucie Arnaz and Robert Klein, one of the funniest actor-comics I ever worked with. He had that irascible New York humor that I was so fond of, and like the two characters in *Barefoot in the Park,* they were hardly nice to each other for a moment in the play until he realizes how much he needs and misses her at the end. Robert Klein was also an excellent musician, sang well, played the harmonica and was very believable as the harassed composer. We added six dancer-voices, who played no actual parts in the show but augmented all the songs and carried out the wonderful movement staged by choreographer Pat Birch.

The show opened at the Ahmanson Theater in L.A., received not only terrific notices, but we paid off the entire investment of the show within three months after opening in New York, where we ran for three years, followed by a two-year national company, a successful London company and worldwide engagements for another few years. So the hits kept coming. I never questioned it and never considered that it might all come to a crashing halt one day.

In California a husband and wife share community property and what I made was half Marsha's, what she made was half mine. The money was rolling in so swiftly, so regularly that neither one of us was paying all that much attention to it. Having lost all the rights to the TV version of *The Odd Couple* some years before after following some advice I shouldn't have, you'd think I would have been more wary of any future investments and advice. I wasn't, nor was Marsha. I had now moved to another business manager, a man whose name became prominent on TV since his number one client was one of television's biggest stars. The *Variety* reports kept telling us how rich the TV star was getting, due to his canny lawyer–investment advisor. He was now the owner and president of a bank in Los Angeles, he now controlled TV and radio stations in Las Vegas, Texas and other places around the country, making huge land deals and oil deals and the money kept rolling in. When you are naive and pretty foolish about such matters, there's no end to the stupidity you are capable of. Marsha and I were too busy making films and doing plays and decided to trust the money managers to manage our destiny.

Within two years we had lost millions in deals that never came through the way we thought they would. It took years more for my mentor and protector, Ray Stark, to straighten me out and to get me back on the right path.

My next financial move wasn't much wiser. I left the fancy-talking business manager and went with a staid and reliable major accounting firm and let them handle my business. Within a year, the bright young woman who handled our business for the major accounting firm decided to branch out on her own, and like lemmings toward the sea, we followed her to the edge and beyond. She was not dishonest and never cheated us, but the results of our business dealings again were not successful. It was nearly too late before Ray Stark rescued me from that imbroglio, while my money and savings were diminished once again.

But why worry about such things when you have another project coming up? I was writing shows and screenplays with such regularity that I have no memory of exactly when I wrote them, and how, because they were usually squeezed in between two other projects with which I was deeply involved.

On the heels of all this financial upset came another play, *I Ought to Be in Pictures,* presented first at the Mark Taper Forum in Los Angeles. It was the story of a young girl from New York, abandoned by her father when she was a mere child, left to be raised by her mother. The father has become a screenwriter, and although his best years—and they were few—are far behind him, his daughter believes that he can not only get her a career as an actress in films, but that it's her birthright to be helped by him, as repayment for the callous and unloving way he treated her as a child. The minute I finished the script, I had a very clear idea about who I wanted to play the failed screenwriter.

Tony Curtis was an unusual star. Certainly he was not the greatest actor in the world, but he possessed a world of charm, sex appeal, humor and on quite a few occasions had shown the ability to get deeply into a part and come up with a remarkable performance. His performance in the film *Sweet Smell of Success* may have been one of his best. To play the daughter, I hired Dinah Manoff, the daughter of actress Lee Grant; she was a perfect choice. It was to be a love story of another kind, one between a guilty but put-upon man who never achieved the success he thought was coming to him, and his angry, mistreated-but-anxious-for-approval daughter from New York. In a sense, it was another odd couple story. I called agent Irving Lazar, who represented Curtis, and told him I was interested in Tony playing the lead in the new play that I was preparing for L.A. and eventually moving on to New York. Without a beat, Irving said to me, "Neil, you're my friend, Tony is my client. My advice is not to take him." I was astounded at his quick reaction. "Why not?" I asked. "Is anything wrong? Is he ill?" "Don't ask me any questions, Neil," Irving continued. "I think Tony is a wonderful guy and a terrific actor, but I just don't think this will turn out well." "So what are we talking about here, Irving? Is it drugs? Is Tony having a substance problem?" "I never said that," Irving responded quickly. "Listen, I've said my piece," he continued. "If you really want him, if you think he'll be good for your play, then I will highly recommend Tony to do it."

Given Irving's words of advice, I knew I was headed for trouble, but I had a naive, almost unshaking belief that Tony Curtis would not only be news on Broadway, but that he would be the absolute perfect man to play the part. I knew he could charm the pants off a mannequin. "I'll send him the play. If he likes it, let's talk business," I said.

A few days later Tony Curtis, director Herbert Ross and I met, and Tony made it clear that he was excited and delighted to play the role. He saw a new career for himself—the stage, something that eluded him in his meteoric rise to Hollywood stardom. Within a few months we were into rehearsals. Tony was not used to having to learn an entire script before, since films are shot, as we all know, mostly at the rate of a page or a few lines at a time. He asked for a driver to pick him up for rehearsals each day, one who would not only drive but would coach him on his lines going to and from work. It was clear from the outset that Tony was very nervous, which we expected, but he also showed a need to be loved, to be wanted, to be the focus of our attention. He started to call me at home at night, at all hours, wondering if he was doing well, asking if we could spend more time together, becoming pals, close friends, so to speak. It was disconcerting for me, yet I felt not only a sadness for him, but a genuine fondness. He was not afraid to tell you he needed help, that he wanted to be wonderful in this part and that together we might all pull it off. He was always cooperative and hardworking, but it was obvious that the learning of the long pages of dialogue was giving him problems.

Four weeks later, after arduous rehearsals, we were ready for our first preview performance. I had no idea what to expect and had mixed feelings: I knew that if we had hired a more experienced stage actor, we would not be as worried as we were; at the same time, if we hired a more experienced stage actor, he probably wouldn't come close to the charm and warmth that Tony was showing on the stage.

We got through the first preview. On the whole, I was optimistic. Tony held up pretty well, Dinah Manoff was delightful, and the ever dependable Joyce Van Patten, whom I used in play after play in those days, was the perfect makeup girl from the studio who was having a sometimes live-in relationship with Tony's character. After the preview we quickly retired to Tony's dressing room and Herbert Ross was ready with all sorts of comments. What I was thinking above all was that the play basically worked, but still had a lot of rewriting to do, which I would undertake as I did with every play I ever mounted in my career. After Herbert's encouraging notes, Tony looked at me and said, "What do you think, Neil? You happy?" "Very," I replied. "I think we're really on the right track here. I see all the things I've done wrong and once I do the first rewrites, I think we'll begin to shape up very quickly."

Tony looked at me as if I were suddenly speaking a foreign language. He was hearing words he never heard before, not understanding the meaning of them, not getting the very concept. "What do you mean, rewrites?" he said. "I thought this was the play. I thought what I learned was the play we're going to do."

The other actors looked at me, then put their heads down, knowing that Tony was going to suddenly learn the do's and don'ts of the theater.

"Well, Tony, it's just the beginning. I can't write a play and get it all correct in one draft. There are things that don't work. Things that I have to rewrite. We could never go into New York with the play as it's written now."

His face turned white. He wiped his brow with a towel, then shook his head adamantly. "No. No way. I learned one play, that's all I can learn. Either we do this or we forget about it."

Herbert Ross tried to tactfully explain the realities of the theater, but he also knew this was not the time to bring things to a boil. "Well, let's discuss this tomorrow, Tony. You did very well for tonight."

Herbert and I went out for a drink and knew we were in trouble, that Irving Lazar's warning had finally brought home the essence of our plight. It was clear to us both that Tony Curtis was never going to make it to Broadway with this play nor would we make it with Tony Curtis. Still, we didn't want to give up. We couldn't. We still had four weeks to play out in L.A., and one never knew what miracles could happen in four weeks.

Until one day at a weekend matinee, all hell exploded. When Tony came out for his first scene on stage, all did not seem well. He was edgy, fidgety, even surly on the stage in his scenes with young Dinah Manoff. It was a play that had no four-letter words in it, since there was still a great deal of aspired love and respect between the father and his daughter. Then toward the end of the first act, Tony lashed out at Dinah with a barrage of language, a string of obscenities, of furious anger. She was stunned and didn't know how to react. He was still playing his part, but it seemed as if Mr. Hyde had emerged from his soul and Dinah was bearing the brunt of his tirade. The audience, although they had not seen the play before, sensed there was something wrong. The language that was now being flung around on stage did not seem compatible with what I had written so far. Tony stormed off the stage as the act drew to a close. Dinah ran into her dressing room, bathed in tears and frightened at what had just occurred. The stage manager waited for things to cool down, then at the appropriate moment, knocked on Tony's dressing room door and said, "Five minutes, Tony." There was no answer from the dressing room. The stage manager repeated his call. Still no answer. He knocked on the door, then opened it to see if Tony was all right. He was getting dressed, changing his clothes, but he was not putting on the clothes he was to wear in the second act. He was putting on his street clothes, his civvies, to be exact.

"What are you doing, Tony? You're putting on the wrong clothes."

"No," said Tony. "These are the right clothes. These are my going-home clothes. I've had enough acting for today. Get someone else to do the play today," and he was out of the theater in a minute. The dazed stage manager quickly ran down the hall to find the understudy, told him to get ready, and then rushed to Dinah Manoff's room, knocked, walked in and said, "Tony's not coming back for the second act. You'll have to do it with the understudy."

But Dinah was too far beyond upset to even get the meaning of what he was saying. She was crying, leaning in the arms of the protective Joyce Van Patten, mumbling she couldn't go on. She couldn't face the audience after what just happened. The befuddled stage manager walked out to the stage, never having been in this position in his entire life. He did the best he could when he announced, "Ladies and gentlemen, unfortunately Mr. Curtis and Miss Manoff have suddenly taken ill during the intermission. Their parts will be played by their understudies. Thank you," and he walked off the stage, probably wishing it could have been off the Oakland bridge. The audience began to boo, not only at their disappointment at not seeing the stars, but sensing what must have happened during the end of the first act.

In truth, I can't remember if Tony Curtis ever came back to finish the engagement. Perhaps he did, perhaps not. In a way I felt badly for him because he was coping with a lot of things in his life. In his book a few years later, he referred to Herbert Ross and myself as "those two terrible men," as if we were the cause of his troubles. Eventually Tony was replaced by actor Ron Liebman for the New York run and Ron is a first-rate, exciting and complex actor. He did extremely well for us. Dinah Manoff went on to win the Tony Award for her performance on Broadway in *I Ought to Be in Pictures*. She later repeated the role in the film opposite Walter Matthau. But the next time an agent advises me not to take his client for a role we just offered him, I would think my answer over much more carefully.

GOT TO DANCE
19

IF YOU'VE EVER SEEN a documentary of Fred Astaire's film career, you would think the man never slept a night in his life. He performed one unbelievable number after another, in every fashion, every style, every mood, with almost every beautiful actress in Hollywood as his partner, not to mention a variety of inanimate objects including drums, canes, golf clubs, gym equipment and roller skates, all of which seemed to serve him as well as his human partners. Did the man ever just walk? Did he ever sit still, read a newspaper? Did he ever see a dentist? No, he just danced. Well, that was the vision I was beginning to get of myself, dancing frantically through every day, only without the tap shoes.

Whatever I did in life, it seemed that most of it was writing. There is a drug, given in recent years, to patients who undergo surgery, and although they experience postoperative pain, the drug prohibits the *memory* of the pain. In other words, as soon as the pain appears, you forget it, although you just experienced it, so the lasting effect is as if no pain ever occurred. In terms of my writing, I was under the influence of something like that drug. A screenplay would pour out of me almost without my knowing it. Thirty pages of a new play appeared neatly typed in front of me and I never knew where it came from. I would open a drawer in my desk, take out a draft of something I wrote a week ago or a month or two years ago, and since I had no memory of doing the work, I'd look at it and wonder if someone sent it to me through the mail, asking my opinion of it. I sat in the screening room at Columbia watching the first assembled cut of a movie called *Seems Like Old Times,* and although I really liked it, I found it hard to focus because I had spent the entire morning prior to the screening working on something else. Yet there were Goldie Hawn and Chevy Chase, sitting in the screening room with me, and I remembered how much I enjoyed watching them work every day, but when did I write this screenplay, when did I find the time?

The picture was a hit and twenty-some odd years later I see it playing on a cable station and I laugh, surprised that I don't know what line or scene is coming up next. I was working, I suppose, on automatic control, and like a well-made toaster, I was popping out crusty English muffins that everyone seemed to enjoy. But I never stopped long enough to really taste them. At dinner Marsha would start a conversation and I would try to pick up the thread of what she was saying, but my mind was on something called *Actors and Actresses,* a new play that seemed to be writing itself while I watched over it like a shepherd, seeing that it didn't stray too far from the corral that I was keeping new plays in for that week.

Did I care about what I was writing? Yes, very much so. Oh, I cared about some less than others, but some meant a great deal to me. I liked *Actors and Actresses* because it was bleak and sad and yet had a kind of fragile humor (sometimes tough and biting) that I was dealing with in that period. It was about a group of over-the-hill actors coupled with a few not-ready-for-prime-time actors who traveled the highways and byways of America's small theatrical stopovers, playing one-night stands in small cities like Duluth or Peoria and sometimes the semi–big time in a place like Cincinnati. The actors traveled in a bus, the scenery went in a truck, thus it was called a bus-and-truck tour.

Where was I when I wrote this play? I don't know, but I actually tried it out some months later, either in the Hartford Theater in Stamford, Connecticut, or the Stamford Theater in Hartford, Connecticut—I don't remember. And how did I get there? Plane? Train? Bus? Or did I just wake up in some hotel room one morning and ask the desk clerk to direct me to the theater?

The play had its good moments and its not-so-good moments and we never brought it to New York, but I have no recollection of the struggle, the disappointment, the energy spent and the promise that went unful-filled. The nonexistent pain remover was working its magic on me and I could write day in, day out, weekends or holidays without any strain or harm to my psyche. Or so I thought. The bill that was mounting up would have to be paid later (and pay it I did). But until then, the started plays, the half-finished musicals, the outlined films were all waiting on the assembly line, but now I felt I wasn't even pushing the buttons. At the end of each day I just picked up the finished pages, made a correction or two—or twelve or fifty—and then put them on top of the pile that the category dictated.

What was going on in Marsha's mind, I wonder now, and did she as-sume that I thought I was perfectly in control of a perfectly uncontrolled life? Was I manic? Was I depressed? Was I euphoric? No, I was just writing, and as I recently read in an article by playwright David Mamet, "Writing is the thing you do so that you don't have to think about the things you'd rather not think of." That was me, or a version of that. If there were things I didn't want to think of, they must have been infinite because the writing never slowed up. I had empty notebooks strewn everywhere around my of-fice, all fighting for a place on line to receive a portion of my daily atten-tion. Pens of all kinds and colors were sitting on tables, in jars, on my desk so that no matter where I stepped or turned, there was always something to write on and something to write with. I was like Chaplin in the classic comedy *Modern Times*. He played a factory worker with a wrench in each hand and his sole job was to tighten any bolts that came out of a huge ma-chine. He had been doing it so long and so repeatedly that he tightened any bolts that went by him, passed him, under him, over him or through him. Instead of bolts, I tightened scripts, and like the tireless factory worker, I never heard the five o'clock stop whistle any more than he did.

Again, to clarify the picture for you, don't suppose that if you were in my office when I worked that you would see a blur, a whirling dervish of pages flying and writing utensils brandished like knives in a duel. I sat qui-etly, hardly moving, very deliberate, thinking things out carefully. If you tried to watch, you'd be bored in five minutes. It was the slow, rhythmic but steady pattern of a mind at work, fingers typing and stories silently

1

Nancy and me. Am I lucky, or
what?

Ellen, my first daughter. How
pretty is that?

2

Nancy on the left, Ellen on the right in New York. They're still that close today.

Chips, the dog that Joan and I raised in New York.

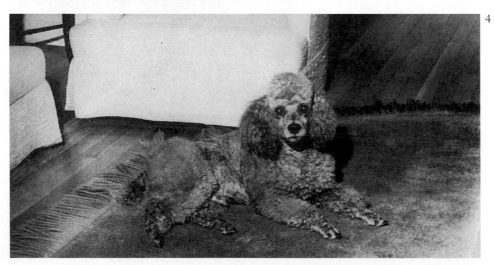

Marsha's incredible film debut in *Cinderella Liberty*. Her first Oscar-nominated film.

Marsha and me in New York, backstage on an opening night of one of my plays.

With Marsha and Nancy, early days in Bel Air.

The house on Chalon Road in Bel Air. It was more Connecticut than L.A.

9

On the set of *The Goodbye Girl* (me, Marsha, Ray Stark, Herb Ross, seated).

Marsha with Jimmy Caan in *Chapter Two,* a scene close to our own life.

10

11

Marsha with Herb Ross, who directed *The Sunshine Boys, The Goodbye Girl, Max Dugan Returns,* and many other films of mine.

Me happily surrounded by the stars of *The Cheap Detective*.
Top left to right: Madeline Kahn, Louise Fletcher, Eileen Brennan, Ann-Margret, a blonde Marsha Mason, and Stockard Channing.

A guest lecture with Walter Matthau at UCLA. He laughed at everything I said.

At a press conference with
Maggie Smith in London.

On the set of *Murder by Death*.
Behind the makeup is Peter
Sellers, who always made me
laugh.

16

Diane and me on our wedding day in L.A., first time around.

OPPOSITE:
Top, happier days with Diane and Bryn.

Bottom, on vacation with Diane and Bryn

17

18

Bryn and me. Bryn is the beautiful one.

OPPOSITE:
Top, with Diane at the Kennedy Center honors, 1995.

Bottom, a very proud father with his beautiful daughter Bryn.

20

21

23

24

Opening night in New York for *Lost in Yonkers* with Mercedes Ruehl and Kevin Spacey.

Office in Chalon house.

Office in L.A.

Ellen on the left, Nancy on the right. Both as pretty as their mother.

Nancy, me and Ellen *en famille,* East Hampton, NY, 1998.

being told with no one but my imagination to hear the words. Still another play appeared, this one more of a fable. I called it *Fools*. It was based very loosely on the stories of Sholom Aleichem, wherein he wrote about a fictional village in middle Europe called, I believe, Chelm. (For those of you who don't happen to have friends of the Jewish persuasion, the "Ch" in Chelm is made with a slight coughing sound.) Chelm had one great distinction. Everyone who lived there was stupid. My Chelm was located in Russia, and I called it Kulyenchikov, a name that no one in Kulyenchikov could spell or pronounce. *Fools* was a play that I finished and loved writing, but I never thought it should go to Broadway. As a fable, and almost a children's fable at that, I thought it was more suited to off-Broadway, but in those days it was unthinkable by others that Neil Simon should appear off-Broadway.

Fools was pure vaudeville couched in the guise of a fable, the story of peasants who were so sweet, so innocent, so pure that their inability to put two coherent sentences together was as touching as they were silly. Leon, a schoolmaster from Moscow, wanders into this remote village looking for employment and instead finds love and no one to talk to who makes sense. He meets the local doctor and his wife, and their daughter, Sophia. When the doctor asks a patient to read an eye chart, the patient would read the letters aloud, "O . . . R . . . K . . . M . . . Z . . ." Then he'd say to the doctor, "Did I get them right?"

"I don't know," the doctor replies. "Sounds good to me." You get the drift.

Then Leon proceeds to question Sophia:

LEON

May I call you Sophia?

SOPHIA

Why?

DOCTOR

It's your name, darling. Remember?

LEON

Would it please you if I called you Sophia?

SOPHIA

I don't know. Try it.

LEON

Tell me, Sophia, what is your favorite color?

SOPHIA

My favorite color?

DOCTOR

Oh, I used to know that one.

LEON

Once again, Sophia, what is your favorite
color?

MOTHER

Why is he being so hard on her? This isn't a
university.

SOPHIA

My favorite color is . . . is . . . is yellow.

LEON

Yellow! Very good, Sophia. And why is
yellow your favorite color?

SOPHIA

Because it doesn't stick to your fingers as
much.

DOCTOR
(To Leon)
I think she's wrong. I think it's blue that
doesn't stick to your fingers.

Well, if it was laughs, love and a two-thousand-year curse put on a village you were looking for, we had two hours of it. If it was a hit show you wanted, try *Mister Roberts*. We ran about six months in New York and the play is still performed today in theaters everywhere from Bangor, Maine, to possibly a village in Russia called Kulyenchikov.

Not all the decisions to undertake a new project started with me. For example, I received a phone call from Frank Price, then the studio head of Columbia Pictures, a bright, amiable man who came out of television with a reputation as someone who knew a good story when he read it. He invited me to breakfast at the Beverly Hills Hotel where so many other actors, agents and studio folk were making deals at the same time, you could practically order what film you wanted from the menu. Frank was not much into small talk and in his soft-spoken manner he got right to the point.

"I just wanted to know what you're up to, Neil. Is there anything you'd like to do? Any ideas kicking around?"

I was prepared. I didn't think he wanted to see me just to watch me eat French toast.

"Actually there is something, but I never brought it up to you because it's a bit offbeat."

"I like offbeat," he said. "What is it?"

"It's something I've already done as a play a few years ago, but I always thought it would make a much better movie." Perhaps the reason I never pushed it was because I thought it had a great starring role for Marsha and never wanted to put the studio in the position of having to take Marsha as part of the deal. I would hope they'd want her, of course, but I wanted it to be because they'd feel as strongly as I did that she was the best actress for it. I then told him about the play, *The Gingerbread Lady*.

For me it was a breakthrough play of sorts, one that dealt with the drama of the story even more than the comedy. It came close to failing in Boston where it previewed; it starred Maureen Stapleton. The critics were not too kind to it and said plainly that what they wanted from me was *The Odd Couple* and *Barefoot in the Park,* while I wanted to press on in other directions. When the reviews came in at the small, bleak opening party we were all attending, Maureen sensed it was over for all of us. She grabbed me by the collar and said, "If you close this play, I will personally stab you in your sleep with a fork." The next morning, buoyed by our one good review, I told the producer that I wanted the rest of the four weeks in Boston to try and save the play, then I got on the next train to New York and wrote intensely for the four-hour trip back home. The play eventually made it to Broadway, ran a year and Maureen won the Tony Award as Best Actress. I briefly outlined the story of the play to Frank Price and told him what I intended to change for the film. He nodded, more intrigued than enthusiastic, but said if I sent him the play, he'd read it by the weekend. Three days after our breakfast, Frank called me and said very simply, "I like it. Let's do it."

As simple as that. In today's world, that breakfast wouldn't have gotten past the first cup of coffee before a studio head would say, "Where's the stars? Where's the action scenes? Where's the songs? How do you get kids in to see it and who'll understand it in Europe?" In today's world, I guess I would say, "Well, we could show it on a double bill with *Twister.*" I was, however, lucky enough to still be living in an era and a theatrical climate where all a studio wanted to know was, is it a good story or not? With a green light from Frank, I began writing the script, which I would produce along with director Glenn Jordan. The three leads in the film were Marsha, Joan Hackett and Jimmy Coco, and aside from a young Kristy McNichol, Marsha was the only real name that meant anything. She was going to play an alcoholic who is trying to dry out, get her acting career going again, finding herself a nonloser boyfriend and hoping to regain custody of her young daughter. In today's world, I would have been shown the door and the studio gate quickly as they ordered me off the lot forever—unless, of course, I could get Jim Carrey to play Marsha's boyfriend, and give his character this problem of having to tell the truth for twenty-four hours. But this was 1981 and we made this small picture—having changed the title from *The Gingerbread Lady* to *Only When I Laugh*—on a smaller budget. The picture probably made its money back thanks to video and cable sales, but what pleased me so much was that we were nominated for three Academy Awards: one for Marsha, her fourth Best Actress nomination in the eight films she made, possibly a record, and one each for Joan Hackett and Jimmy Coco in supporting roles. Those were still innocent times and we were all fortunate enough to be part of it before the phrase "mega-hit" was invented.

IRELAND, SANTA FE AND OBLIVION
20

SOMEHOW, before filming started, Marsha and I squeezed in a trip to Ireland with my good friend David Picker, former head of United Artists and his then wife, Nessa Hyams. We decided to rent a car and follow the Irish road maps wherever they took us, with some planned stops along the way at hotels that were recommended to us. Following the map wasn't hard. Pronouncing the names of towns and small cities was the difficulty. David, happily for all of us, elected to do all the driving and the finding of places called Broughmohal and Collygrud and Mollybulech, which after a while I began to think weren't towns at all but rather names of the local ale. David's mistake was asking strangers where he could find such and such a town, only to have a very kind and generous farmer rattle off directions sounding like a man who had his tongue tied very tightly to his tonsils. I told David to be careful because if he pronounced these places in the proper Irish brogue, he could possibly asphyxiate himself.

Ireland is as beautiful a country as you could find in the world but you'd better dress right for the weather. At one point we drove through a rainstorm for over two hours, but every time we looked behind us, there was no rain falling. I told David to drive slower so that we'd always be in the sun that was following us right at our heels, but it was not in David's makeup to drive slowly or try to make friends with the weather. We played on golf courses so thick with deep grass that to hit your ball was to lose it.

If you swung and missed, you lost a stroke but saved a ball. There were, I believe, many charming small cottages in the vicinity made completely out of lost golf balls, sort of adobe huts with dimples in them.

Since we were two couples, we had to make unusual arrangements for the booking of rooms in hotels. David wisely suggested that since it was unlikely we'd each get comparable rooms, the fairest thing to do was to switch first choice at each hotel so that by the end of the trip, no one would come out the loser. We tossed a coin and Marsha and I won first pick at the first hotel we stopped at. It was a very large manor house, possibly once a small castle, and although we all dream of living in a castle one day, it took an experienced traveler like Cole Porter who told us in a lyric that a castle in Ireland is the likeliest place to catch pneumonia. Nevertheless we were thrilled when we entered the large entrance hall and were greeted by a small contingent of concierges. David graciously told our host to please show the Simons to the most favorable of the rooms, and that they would be happy with the second choice. We were led into a small elevator (sorry, lift) to the third floor, then through red-carpeted hallways, past paintings of some former lord or earl who once called this mansion home, and finally into a corner suite, two extremely large rooms with an old but perfectly suitable bath. They were, however, a bit stingy with the soap. Still, it was decorated simply but tastefully, and you could picture The McGillycuddy of the Reeks, Irish chieftain of note, spending a fortnight in here, next to the warm fireplace and oversized chairs. From every large window, the views were spectacular, where you could see for twenty miles all around, the loveliest green hills and pastures, looking like a Turner landscape. There were sheep in the meadows and ducks in the ponds and whatever else was in that nursery rhyme we still vaguely remembered. We were in heaven—and then our phone rang.

It was David.

"How're your rooms?" he asked pleasantly.

"David, it's incredible. I just hope yours are even half as nice as ours because this is paradise . . . How'd you make out?"

"It's interesting," he said. "You ought to come over and see."

"Sure. We'll come down before dinner."

"No," he said. "It will be dark by then and you can't get the full appreciation of this unless you see it in the light."

"Okay, I'll come now. How do I get there?"

"I'm sending a bellman up to your room. He'll show you."

"Right," I said. "Be right there."

"Take your time," he said. "It's a bit of a walk." And he hung up.

Marsha, tired from the drive, sank into the deep bed, kicked off her shoes and asked me to wake her an hour before dinner. She was asleep before the bellman knocked on the door.

Ireland is still a poor country, and real luxury is not as common there as one would find, say, in France or in America, but its simple beauty and gracious hospitality made me feel fortunate to be where we were on this cool, sunny July afternoon.

I followed the bellman across the red-carpeted hallways, down the lift to the Great Entrance Hall, then through a side door paneled in exquisite wood, then to my surprise, down a flight of stairs. Then through another door, this one not paneled, and more of a surprise, down another flight of stairs. There was no further natural light coming from anywhere. It was all wall lights, and dim ones at that. There was no doubt that when the first lords and earls inhabited the mansion, the only way through these passages would be to carry torches, which I thought would come in handy on this present trip as well.

"Is this some sort of shortcut?" I asked the bellman.

"Shortcut? No, sir. This is the only way."

I suddenly felt this man's name was Igor and I was following him through passageways from which no human was known to return.

"Where are we?" I asked the bellman with some trepidation.

"These used to be the servants' quarters in the old days," he said as the passageway now began to curve. "In recent years, when the manor became more popular, these were redone and turned into guest rooms. They're not always used, but when we're full up during the height of the season, as we are now, we open them up again. Actually, they have a certain quiet charm of their own."

"To whom?" I wanted to say. "Rabbits?"

He stopped suddenly and I had to brace myself to avoid bumping into him. He knocked on the door and called out, "Bellman."

A familiar voice, sounding more dour than usual said, "It's open. Come in."

The bellman opened the door. Two dismal lamp lights were on either side of the bed. David and Nessa were sitting on the bed, their unopened luggage on the floor in front of them. The windows—there were two of them—were high up on the wall, making it quite clear that this room was below ground level.

The room was damp and dank, and clearly was more a part of the earth than of the hotel. When you looked up to the windows above, you could only see the shoes and ankles of people passing by. I felt a chill and wished I had worn a sweater. David and Nessa obviously wished they were on a sunny island in Greece. If Marsha and I had a Turner landscape, David and Nessa had the back of the canvas, nails and all.

"Is there anything I can get you, sir?" the bellman said to David.

"I can't possibly see what," said David. "I think everything we need to survive for two days is right here."

David gave the bellman a tip and the bellman looked for a moment as if he was going to give it back, out of respect for the situation. He left. I didn't know what to say. I felt enormously guilty and upset and miserable, coming in only second to David's and Nessa's misery. David had arranged the trip, he had found the hotels, he had been driving us everywhere, telling us the history of this hotel, of its incredible food and, above all, their magnificent gardens, which at the moment were growing directly above their room. I had to restrain myself to keep from laughing, because it was an awful joke. But then those are usually the funniest kind.

"No, David," I said quickly. "This is no good. We have to do something."

He shrugged. "There's nothing to do," he said. "This is the only room they had left. We tossed, you won. We'll manage fine."

He also managed a smile and I bit my lip hard to prevent myself from falling hysterical on the floor, which proves to you that people who write comedy don't always know the parameters of decency.

"What if you stay here tonight and tomorrow night Marsha and I will exchange rooms with you?" I offered.

"No. Really. It's only for two nights . . . Does Marsha like your rooms?"

"Actually, not that much," I said with all the sensitivity I could muster. "It's really cold up there. And you can hear the people in the next room. It's okay, I guess."

David grinned. "Yeah, I'm sure," he said with more irony than was necessary.

"It'll even out," he said. "I just didn't want you to miss seeing this. We would have taken a picture of it, but there's no flash camera that's bright enough to make anything visible."

I found my way back to our room, but only before stopping every twenty steps or so to release the pangs of laughter that were building up inside of me. The worst moment came as I entered our room just as Marsha was getting up. I prayed she wouldn't ask it. I prayed she wouldn't think of it. I prayed the words wouldn't form on her lips. My prayers were not answered.

"How's their room?" she asked innocently. She must have thought I just had a stroke because I fell across the bed, laughing indecently. I never could get to describing their room. Every time I started, I was overtaken with insanity.

After dinner, David couldn't resist, and said that Marsha had to see their room. When they opened the door with their key, Marsha stepped in and her hand went to her mouth as if she had just seen the *Hindenburg* burning. Tears came to her eyes with compassion bordering on grief. She hugged Nessa like a mother would hold a child who just broke her favorite toy. Marsha was an angel. I was a fiend because I was still laughing three days later as we drove to the next hotel. That's when things evened up. David and Nessa had a sun-filled suite with a magnificent view of the sea and the Irish coastline; Marsha and I got a bleak, tiny room that looked out on the parking lot. I wondered, at two o'clock in the morning, if that was David honking the horn in his car or was it just my imagination?

IT WILL SURPRISE no one, I'm sure, to hear that somewhere between the trip to Ireland and the start of shooting *Only When I Laugh,* I wrote another screenplay. Did I write some in Ireland? Perhaps. On the plane or waiting in airport lounges? Probably. I could get a half a page in while waiting for Marsha to get dressed for dinner and sometimes the writing was done only in my head while watching a film or a play that didn't particularly interest me. I did that a lot in musicals where the number on stage held no one's attention including the person who was singing. I couldn't keep the exact dialogue of the imagined scene in my head, but the gist of it was clear enough to remember, and I emptied the contents of my memory into a typewriter the following morning.

This film turned out to be *Max Dugan Returns,* and it concerned a widowed schoolteacher, played eventually by Marsha, and her fourteen-year-old son. Her plight was to make her meager salary cover her bills when a mysterious stranger appears at her doorstep on a dark, misty night. The stranger turns out to be her estranged father who had abandoned her as a child, and now has come back with a suitcase filled with six hundred thousand dollars in cash, which he skimmed off the top as a blackjack dealer in Las Vegas. He is a man with a heart condition and about six months to live, and he wants to pay back his debt to his daughter and to the grandson he has never seen. Did it occur to me that this was the second time I had written about a child abandoned by a parent, in both cases, a father? Not consciously perhaps, but nevertheless, there it was, popping up again. It appeared in a later play as well, *Lost in Yonkers,* where a father unwillingly leaves his two sons in the charge of their grandmother, while he goes off to earn money to pay off hospital debts accrued during his wife's bout with cancer.

I always knew you could trace my life through my plays (not all, but many) and in the above paragraph there are listed three common themes that show up in various forms throughout my career: the abandoned child, a father with a failing heart (my father died of one) and a mother dying of cancer, which of course was Joan. Always abandonment in one form or another. It shows up in *Chapter Two,* in *Jake's Women,* in *Broadway Bound* (in that one, all three are present, since the mother knows her husband will leave her, the father has a heart attack, and the father still sees a woman he once had an affair with but is now dying of cancer). Even in *Proposals* the father dies of a heart attack and both he and his daughter feel abandoned by the mother who left them. And in the comedy *The Odd Couple,* the wives of both Oscar and Felix have left them. Oscar copes but Felix is almost suicidal. Abandonment, of course, doesn't always mean someone actually leaving you. They can be there *with* you, but not be there *for* you. My mother's inability to deal with my childhood illnesses made me feel just as alone as if she were the one who packed up and left instead of my father, who did it time and time again. Obviously, the ultimate abandonment in my life was Joan's death. It was a clue, even the key to why I wrote so much, always in pursuit of putting these ghosts in their place and coming to closure with my childhood fears. Apparently I didn't succeed, since the same themes keep coming up, albeit in different forms. The writer plays mind games, trying to trick himself into thinking he is moving forward in his life, but the words he puts down on paper betray him.

Knowing why you do something—in my case the enormous amount of writing—and doing something about it are not the same thing, and recognizing the "problem" doesn't necessarily mean fixing it. On the contrary, since the writing *always* makes me feel better, always improves my moods, I not only have continued to deal with my fears that way, but eventually I have become addicted to it. It's also why I rarely answer the phone in my office (since I rarely give out the number), because I'm in a safe place. No phone calls of goodbye, no messages of farewell. If it's important, they'll eventually get to me but while I'm there, in my impregnable cocoon, I am, paradoxically, free.

It's interesting, I think, that I've become extremely successful by feeding off my own insecurities and sharing them with a world of people who, in many, many cases, identify with them from their own experiences. I've also been able to find humor in my pain, and if that humor touches those who watch my work, then they find an alternate way of dealing with their own problems. I have been accused by critics of trying to sugarcoat the pain with laughter, but I never thought that was the case. I always thought the humor was the instrument I used to first reach people, and then, as an extension of the characters and stories, I would deliver the underlying issue, the pain that so many of us want to avoid at any cost.

I myself *never* wanted to avoid it. I wanted to take an audience by surprise, to be sure they never saw the pain coming, and when it came, they were pulled into dealing with it and consequently realized that none of us are really that different. This inevitably led critics into accusing me of being middle-class, of pandering to the petty problems of the middle class. Sorry, but I never knew there was a class distinction between those who were abandoned and those who weren't, or between those who were abused or alone or discarded.

By that criterion, then, Shakespeare's kings, queens and princes were no less middle-class. Who felt abandonment worse than Hamlet? Who felt discarded more than Ophelia? And what delights us more than Shakespeare's comedies, the aim of which is not only to make us laugh, but to show us what asses we mortals are?

The final abandonment for the writer, I'm certain, is when he feels he has lost his power to convey himself through words, or even worse, has lost his enthusiasm even to try. And the final humiliation, of course, comes when backs are turned and ears are covered so that people can even avoid listening.

IT BECAME APPARENT, despite the fun we had in Ireland, despite the two new projects that would enable us to work together again, that a change was taking place between Marsha and me. It was not so bad, I thought, that it threatened our relationship, but something had shifted; it wasn't tangible, though, and since it had no name and there were no words to describe it, I let it pass. But something in the shift must have left enough of an impression on me to suggest we might consider finding a place where we could go for weekends and holidays and vacations—a retreat for just the two of us, far from the maddening pressures of our life in Los Angeles.

THE NAME Santa Fe came up. The city was only an hour and thirty minutes by plane from Los Angeles, and its natural and exotic beauty appeared almost monthly in full color in every chic magazine in the country. I had to fly back to New York to meet Manny Azenberg to discuss a proposed revival of the musical *Little Me,* and I told Marsha I would stop off in New Mexico first, and if I wasn't carried off by a pack of coyotes, I would see if I felt comfortable living where the buffalo used to roam.

When I arrived there, I realized why the buffalo disappeared. Santa Fe was just too expensive for them. Someone forgot to tell me that the hour-and-a-half flight only got you to Albuquerque. It was an additional hour-and-a-half drive from there to Santa Fe. I rented a car and as I moved through the prairie and then into the red-clay hills, I was seeing some of the most beautiful country in America. Santa Fe tried desperately to hold on to its simple and historic past, and although it had too many tourist shops, the city had charm, a warm ambience, clean air and the pleasing aroma of mesquite wood burning in fireplaces almost everywhere. It's situated a little over seven thousand feet above sea level, and it took my lungs by surprise.

Since no one was expecting me, I wandered into one of the many adobe real estate offices in town. The man in the bolo tie looked up from his desk and said, "Can I help you, sir?" The four other estate agents suddenly looked up as well when I said, "Yes. I'm looking for a house. Something with a great view." The man in the bolo tie smiled, knowing his work was already half done; I had done the other half by indicating I was in a shopping mood.

As we drove around the city of Santa Fe, I said, "I love the town, but what I am looking for is a retreat, a place for my wife and myself to be alone."

"Privacy," he said as though he had just invented the word. "Know just what you're looking for," and he shifted his four-wheel-drive into high and we headed not only further away from Santa Fe but higher as well. The air got thinner and even clearer, if possible, and I began to feel giddy. "It takes a day or two to get used to the altitude," he said, no doubt noticing that I was taking four breaths to his one.

We soon ran out of asphalt and were now driving on terrain so rough, bumpy and dusty that I was sure even the deer and rabbits looked for alternate routes. We were seeing fewer and fewer houses, and the ones we saw became further apart from one another, until they seemed to disappear entirely, in part because the houses were built to blend in with what nature had built eons ago. We kept climbing until he pointed to the highest point we could see and said, "There's one I think is just what you're talking about."

I could barely see it; I could make out the few geometrical lines of the roof but nothing else. I saw no visible roads leading to the place, and wondered if you just drove up there by instinct or had to attack it with a plan like scaling something in Nepal. "Is there an actual road that goes up to this place?" I asked.

"Oh, yes. Folks who owned it cleared this out when they built it two years ago. You'll get the hang of it."

We were now moving out of the realm of "privacy" and into what would be better described as "isolation." I was now questioning my judgment; did I really want to live in a place you couldn't find or breathe in? And suddenly the house appeared before me, as if rising behind a hill and revealing itself. I stepped out of the car and even if we had been at sea level, my breath would have been taken away. I had never seen views like this in my life.

All around me were three hundred and sixty degrees of the most magnificent vistas, from distant snow-capped mountains to prairies a hundred miles away, to rolling hills and rivers that moved like an endless snake glistening in the sun. Above us the sky was so blue you felt you could see the end of the universe. No matter in what direction you looked, the mood was different. Ahead of me the dark clouds seemed cold and threatening, behind me the sun looked as if it would shine there forever. To my left the trees were green and young, and to my right, the leaves were changing. If you just turned your head slowly, you could see all four seasons at the same time. The wind that blew through the canyons below whistled softly as the leaves on the trees and the tall grass swayed gently in a rhythmic pattern that lulled and quieted your thoughts as you realized you were experiencing, for the very first time, a true glance at tranquillity.

Eventually I walked through the house, merely glancing at the rooms. As charming and inviting as they were, I couldn't wait to go back outside and sit on the old bench that looked out on the horizon, knowing I could get lost forever in the kinds of sights and sounds I had never experienced in all my urban life.

As we drove back into Santa Fe, I realized neither one of us was talking. The realty agent knew he didn't have to. He could never be as good a salesman as nature was. I kept hearing the wind as I heard it from where the house was perched on top of the world, saying, "If you turn your back on this house, on this place, on this day, you'd be the biggest fool alive."

I sat in a small room in the realtor's office, talking on the phone to Marsha back in Los Angeles. I rambled on and on, trying to capture in words what my eyes and ears and all my senses had experienced twenty minutes before. Her enthusiasm and excitement were fired by my energy and she was as anxious to see it as I was to describe it. If our relationship had shifted off center by a few degrees, her voice was telling me that maybe we were back on line. I told her I was going to make an offer on the house, contingent on her seeing it and wanting it as much as I did.

Now another common thread was winding itself through my life. It was almost ten years since I drove myself up to Bedford Village, New York, to look for a summer house that might cheer up and possibly heal Joan in her fight against cancer. I bought that house on my own since Joan was in no condition to be driving through the countryside looking at houses. Now, years later, I was looking at another summer house alone, hoping that by my taking the initiative toward something positive, it would heal an ailment of another kind. It was a matter of days before Marsha and I stood together atop that perfect spot a few miles outside Santa Fe. The winding, bumpy, dusty roads never bothered Marsha for a moment. In fact, I think she preferred it that way, just as she never thought it was an "isolated" spot. I watched her face as she stepped out of the car and saw what was waiting. One hand went over her mouth and I could see the tears of pure joy filling up her eyes.

"You mean we could really have this?" she said to me, a variation on her question, "Do we deserve this?" when she first saw the house in Los Angeles.

After filling out the appropriate papers regarding the house, we checked into a nearby hotel. Marsha was animated, discussing how she wanted to furnish the place, and how she wanted to leave the land untouched, preserving its natural state. From the small balcony outside our room, we could see the huge bolts of lightning miles away, turning night into day every few seconds.

On that night in Santa Fe, was I conscious of the identical scenario of those two events, that "common thread," the search for a house on my own, first in an effort to save the loss of a wife and now to save the loss of a marriage? No, I was not. The first time it occurred to me was this very minute, as I write these words on these pages. I find that the writing of a memoir has two functions. One is to pass on, as much as you're willing to tell, the facts and deeds of your life to those who might be at all interested. The other function is to discover a truth about yourself that you never had either the time or the courage to face before. You will never investigate yourself as vehemently as you do when you put one word after another, one thought after another, one revelation after another, in the pages that make up your memoirs, and you will suddenly realize the person you are instead of the person you *thought* you were. To force memory is to open yourself up to that which you have chosen to forget. It's your own Rashomon. You begin to see all the different sides of your own story.

TO PUT THINGS in perspective, I have to back up a little and bring my daughters, Ellen and Nancy, into the picture again. In 1980 Nancy was graduating from the Westlake School. I was asked to give the commencement address for her class. I had long since given up my fear of public speaking, but it returned with a vengeance on that day. The last thing I wanted to do was embarrass Nancy and I worked as hard writing that speech as I would on the first act of a new play. In the fall, she was off to Williams College in Massachusetts and as all parents who put their child on a plane that will carry them away from their childhood, we think to ourselves, "Where did the time go and what will replace those incredible years for me?"

To go back even further with Ellen, she had already given two schools a chance in California, searching for a clue to her future. She moved back to New York on her own, found an apartment, reunited with her former girlfriends from the Dalton School, then attended New York University for a while. She soon found a job in the Holly Solomon Art Gallery in SoHo, but still worked out regularly in dance classes. One of her aspirations was to become a choreographer. Her inspiration was Bob Fosse and eventually she presented an evening of her work at New York's prestigious Lotus Club on Park Avenue.

But there was something pulling Ellen in a completely different direction. As many young people were doing then, she soon found herself looking to fulfill the spiritual side of her life, possibly influenced by Marsha's own interest in Eastern religion and philosophy. I was surprised how deeply Ellen's interest ran when she decided to fly to Bombay, India, to study under the tutelage of a master guru, Swami Muktananda. Neither Ellen nor Nancy had much religious training, and this trip to India must have come from a very deep need to search for something she was missing. When she finally arrived back in California, Ellen seemed more centered than I ever remembered her, and she seemed ready to take the next step in her life. When Muktananda made one of his few pilgrimages to America, he set up an ashram in Santa Monica, just a fifteen-minute drive from our house. She and Marsha went down there quite often and Nancy and I were invited to come to one of Muktananda's sessions. I was amazed to see how many devotees he had. It seemed to me there were almost two thousand happy people squeezed together on the floor, made possible, I suppose, because they all left their shoes outside the main hall.

Nancy and I were respectfully quiet as we listened to Muktananda speak through his interpreter, and what he said was quite inspiring; I could see why he had so many followers throughout the world. Nancy and I, however, did not become converts. It was not because of any lack of faith in his sincerity and his wisdom, but like so many good things that are offered to you in this life, it either has something for you or it doesn't. Through this guru, Ellen not only found the answer to some questions that needed clarifying for her, but she also found a tall, lanky devotee with a warm smile named John Leland. It eventually led to marriage and in December of 1980, she gave birth to a son, Andrew Leland, my first grandchild. Nothing could please a father more or make him feel older than becoming a grandfather.

When one looked at both Ellen's and Nancy's faces, you couldn't help seeing the face of Joan, the same color hair, the same smile, the same special aura that was part of Joan's nature. There was no doubt in my mind that Joan found a way to attend the graduation, the wedding and the birth of her first grandson.

ELLEN DECIDED after living almost a year in Los Angeles that she wanted her son to grow up in the same environment as she had. She and John found a house near Nyack, New York, and from her back porch she could see the Tappan Zee Bridge and the Hudson River. Downriver a few miles was the George Washington Bridge, the same bridge that I passed every day as a boy on my way to school. With my family all now living back East—since Nancy also made it clear that after she graduated from Williams, she wanted to find a place of her own in New York—I was wondering what I was doing in California, and now in New Mexico as well. I never seemed or felt comfortable in any other environment than the one I was conceived in, and I'm sure I must have been born with an umbilical cord so ferociously tied to New York that I thought someone in the delivery room never took the time to sever it. This was especially so on the nights I had to drive myself from Santa Fe to our hidden house in the hills without the benefit of a full moon. I never did get the hang of it as the bolo-tied salesman had told me I would, and I wondered if Marsha would mind my installing eight miles of ground lamps that, while they might have bothered the local naturalists, sure as hell would have helped me find home before dawn.

WHEN WORK ON the house in Santa Fe was finished, when Marsha had planted her last tree and hung her last picture, when the last towel rack was in place, hung with the appropriate towels, I stood by in awe. In the early morning she loved sitting on the bench outside, wearing a robe and holding a large mug of coffee, her legs crossed, contemplating the beauty that surrounded her. Perhaps her studying a different way to view life on her trips to Muktananda's ashram in India had prepared her to look within herself and to connect with nature. She found something to do there that I found almost impossible to achieve: she relaxed. I could read a book, I could watch a basketball game, I could play tennis, but I could not sit for two hours or even twenty minutes and just let my mind wander. It had nothing to do with achievement. I was not looking for ideas—they came on their own, and when they did, I sifted through them, tossing out the worthless ones and holding aside those that had a sparkle. Do artists look at a mountain or a sunflower without thinking of how it would look on canvas? I don't know. I must ask one.

I never became disenchanted with the house, but after a while I found that a beautiful view is always just a beautiful view, and my restless mind was suddenly searching for new ways to achieve satisfaction. The day I told Marsha I was going to Connecticut to try out *Actors and Actresses,* the look on her face went from surprise to anger as quickly and as threateningly as the lightning bolts that were almost a nightly occurrence.

"You said you weren't going to do a play for a while," she said with a look of irritation and disbelief I can still remember.

"I'm not doing a play," I answered defensively. "I'm just going to try it out. See how it goes."

"We've just done the house and you're going off to try out a play you may never even do?" she said, her tone incredulous.

"I can't tell unless I try it out. I'm getting restless. I can't paint or plant or just hang out all the time. The fun was doing the house; now it's finished, isn't it?"

She looked at me with a coldness that was chilling.

"Yes. You're right," she said almost calmly. "It is definitely finished."

The word "finished" resonated through the hills and the canyons, making an impact that was all too clear to me. I should have stayed. I should have called off the tryout. But the show was cast, the theater was booked, the director was waiting for me. Whatever compelled me to be in a theater again obviously was more powerful than watching the clouds roll by or staring at a billion stars at night. The stars didn't need my help, but a play about to be born did. My newfound passion for the great outdoors was short-lived. I was an indoor person who thrived in a world where I never got lost trying to find my way home. I was hoping that once I got back from Connecticut, Marsha and I would be able to work things out. I was as wrong as I could be.

I MET MARSHA at the appointed time in the office of her therapist. He was an attractive man in his late forties, extremely bright, but without a trace of warmth or compassion, which I was hoping to find. He was there as an arbiter to help reconcile us. He was, in fact, not a therapist for individual cases any longer, but was now doing something called corporate counseling. I could only picture sixty-seven executives in suits, lying on sofas in a huge gym, where he counseled them from atop a lifeguard's stand, bellowing cheerful clues to more productive gross output through a bullhorn. Marsha was one of his last remaining individual patients. He sat behind a large desk, Marsha and I opposite him but not close to each other. The look on her face, as I recall it, was pained but determined. Her therapist opened the proceedings by explaining to me the state of Marsha's emotional stress, her pain, her dilemma, her sorrow, her regrets and her determination to do what she thought was the only solution to our situation. I was hoping for a reprieve, a last-minute stay of execution. It seemed unlikely. He summed it up in one sentence.

"Marsha would like a separation of six months."

I thought he said six years but six months sounded just as long to me. I nodded that I understood but not that I necessarily was in agreement.

"And how do we accomplish that?" I asked, not knowing what it's like to be separated for six months.

"Marsha will leave. She would like to do this as soon as possible."

I looked at her. She glanced at me to see my reaction, then put her head down. I had screwed up and I knew it, but I was still in love with her and naively thought that a dinner alone with her that night would straighten out everything, clearly another example of the overconfident playwright who thinks he can rewrite anything. I turned back to the therapist, facing reality for the first time.

"Six months?" I repeated as if it had just sunk in. "And how do we live our lives? Does Marsha see other men? Do I see other women? Because I think that six months would be disastrous. It's the same as saying it's all over."

"Not necessarily," he said. "I did it myself," he continued, revealing his own life, which I always thought was anathema to therapists and analysts. "My wife and I separated for months. It can be done."

"And how did it work out?" I asked.

"Not well, we eventually divorced."

I was stunned by his answer. Then I laughed because what else could I do?

"Gee, that really worked out swell, didn't it?" I said with needless sarcasm. It was quiet for a moment. No one chose to speak, so I guessed it was my turn again.

"Is this your recommendation?" I asked him.

"It is," he said. "But more importantly, it's Marsha's wish. The situation is regrettable, but it's not negotiable. Still, you never know how these things work out."

I knew how they worked out if he was any example. I looked at Marsha again. I could see the tears about to surface and she turned away again; the look of determination, though, was still there. The meeting was over. I was instructed that Marsha would need the next two afternoons to get her clothes and belongings out. The house would remain the way it was, at least for the time being.

I left the office first. Only in movies would the two of us go down the elevator together. When I got outside, the sun was beating down on me like everything else was, only it didn't warm me. Inside I was as cold as a dead man. Marsha packed up during the next two afternoons and I stayed away in my office. I came back to the house after calling to make sure she had left. I walked around in a daze and wondered what Marsha was feeling at that same moment. I went into her dressing room and opened the closets. Some of her things were still there, but enough was gone to make the emptiness more vivid than even I anticipated. Nine years before I had opened Joan's closet on the day after she died. Everything was still there exactly as she left it, which made her absence even more acute. In both instances, I felt guilty about opening their closets, knowing then that Joan was never coming back, and now that Marsha might never return as well. I felt I was invading their privacy, because in some sense the space was still theirs, even after death or separation. I closed Marsha's closet door, walked into my office, sat at my desk, picked up a pen, looked at it and realized that for the first time in years, I had no desire to write a single word.

Marsha's request was fulfilled. We didn't see each other again for well over six months, and by then, as anticipated, it was too late for both of us. The awful thing about losing a spouse is that, unlike any other bad day you've had at the office, when you come home, there's no one there with whom to share it.

THE SHOT HEARD 'ROUND BEL AIR

21

AFTER FOUR MONTHS of separation, I filed for divorce. There was no word, no sign from Marsha that she wanted it any other way. In California, you have six months after filing to change your mind; during that time, if both parties are willing, you could call off the divorce and return to your marital status. This never happened. As I look back on it, I don't believe my going to Connecticut to try out a play was the only reason for the breakup. It's my belief that some marriages end because they have run out their time. If there are genetic faults in our systems that determine the length of our lives, I believe to some extent that holds true for marriages as well.

From my point of view, Marsha and I had seven incredible years together, but in the eighth year, something terminal infected our marriage, and there was nothing either one of us could do to save it. This is not to say that there weren't other specifics that led to the breakup, but I think even those were inevitable. We simply could not fulfill each other's needs past eight years. In the heat of any marriage that is heading for destruction, it's amazing how many things remain unsaid, unspoken, and it's probably those silent issues that are the ones that do you in. In time, at least in my case, you may even forget what they were. I put no blame on Marsha nor do I accept full responsibility. It takes two to untangle.

Now, almost two decades later, Marsha and I remain friends. We still have the Nancy and Ellen connection, and I have often gone to see plays or

films that Marsha is in, always happy to see that she's doing well. This benign state, however, did not exist at the time of our breakup. I was bitterly
and ferociously angry at her for leaving. Once obsessed by an abandonment complex, as I was, there was nothing that could defuse the bomb
within me to keep it from exploding. Perhaps it was that the split came so
soon after Nancy went off to college and Ellen moved back to New York
with her new family, that triggered my anxiety. I was now living alone in a
house that was too big for two people, let alone one. I at least had our dog,
Duffy, the sweetest friend a man alone could have. He was, legally, community property, but fortunately I had him for a few years, until Marsha
bought her own home and then he spent the rest of his days with her. It's
amazing, when you're alone, angry, dismal and fairly neurotic, how much
you will talk to your dog. I told him things I wouldn't even reveal to my
analyst. He always listened attentively, never interrupted and, above all,
never disagreed with me. I let him listen to all my phone calls. I had nothing to hide from him. He occasionally heard some foul language from me,
but I always assured him it was never directed at him. And every night he
slept with me in my bed. In the early days of bachelorhood, his licking my
face could be very comforting.

If Marsha thought I was needy, I don't think she had any idea how
deep the bottom of the well was. Abandonment, in my case, only applied
to women. When my father died, I accepted it as the natural fate of man.
Joan's death probably set the stage for the intensity of my rage at Marsha's
going, because, in a way, it was not much different than a death. I knew intellectually that time heals everything, but the bitter weeks and months
that followed brought no relief, and suddenly I had no time to allow time
to pass.

Marsha was gone from the house; now I wanted her out of my mind.
She refused to move, though; in fact, she took over every foot of the house,
and even sat staring at me as I ate my meals. She invaded my office as well,
sat on my typewriter, made disapproving looks at whatever I had typed on
the page, and finally she became the first person ever to find out how to
stop me from writing.

Finally, one night, I felt I had to do something so outrageous, so unlike
me, so close to madness, that I might be able to stem the tide. I remem-

bered that I had a .38-caliber pistol in the house and a small box of bullets. I had bought the gun right after we had moved into the house, and, for the first and only time it ever happened, someone tried to break in through a back window while Nancy, Marsha and I were at home. The alarm went off and so did the would-be intruder, but the vigilante in me, the protector of his family and his goods, decided to arm himself against any more attempts to harm his loved ones. A while later, I was told by a police officer that a .38-caliber gun was the worst protection I could have had.

"It's a good way to get yourself killed," he said. "Chances are any burglar with a gun knows how to use it better than you. If you feel you really need a weapon, get yourself a double-barreled shotgun. That usually stops them."

This conversation was getting too Wild West for me, so I tossed my small gun far back on the top shelf of a closet, deciding against arming myself for an outbreak of war. But now, years later, I had the gun in my hand, and I loaded two bullets into the chamber. I wasn't quite sure what I was going to do, but there was no chance I was going to empty those bullets into my head. I was angry, but I wasn't crazy. I left Duffy in the house and heard him whimpering as I walked down the steps that led to the pool. I turned the pool lights on. It was about eleven at night and the darkened windows in the large house next door above my hill indicated my neighbors must all be asleep. I sat on the cold brick steps that led down to the pool and just stared into the water. How long I sat there like that, I can't remember, but finally I took one bullet out of the chamber, put it in my pocket and then clicked the other bullet into its firing position. Then I slowly raised my arm, gun in hand, feeling the heavy weight of the barrel; I aimed it carefully, squeezed the trigger ever so slowly . . . and shot the pool. I got it dead center, about where the four-foot part drops off to the deep end. The blast was deafening. I was sure it reverberated all through Bel Air and over into Westwood. I looked up to see if the neighbors' lights had come on, but they hadn't. I waited for two or three patrol cars to suddenly pull up, but they didn't. Actually nothing happened. No one called; no one came. The only thing I heard was my own voice saying in astonishment, "Holy shit! You are nuts!"

Perhaps I was, but sudden calm came over me, a release of all the pent-up anger that I had been storing inside ever since Marsha had left. Firing the gun had set off a noise infinitely louder and more powerful than I could ever have made myself, and I felt like some gorilla in the wild, pounding his chest at what a fearsome creature he was. Then I started to laugh at the idiocy of it, thinking of what would have happened if the police had shown up.

"We heard a gunshot, sir. What happened?"

"It was me, officer, I fired the gun."

"Someone try to break in?"

"No. Someone broke out."

"Broke *out?* Who was that, sir?"

"My wife. But it's all right. I shot the pool."

"You shot the *pool?* Why would you do that?"

"Well, for one thing, I knew I could hit it . . . I had another bullet but I didn't need it. It was dead."

"The pool?"

"No. The pain."

And it was. I went back into the house, tossed the gun into the back of the closet, got into bed with Duffy at my feet and had the best sleep I'd had in months.

THE PAIN was gone but the complaining lingered on. I no longer made Duffy the sole, dutiful listener of my residual anger. I now turned to my friends, who would nod politely at my daily harangues about the pitfalls of marriage while they tried to eat their Caesar salads and listen at the same time. I was extremely boring for about three and a half months, and then I eased off to being just plain annoying. I had only reached the point of being better than somewhat bearable when the most unlikely person put an end to all of my complaining with one devastating sentence.

I first met Sean Connery and his wonderful wife, Micheline, at a party when Marsha and I were still together and happy. My friendship with Sean developed more fully on a Sunday afternoon at Barbra Streisand's home in Malibu Canyon. It was a fun, games and sports party, and somehow I ended up playing tennis singles with Sean. He was new to the game and I had been playing for about twenty years. As we rallied before the game started, I thought I was the superior player. I decided I was not going to use my A game against him because that would have been poor form, and also because I didn't *have* an A game. At best, I had a B-minus game, although on occasion, I had an A version of a B-minus game, which meant I could sometimes beat B-minus players but was helpless against genuine A players. What I didn't take into account was Sean's competitiveness, his skill as an all-around athlete (he was, I heard, a first-rate soccer player), and that he had learned to play golf to make the *Goldfinger* film and turned into a low handicap player. He also had twice the stamina I did. Still, I was able to keep up with him, and if I won the match that day, it was by the narrowest of margins. I knew that if there was going to be a next time, he already would have taken lessons, and by then would have been a B-plus player, and my fight would be uphill.

After that we began to see each other socially—although only occasionally because he spent most of his time living in Spain—and we had dinners out or dinners at our house. One night we got into a private conversation and I began to tell him what it was like growing up in New York during the Depression with two parents whose behavior with each other was anything but normal. I told him how my mother was playing gin rummy in the kitchen with her lady friends one night, and my angry father, who had not been speaking to her, walked into the kitchen in his pajamas, drank a glass of water over the sink, and then, having said nothing, left and turned off the lights, leaving them all in the dark. Or how he left his suit, shoes and a hat laid out on the floor near the front door looking like someone who just died, just to give my mother the fright of her life as she came home from her sister's one night. Sean laughed uproariously. He loved those stories and wanted more.

He then told me what his Dad and brother were like, all growing up in Scotland and how his mother dealt with them. Amazingly, his stories of family life weren't that much different from mine, and we realized how much we had in common in our youth. I was about three years older than Sean. I enjoyed his company enormously and told him it always had been my hope to write a film for him in which he could co-star with Michael Caine, with whom I had already worked in *California Suite*. Sean was eager to do a comedy, although I think audiences preferred him in his action films or in the darker dramas he sometimes undertook.

One day I called Sean in his L.A. apartment that he used as a pied-à-terre, to tell him I thought I had an idea for the film. He asked me to come over and tell him the story, but he warned me that he didn't have too much time since he had a golf date at the Bel Air Country Club. Sean got his golfing clothes ready as I talked and he listened, smiling his broad smile at the parts he liked. When I was halfway through my story, he realized he was going to be late for his match, so he asked me to finish it as we went down to get his car. He closed his apartment door, which was high up on the seventeenth floor or thereabouts, and crossed to the elevator. Suddenly he realized he had left his clubs back in the apartment and didn't have his keys with him. I suggested going down to the concierge and getting an extra key.

"It will take *tew* long," he said in that inimitable Scottish brogue. "I'll get them. I'll be right back."

I watched as he walked down to the end of the hall and opened the window. When I saw him climb out, I rushed down to see where he was going. There he was, climbing along the ledge, seventeen stories above the earth; he eventually found a window open in his apartment and disappeared inside. *Tew* minutes later, he came out of the apartment, his golf clubs slung over his shoulder, and without any comment on what he had just done, said to me, "Go on. Tell me the rest of the shtory." The SH sound was his trademark. He didn't just act James Bond. He *was* James Bond.

Months after the split with Marsha, I was up in Sean's apartment waiting to go out to dinner while Micheline fixed us both a drink. As I had been doing for some time, I continued my harangue about the breakup of the marriage. Sean obviously had had enough of it, and the expression on his face turned as stern as that of a sergeant major in the British Special Forces. He fixed his eyes directly on mine, practically piercing my pupils. He then said to me, making it clear he was going to say it once and *only* once, "Get *off* it, Neil." Then he looked away and finished his drink.

I was shaken but not stirred. I understood immediately that what he was saying was not only that he didn't want to hear it again, but that it was time for me to give it up. The only thing he spared me was not saying, "Be a man, fer Crise sakes." His remark was spoken in a low, almost threatening voice that packed so much power it came at me a thousand times louder than the gunshot that killed the pool.

I finally moved on with my new life, looking to a brighter future, when I suddenly realized that while I had been busy brooding away my time, something awful had been happening to my career.

FROM THE BOTTOM UP
22

ACTORS AND ACTRESSES never made it out of Connecticut. *Fools* ran a few months and closed. The revival of *Little Me* was short-lived. Suddenly the rumor around Broadway was that Neil Simon was through. He had lost his touch. The long consistent ride to the top was over.

If I looked closely for clues as to what went wrong, the answers could be found just in reading the titles of the three failed plays. I had gotten away from my roots, away from the kind of plays that audiences so closely identified with, plays like *Barefoot in the Park, The Odd Couple, Plaza Suite, Chapter Two, California Suite,* and *The Sunshine Boys.* Those plays expressed my own feelings about people and experiences that I knew well, and since writing those plays I had gotten far off the track. Recognizing it was one thing. Getting back on wasn't so easy. I now knew what direction to take, but I wasn't sure what vehicle would be the one to carry me there. There were no ideas flowing freely from my mind as they had done in the past. I felt shaky, and loss of confidence can rob you of the ability to tell a good idea from a bad one. You find yourself staring at a blank wall, one that had never been blank before.

I sat for days and weeks wondering what would happen to me if my playwrighting career truly was over. I was not trained for or experienced in any other kind of work, and like Job, I was wondering if God was testing me or just bored with me. I started to think about the classic, older plays and movies, trying to take them apart, scene by scene, so I could see what made them work, only to reach the conclusion that what made them work was an inspiration on the part of the author. There isn't a writer alive who hasn't gone through this experience. It was especially frightening to me, though, because this was my first time. Was I drying up or had the gunshot explosion clogged my ears, blocking all thoughts from getting through to my brain?

One afternoon, out of sheer desperation, I started to rummage through the drawers of my desk, looking for some idea that I had discarded, but now might spark me if I saw it in a better and fresher light. There was nothing there that was any good, though, and I couldn't think why I even saved them in the first place. I looked in my files where I kept my original first drafts of plays. *Barefoot in the Park* was there, typed originally on cheap yellow paper that was now drying up and beginning to disintegrate, looking something like the Dead Sea Scrolls. (I eventually put it in airtight plastic bags.) I found *The Odd Couple,* drafts one through twelve. I didn't remember doing it over so many times. I was about to close the file when I noticed that in a faded manila envelope, unmarked, was another script. I took it out and read the title: *Brighton Beach Memoirs.* I looked at the date on the lower right corner. I had written it nine years before and had never even looked at it since then. There were thirty-five pages, held together by a small paper clip. I remembered how much Ellen and Nancy had loved those pages at the time, and how they prodded me to finish it. I was unresponsive; I had hit a wall with the play, so I just filed the pages away.

I sat back and read it slowly, surprised by how much I was smiling, even laughing at it. When I finished, I looked up at the blank wall and said to myself, "Wait a minute. I think this is good. *Really* good." I read it once again, and whatever block that stopped me from going on nine years ago had mysteriously disappeared. I knew at that instant in what direction the play should go, and the years that had passed seemed as if they never happened at all. I put a fresh sheet of paper into the typewriter, and seven weeks later I was finished with the first full draft of *Brighton Beach Memoirs.* The mistakes I had made in planning the play the first time became clear. The play took place in 1937, just as the clouds of war were gathering over Europe. I wanted some depth to the characters, to show their anguish and fears in the face of hard times in America during the Depression, and their worries about their relatives in Poland, who might never get out in time. I had tried to write the first version with some humor, but it felt strained and forced. This time I decided there would be only one character in the play with humor, and that would be fourteen-year-old Eugene Morris Jerome, no doubt my own alter ego. The Depression didn't really affect him, and the impending war was a million miles away. He was going through puberty and all he had on his mind was sex, baseball and his annoyance at always having to go to the store for his mother. Fourteen-year-olds have no idea that anything in the world is important except their own immediate needs. To get his own thoughts across to the audience, I had him quote to them from his diary, which he called, "The Unbelievable, Fantastic and Completely Private Thoughts of I, Eugene Morris Jerome, in this, the fourteenth year of his life, in the year 1937, in the Community of Brighton Beach, Borough of Brooklyn, Kings County, City of New York, Empire State of the American Nation." I think I may have borrowed a little of Thornton Wilder's *Our Town* in that description, but if you borrow, borrow from the best.

I sent the play to Manny Azenberg and waited anxiously for his reaction. Manny was ecstatic but also guarded, and even though I thought this play was one of the best I had written, I was extremely tentative about investing my own money in it, as I had done with every play since *The Odd Couple*. Our faith in it dropped still more when the Shubert Organization, who owned most of the theaters in New York, turned the play down. They read it and said it was too episodic. This news invariably would get around Broadway, making our task only more difficult. We then sent the play to James Nederlander, who, with his brothers, were the second largest theater owners in America. I'm not sure if they were crazy about the play, but they took it on, in part, I think, because they were happy to get me away from the Shuberts, whose theaters were the ones I used for almost all my early successes. The offers from investors to put money into the play didn't come quite as freely as they did when I was riding high, but we did have our supporters. One was Bernard Gersten, now one of the guiding lights of the Lincoln Center complex of theaters, but then he was working for Radio City Music Hall Productions. On Bernie's recommendation, they put in a hundred thousand dollars and became co-producers with Manny, along with actor Wayne Rogers, who had his own group of investors.

The pressure on me to succeed was now even greater than it had been with my first play, *Come Blow Your Horn*. One more flop and I would be worse off than a newcomer. I would be a has-been, and a has-been is nothing more than a newcomer whose promise has eroded. On the upside was our choice of director, Gene Saks, who last did the hit *California Suite* for me. For *Brighton Beach* we gathered a wonderful ensemble cast featuring a young teenage boy who was soon to become a major star named Matthew Broderick. Matthew was everything I hoped Eugene Morris would be— shy, intelligent and funny without ever trying to be. Our tryout was to be at the Ahmanson Theater in Los Angeles and then, barring disastrous notices, it would be on to San Francisco and then the Alvin Theater in New York.

The set of the small Brooklyn house was perfectly done by designer David Mitchell. It was small enough to be claustrophobic, especially since it had to house seven people. The walls were paper thin and there were no secrets in the Jerome household. I created the family by doing the exact opposite to what happened to me in my own life. My father left my mother when I was Eugene's age and she and I were taken in by my cousins, Ceil and Martin Klein, who then lived in a small apartment in the East 60s. They later moved to their first home, a little house in Forest Hills, and my mother and I were given a tiny room together, sleeping in the same bed. For a fourteen-year-old boy to be sleeping in the same bed with his mother gave me more emotional scars than I like to think of. I literally slept in the small crack between the bed and the wall, for fear of touching her during the night. That episode was worth at least a year of analysis. My brother, Danny, was taken in by my mother's brother and his wife, Sol and Marie Levy. He did not have the same trouble, since they did not invite him into their bed. With all this happening in two separate houses, I had to rearrange our lives to fit us all into the same house for the sake of the play. What happened in the play was that my mother and father (actually Eugene's) lived with their two sons, Eugene and Stanley, and took in the mother's sister Kate and her two daughters, Nora and Laurie, since Kate's husband died from cancer. When I was a boy, the word "cancer" was never uttered unless spoken in a whisper. This is how Eugene explained it to the audience:

> EUGENE
> . . . Aunt Blanche's husband, Dave, died—
> from this thing. It was . . . *(he whispers)* . . .
> cancer. I think they were afraid if you said it
> out loud, God would say, "I HEARD
> THAT! YOU SAID THE DREADED
> DISEASE! JUST FOR THAT I SMITE
> YOU DOWN WITH IT" . . . There are
> some things that grown-ups just won't
> discuss. For example, my grandfather died
> from . . .
> > *(He whispers)*
> . . . diphtheria. Anyway, after Uncle Dave
> died, he left Aunt Blanche with no money.
> Not even insurance. And she couldn't
> support herself because she had . . .
> > *(He whispers)*
> . . . asthma . . . My father thought it would
> just be temporary, but it's been three and a
> half years so far and I think because of
> Aunt Blanche's situation, my father is
> developing . . .
> > *(He whispers)*
> . . . high blood pressure.

Since I was raised in Manhattan, why was this semiautobiographical play taking place in such a distant place as Brighton Beach? The answer: because it was such a distant place. I wanted my father to be beleaguered with problems like a) having to hold down two jobs to support seven people, b) after a hard day's work, having to hear the problems of everyone else in the family, and c) being expected to give advice as sage as that of King Solomon. That responsibility and pressure was enough to give him (whisper) a nervous breakdown. To travel by subway from Brighton Beach to the garment center in New York in the freezing winter or in the brutal heat of summer was more than one man could handle. But Jack did his duty without complaining, and his lack of complaining is what leads to his heart attack in the second act. Troubles beget troubles and to me, this was the stuff that good plays are made of.

During the rehearsals of the play in Los Angeles, a situation arose with our cast of actors that I had never seen before. It was an ensemble company, meaning there were no prominent stars in the cast and no one role more important than anyone else's. There was one exception, however, a very good actress, who was once pretty well known in films. To her credit I'd say she asked for no special favors, no higher salary or more prominent billing. She worked as hard as any other member of the company. But as we got to the beginning of the third week, meaning we had less than two weeks to go before we started previews in front of an audience, the woman in question seemed to get nervous. During rehearsals she would stop the flow of a scene to ask Gene Saks for an interpretation of a different move on stage. Or she might ask, "Wouldn't it be better if I did this or that?" All actors do this kind of thing, but there must come a time when they start to act as a group, and I could see the rest of the cast losing their patience. They were now at the stage where they wanted to rehearse the play without stopping, waiting to hear Gene's comments after they finished the scene. We never could get that far. The actress continued to interrupt, stopping the flow of the other actors' performance, always to ask about *her* part, *her* motivation, *her* position on the stage.

Finally, during a break one day, I talked to Gene about this problem and he agreed that he foresaw trouble ahead, but he is a patient man, and directors always feel they can correct the situation through their own efforts. Another day went by and things did not get any better. That night I left the rehearsal hall shortly after all the actors were gone. It was quite dark, and I started to look for my car parked on a side street in a fairly questionable neighborhood. Suddenly, from across the street, I heard a hissing sound, like four tires going flat one after the other as the air escaped in fits and starts. I turned and looked. From behind a car, I saw shadowy figures beckoning to me with their hands, all hissing to get my attention. I couldn't make out who they were, and was understandably hesitant to re-spond to hissing and shadowy figures, especially in an area that required cautious people to walk quickly to their cars and drive off with the doors locked. Curiosity, not prudence, got the better of me, however, and I crossed over. Behind the car were six members of the company minus the actress who was causing us so much worry. Their spokesman said to me that it pained them to say what they had to say, that they felt guilty talking about one of their own, and he made it clear that none of them had ever done this kind of thing before in their careers, ever.

Their spokesman continued: "Neil, none of us here wants to hurt a member of our profession, but we also want to protect this play. We all feel this actress is hurting us, hurting Gene and ultimately why we all wanted this job. We've been as patient as we could, but things are not getting any better, and if a move is not made soon, everybody will suffer for it. We're saying this not only as actors, but as the characters you created, the Jerome family, because that's who we feel we are. Obviously the decision is yours and Gene's, and we'll abide by whatever you decide. We love this play and it's the only reason we're standing here whispering in the dark behind a parked car."

With that, they all dispersed into the darkness and went their separate ways. That night I called Gene Saks and he agreed that something had to be done. Our only worry was who could we get to replace her on such short notice. A favorite actress of mine and Gene's was Joyce Van Patten. I had already used her in *I Ought to Be in Pictures,* in which she was superb. We called her, found she was available, and she showed up early the next morning, read the part for us and we signed her on the spot. We did more good work with her in the next ten days than we did in the previous three weeks with the other actress. It may sound cruel to talk so frivolously about dismissing (aka firing) another actress, but the move was made for the betterment of all concerned. It wasn't only Shakespeare who said, "The play's the thing."

When an actor or actress is replaced, the actor who leaves is entitled to their full pay for as long as their contract has stipulated. I've always thought this was grossly unfair to the other actors. One actor who doesn't work out leaves and gets full pay for nine months, while the actor who is a major plus for the play has to perform eight shows a week for nine months to get the same salary. I never thought the producers should benefit for their error in judgment in casting the wrong person, but I did feel a fairer arrangement would be that the fired actor receives full salary for half the term of their contract while the other half of the money should go to the Actors Fund or to Equity, the actors union, for those actors who are in need. I doubt that this change will ever happen but I'm just throwing it out on the table for someone else to examine.

THE PLAY received excellent reviews in Los Angeles and then again in San Francisco. This was still no reason to feel optimistic, however. Success in the New York theater is almost wholly dependent on receiving praise and support from two sources: a good review in the *New York Times,* and a healthy advance sale from the agents who book theater parties, the latter being those large groups of people who buy out half a house or more for a specific night in the future, usually to raise funds for charitable organizations. The largest advance sale in history was the twenty million dollars booked for *The Lion King.* A play, any play by any author in today's world, is lucky to get a million dollar advance sale. In the early 1980s, when I had a play coming in that was preceded by three hits in a row, we often had as much as a two million dollar advance sale. But after two failures in a row, the agents had backed off, and waited to see if the *New York Times* would be favorable to our play. Many people often say to me, "Oh, you don't have to worry about the reviews. You're Neil Simon. People will come to your plays no matter what." Unfortunately, that's not true, and to be perfectly frank, why should it be? The two failures that preceded *Brighton Beach Memoirs* were proof enough of that. We arrived in New York with nowhere near the advance we had had in the past, and the negative review we got from the *New York Times* on the opening of *Memoirs* was certainly no help.

If I can stop the action here for just a moment, I'd like to make a point about the relationship between critics and playwrights, or, more to the point, *this* playwright. Of the thirty plays I've done to date, I can barely remember what the critics in New York wrote about them, with the possible exception of five or six of the plays. I imagine most playwrights would best remember what they said about his or her *first few* plays; the ones that would make the most impact on his or her career. Three strikes and you're out. Your first play, of course, would be the most important. An out-and-out pan could send you scurrying to the nearest community college in hopes of finding a career that would pay you a decent salary and keep your name out of the papers forever. An overwhelming rave review will, of course, keep you temporarily euphoric. After the hoopla recedes, after the parties you're invited to dwindle down to a precious few, after you've heard the question "What are you writing now?" for the thousandth time, the paralyzing fear of having not only to repeat your success, but to surpass it, causes you to lose the strength and confidence to pick up a pen again and aim it at a blank piece of paper. I was lucky. My first play was a moderate success. It bought me time and courage to go back to work immediately because no one out there knew I was out there in the first place.

By the time I had done my tenth play and even the twentieth play, I literally scanned through the opening night reviews, looking for the phrase or two that would predict the future of my latest work. It was a pass–fail business and you took the news stoically or happily. The reviews were obviously important, but only on *that* night, for *that* play, for *that* moment in time. Ask me today what *Times* critic Frank Rich had to say about *Brighton Beach Memoirs,* I'd have to think hard and probably come up with, "I think he didn't like it but he said some pretty nice things about it. I'm really not sure." The point is that time throws all your reviews into a blender and you get no special joy or disappointment in drinking the concoction that pours out because by now your doctor told you you are lactose intolerant. The past is past and you get on with your life because a review that was written ten years ago is only important to some theater student who looks it up on a Web site for an article he is writing about you. We have all of Shakespeare's plays but only a smattering of his reviews.

Now then, back to 1983. With two flops behind me, a weak advance sale and a not-so-good review from the *Times,* it seems implausible now that *Brighton Beach Memoirs* would go on to become the highest-profit-making play in the history of the New York theater, at least up until that time. The audiences simply adored it, and from the day after opening night, they came in droves. What *did* help, of course, was excellent word of mouth and a strong contingent of critics that *did* support the play, so much so that there was almost an out-and-out war among the critics themselves when it came to voting for the New York Critics Circle Award for Best Play. Led by Clive Barnes of the *New York Post,* formerly of the *New York Times,* he and his associates championed our cause, and our play won in a close contest. It was my first New York Critics Award ever. I have this award hanging on the wall of my office and as I was writing these pages, I looked closely at the award and at all the signatures of the critics. I am not a handwriting expert, but it's obvious that one hand signed the names of all twenty-two critics. Was that done not to embarrass those who did not wish to sign the award just because it was given to me? Or is that the way it's usually done? I have a similar award on my wall from the Dramatists Guild and it is clearly signed by each individual playwright—Arthur Laurents, Stephen Sondheim, Peter Stone, Wendy Wasserstein and so on. Is that because writers write and critics don't have the time? It's just another one of life's little puzzles to ponder. I do not take exception to critics or their reviews and I admire a great many of them and have often been helped by them. I cannot in good conscience defend all my plays. Some deserve what they got, and some got better than I thought they would. I guess I'm just wondering who signed all twenty-two signatures for them.

It was the grandest opening night party we ever had, and thanks to our investor, it was held in the lobby of the Radio City Music Hall. That imposing staircase alone is so enormous, we never worried that there weren't enough places for people to sit. I not only felt I was back on track, but that I was starting on a new journey, writing in a style I had been searching years to find. I never had any intention of making *Brighton Beach Memoirs* the first play of a trilogy dealing with the life and adventures of Eugene Morris Jerome, because if *Brighton Beach* failed, who would want to see a sequel to a flop? I will say one thing positive for Frank Rich, since that one thing is all I can count at the moment: despite a negative review, he admitted that there was something to admire in the play, and he wrote at the end of his review, "One hopes there will be a Chapter Two to *Brighton Beach Memoirs.*" I did consider that a constructive idea, so one might suggest that these two unlikely people actually collaborated in a way. Talk about Odd Couples.

The play ran for four years on Broadway, a very long time for any play in the post–1950s era; by then I knew where I wanted to get to in my career. My personal life was another matter. I was alone, single and somewhat lost, yet I knew I never wanted to marry again. After one death and one failed marriage, for all the good days it afforded me, another loss was a higher price than I ever wanted to pay again.

SHALL WE DANCE
23

OUR MEMORIES do not always move forward in linear fashion. Our thoughts often jump from real to imaginary, from the present to the past, to better times and to unhappier times, independent of our will. Since I have not planned ahead about what I'm going to write in this book, for some reason, probably a very obvious one, my thoughts suddenly just went back to my mother, now deceased. I miss her today. Not that she was very affectionate, but I always knew I had her full approval—which is what I probably need for an hour or two at this particular moment in my life. I am going through a bad patch as I write this, and the reason why might very well appear in the later pages of this memoir.

I'm not trying to be coy, but merely honest. Just as I never plan what play or film I might write next, I don't plan on what I will write next in these memoirs. As I write these lines at this moment, the "bad patch" I am going through feels as though it might linger, and it might be worth writing about. If it turns out to be a "fleeting pain," it might disappear and not even be worth thinking about. A memoir is in a sense akin to a day-to-day diary, and since I don't know what will happen with my life, I also can't tell as yet what I am willing or not willing to divulge on these pages.

When I think of my mother, I think of two particular days that were unforgettable. This is the first one.

Sometime after the opening of *The Sunshine Boys* film and George

Burns's winning of the Oscar, Marsha threw a fiftieth birthday party for me, upstairs at the Bistro Restaurant in Beverly Hills. There were about a hundred guests and my mother sat at our table, a seat away from Jack Nicholson. She looked her best, as she always tried to do, and was basking in the glory of her son's success. The irrepressible Jack Nicholson, wearing his usual dark glasses, even at night, seemed to be starting his sentences somewhere in the middle of a thought, which did not encourage my mother to attempt to enter into conversation with him. Instead, she was looking down at the far end of the room where George Burns was sitting with Walter Matthau and his wife, Carol.

In a play I had not yet written nor even thought about at that time, there is a scene where the mother (based on my own) talks to her son about the night she danced with actor George Raft when she was a young girl. The scene was based on a story my mother had told me over and over, ever since I was a boy. When she was sixteen years old, living in the Bronx, Mamie Levy (my mom) was known as one of the best ballroom dancers in the neighborhood. A young man would have to be pretty light-footed on the dance floor to have the nerve to ask my mother for a spin around the room. One night, a young George Burns, who was better known then for his fox-trots and his tangos than he was for his comedy, dropped in to look over the new crop of up-and-coming young dancers. In the play I used the name of George Raft instead of George Burns, since a Latin Lover made the story more provocative. But it was George Burns who spied her on the floor that night, and chose her as his dancing partner for the better part of the evening. The next day, Mamie Levy was the talk of the East Bronx. Overnight she had become, at least in that small corner of the world, a star.

My mother played and replayed that glorious night in her life, telling it to me over and over again from the time I was seven, through my entire childhood. I'd nod each time she told it to me and say, "Gee, that's great, Mom." And each time she'd say to me, "You don't believe me." No matter how much I protested that I did, she would still insist that I didn't believe her. Especially when George became a great comic star with his wife, Gracie Allen, my mother was positive that I would never believe her.

Now it was fifty-five or sixty years later, and she was finally in the same room with George again. I knew this was an opportunity not to be missed and I said, "Mom, come with me. I want to introduce you to George." To my surprise, she declined. "No, I'd be embarrassed. He'd never remember me."

"Well, you could remind him," I said.

"No, it's all right. Besides, you never believed that story."

I felt frustrated but I didn't push it. Twenty minutes later, George started to make his way around the room to take a few bows for his Academy Award. With the ever-present cigar in hand, he stopped to say hello to everyone, and never left a table before he got his big laugh, which was always well earned. The six-piece orchestra was playing and people started to get up to dance. I watched my mother's eyes as she watched George getting closer to where we were sitting, never giving an indication of how she would handle it if they were to meet. When he finally came over, he put his arm around my shoulder, and said to me, "Keep up the good work, kid. Someday you'll make it." I laughed, my mother smiled politely. Then he looked at my mother and said to me, "And who is this attractive lady, Neil?"

I said, "George, this is my mother, May Simon."

She nodded, smiled and said nothing more than, "How do you do."

I assumed George would turn and move away to work the next table, but instead he said, "Mrs. Simon, would you give me the honor of this dance?"

She didn't miss a beat. "I would love to," she said as she got up and was led by George onto the dance floor. She danced gloriously with him, and he moved her gracefully across the hardwood as if time had never passed, although he was now eighty and she was just a few years younger. As I watched them, they didn't seem to exchange a word, their feet being more compatible than their conversation. Everyone was watching them as they glided to the far side of the room, sensing something special was happening, but not having a clue as to what. They made their way now toward our side of the room and I was praying the music would never stop. As she neared our table, George gave her a little spin as his back was to our table and she was facing me. She caught my eye, looked at me and said softly so that not even George could hear, "Now do you believe me?"

The tears welled up in my eyes. It is an indescribable moment when a son sees his mother getting the greatest thrill in her life. She handled it with grace and dignity, but I could see she was overflowing with joy. She never once said anything to George about that night sixty years before in a Bronx ballroom, and she never repeated the story to me ever again. There was no need to.

THE OTHER OCCASION was a much sadder one. As my mother reached her late seventies, for the first time in her life she began to show her age. She always had youthful-looking skin, right up to her mid-seventies, but now the ravages of time were taking their toll. It was also evident in her walk and in her lack of energy; by this time, she would not have had the strength to dance around the room with George Burns, even to prove to me that she had been telling me the truth.

I found her a very nice hotel for elderly citizens called Westwood Horizons, just a short drive from my house. I managed to get her an extra large suite, despite her protests that I should save my money, but she eventually luxuriated in it. I spoke to her on the phone every day, and if I missed a single day, she would call saying, "When I didn't hear from you, I thought, God forbid, you were in a terrible accident." I picked her up on as many Sunday afternoons as I could to take her out to dinner along with Marsha. She loved lobster tails, but only once in a great while could I coax her to order them, since she feared it would send me to the poorhouse.

Her eightieth birthday was coming up, and although she frowned on birthday parties, I persuaded her to come to my house to celebrate this very special occasion. She couldn't refuse when she heard that her two sons and her four grandchildren all would be there. On the day, I picked her up at the Westwood Horizons; she was looking particularly frail. Still, when I entered the lobby, she was sitting erect in a straight-backed armchair, looking as regal and as well dressed as she could, a message to the other mothers who were sitting there for *their* children to pick them up, that she was doing just fine. It was, in some respects, a poignant sight to see these aging parents waiting for and depending on their offspring to bring some much-needed joy into their lives. The silk and lace competitions that were waged by these women, wearing their Sunday best, continued every weekend. On some weekends their children couldn't come, but they'd sit there as if waiting anyway, not to allow anyone to think that their children didn't care. Since the men rarely lived as long as the women, they were seen less often in the lobby, choosing either to wait for their family on the street outside the hotel, or to stay in their rooms and play cards rather than face the "indignity" of being cared for.

My mother nodded and smiled when she saw me and always made a point to introduce me as her son, Neil Simon, to all the women I had already met over a dozen times. Her hand was cold and bony as I helped her up and out of the lobby to my car parked out front. She was quiet as I drove, and she seemed not to want her thoughts exposed to me for fear of ruining the party we had prepared. Arriving at my house, she was extremely slow in getting out of the car, even with my help. It was difficult for her to maneuver the few steps to my front door, and she stopped a second to catch her breath.

"Are you all right, Mom?" I asked her.

Before she took the next step, she said to me without resignation or self-pity, "I think I've had enough."

She was telling me that she knew she was going soon and it was the first time she ever admitted something like that to me. In times of sickness or crisis in her life, she would always say to me, "Don't worry. You know me. I'm a fighter." She had suffered in many ways during her life, but she always weathered the storms. I think it was the dancer that still danced within her that kept her going.

The dinner went well, but as she opened the many presents set before her, you could see the anguish on her face. She wouldn't say it, but I knew she was thinking, "Why buy me all these beautiful gifts when I know I won't be around to enjoy them?" When she eventually died, I found her bankbooks. All the money I gave her, all the weekly checks were intact in her account, and all of it was left to her grandchildren.

In the last four or five months at Westwood Horizons, I hired a nurse to keep her company from breakfast till dinnertime. The nurse was an African-American woman in her fifties, whose name I regret not remembering now, but she was very close to my mother. The nurse owned a very small apartment in Palm Springs. The very mention of Palm Springs conjured up images of large, expensive homes of the rich and famous, with a pool for every house and a golf course for every resident. This was obviously not what my mother's nurse owned. My mother was not one to ask for favors, but surprisingly, one day she said to the nurse, "Why don't you take me to your fancy apartment in Palm Springs one weekend?"

"It's not fancy, May," she said. "It's just a studio apartment, but if you'd like to go, I'll take you this weekend."

That Sunday morning I got a call from my mother. "You'll never guess where I am," she said with more vigor than I had heard from her for months.

"Where?" I asked.

"I'm in Palm Springs with all the swells."

It pleased me and amused me. With all the major celebrities she met at the openings of my plays and films, somehow she seemed more impressed at spending a weekend with "the swells in Palm Springs," albeit not in very fancy digs. She called me again later that afternoon sounding even healthier and happier than she had in the morning.

"You'll never guess what I did this morning," she said, sounding more like my daughter than my mother.

"Well, I know you didn't play eighteen holes of golf, so tell me."

"I went to church. The nurse was going to leave to go to her church and I said I didn't want to be left alone. So, I said, good, I'll come with you . . . Well, you know I'm Jewish and I've never been in a church in my life, but it was beautiful and the priest, or whatever he was, made a wonderful speech. When we started to leave, he stood at the door shaking everyone's hand. He blessed them and thanked them for coming. When he took my hand, I said, I have to tell you the truth. I'm Jewish . . . He smiled and said, I'm delighted. We welcome all faiths here. Thank you for coming . . . Can you imagine?" she finished.

She had just had the time of her life, and told the nurse she wanted to go again soon. They planned to drive back to L.A. in the morning. Two hours later my phone rang again.

"Oh, Mr. Simon. I'm so sorry . . . Your mother just passed away. She was taking a shower. I was two feet away from her, holding her robe. But she went so quickly. I'm so sorry, Mr. Simon," she said through her tears.

I was stunned but not grief-stricken. I was happy that my mother died painlessly and quickly, and that her last day of life was such a happy one.

She was buried at Hillside Cemetery, in a plot not too far from where all the stars of her youth were now resting: Al Jolson, Jack Benny, and Eddie Cantor. George Burns would join them later. I knew she'd be pleased, and I pictured her telling all the friends in her building where she was buried.

It wasn't until the day of the funeral that I allowed all my tears to flow. It was not the same enormous pain I felt when Joan died, but more of a re-membrance of how much love I always felt and received from my mother.

Two days after she died, I did the strangest thing. Unwittingly, I picked up the phone, called the Westwood Horizons, and asked to speak to my mother. I hung up before the operator could even answer me.

Some habits are just hard to break.

THERE IS one more story about my mother that I think is worth telling, since it's always been on my mind.

When I was about seven years old, I had warts on many fingers of my hand. Conventional wisdom would tell you to see a doctor, who would painlessly remove them with an acid solution. My mother thought that doctors were only good to marry but not to go to. Like many mothers of that generation, she had her own cure for the removal of warts.

"First," she said to me, "you go to an empty lot." Already I began to worry. "You take a raw potato with you," she said. I was now almost willing to live with my warts into old age. She continued. "You rub the potato on the warts, then drop the potato over your left shoulder. Then you walk away . . . but remember," she said emphatically, "don't look back at the potato."

Some of it sounded, to my seven-year-old mind, almost practical. Per-haps there was a chemical compound in raw potatoes that was able to re-move a wart, which, I later found out, is actually a virus. Where she lost me was when she said, "Don't look back at the potato." This was obviously Jewish voodoo. I was surprised she didn't also add that at the same time I must have a dead owl on my shoulder . . . and burnt plucked chicken feathers in my pocket.

I wondered if this remedy was based on old folk lore. Since my mother came from Lithuania, I didn't believe the part about "go to an empty lot," because *all of Lithuania* was an empty lot, and since all of the Jewish peasants were penniless, no one would leave a perfectly good potato on the ground.

What was more amazing than my mother's frighteningly illogical instructions was that the next day I found myself actually standing in an empty lot with a raw potato in my hand. All alone. I even wore my only tie because I thought this might be a sacred ritual.

The other problem was that there was an apartment house on either side of the empty lot. This meant that if someone in those buildings was looking out the window, they would call their entire family together to watch—and laugh hysterically—while this seven-year-old kid rubbed a potato on his hands and then dropped it over his left shoulder. However, they wouldn't think it odd that I didn't look back at the potato, because who could think someone would tell you not to look back at a potato?

I braved it anyway. I stood there in the middle of the empty lot, looked up and nonchalantly whistled a happy tune as if I were waiting for a bus that drove into empty lots to pick up any children who were holding potatoes.

Then I held the hand with the potato *over* the hand with the warts, and I looked up at the sky, hoping that my audience in the windows would look up at the sky as well, while I quickly rubbed the potato over the warts. Then I yawned, stretched my arm up behind me, and quietly dropped the potato over my left shoulder. I was only seven years old, but I *knew* I was doing something unbelievably stupid. I then slowly walked away from the lot. The temptation to look back at the potato was enormous, and resisting it taught me more about discipline than two years in the Army. I thought if I brought a hand mirror, I could hold it up and look at the potato, without turning my head, thus avoiding the curse that would have followed me all my life. Lot's wife knew what I was talking about. But I resisted, and it wasn't so much that I was afraid of being turned into salt. I just wanted to get rid of warts.

For the next three days I not only looked to see if the warts were gone, but I watched them *all day long.* I wanted to see them actually disappear, proving that my mother had more medical knowledge than Louis Pasteur and Albert Schweitzer together. On the fourth day the warts were still there. On the fifth day, they looked like they were getting bigger. I was afraid I had angered the Jewish Voodoo God by being a disbeliever, and he was now going to turn my entire body into one giant wart. I would be headlined in circuses as Waldo, the living wart. I'd be shown all around the world. I would meet presidents, kings and queens and P. T. Barnum. They all would want to meet me, but they wouldn't want to shake my hand—which I wouldn't have anymore anyway.

Finally I couldn't take it, and I went to my mother and showed her my hand. "Look, Ma. The warts didn't go away." She looked at my hand carefully, then said to me, "You must have looked back at the potato."

The next day my father took me to a doctor who dabbed an ointment on the infamous warts, and they soon started to disappear. I said to him, "Doctor, is it possible to make warts disappear by rubbing a potato on them in an empty lot?"

"My mother told me the same story," he said to me. "That's why I went to medical school."

AFRICA HOT
24

IT WAS TIME to follow up on Frank Rich's suggestion that I write a Chapter Two to *Brighton Beach Memoirs*. I was told by a feature writer at the *New York Times* that Mr. Rich hoped I would write about my days as a young writer on the hit television program *Your Show of Shows* starring Sid Caesar. It was a good idea, but it wasn't time for that play yet. Since I was now planning to do a series of semiautobiographical plays, I wanted to do them in sequence, as they happened in my life. Following the years covered in *Brighton Beach,* the next major event in my life came when I entered the Army Air Force and took my basic training in Biloxi, Mississippi.

In 1943, I was sixteen years old and months away from graduating from DeWitt Clinton High School in the Bronx. Sixteen is young to finish your high school education today, but back then I went through the "rapids" where you could do four years in two, if your grades were good enough. The war was still raging in Europe as well as in the Pacific. I am not brave, not by a long shot. Yet at sixteen, I found myself downtown at the Naval Recruiting Station trying to enlist to be a part of our fighting forces. The petty officer in charge looked over my application, then looked me over from head to toe.

"How old are you, son?" he asked.

"Seventeen, sir," I lied.

"Do you have a letter of consent from your parents to join the Navy?"

That stopped me for a moment, but *just* a moment. "Yes, sir, I do. I forgot to bring it with me. I can have it here tomorrow," knowing I would go home that night and forge a letter from my parents. I would also have to forge some weight on my body because I was skinny as a pencil.

"You look a little thin," he said. "I'll tell you what. You go home, put on about fourteen pounds, then wait till you're eighteen and come see me again in two years. I'll remember you, I promise . . . Next!"

So much for the Navy. When I graduated school that spring the war was still going on, but I thought that in two years it would be over and I'd miss it. My desire to join was not predicated on my patriotism or my desire to fight our country's enemies. It was based solely in what I was seeing in the movies in those war years, films like *Flying Tigers* with John Wayne, *Air Force* with John Garfield and *Destination Tokyo* with Cary Grant. I never thought about dying overseas because every few months John Wayne, John Garfield and Cary Grant were always in a new movie. What I was really looking forward to, though, was walking into a USO dance in my Air Force uniform and meeting starlet Susan Hayward, who was willing to give up her film career to spend the rest of her life with me. I was also looking forward to being wounded (not in a life-threatening place, of course) and cared for by nurse Lana Turner, who spent more time with me than any other patient, including top-ranking officers. It was the medals on my uniform as I walked through Times Square, meeting Judy Garland under the clock at the Biltmore Hotel on my last night's leave and deciding to get married right then, or maybe we'd just take a bus ride down Fifth Avenue, so much in love she thought she would die. For a high school graduate, I was the Most Adolescent in My Class.

Waiting impatiently to grow older and heavier, I spent the next year working in an advertising agency as a messenger boy, writing comedy sketches in my few spare minutes and showing them to copywriters and asking them for opinions and suggestions. They didn't have any. They were too busy trying to come up with a catchy phrase to sell their Black and White Scotch, with the ever-present black and white Scottie dogs in the ad. In the years before television, you could get away with running the same ad in the paper for three or four years. That was why the copywriters were taking three-hour lunches. It was also possible they were imbibing the product they were advertising. I got my best results by showing my sketches to the secretaries, one in particular. I had an incurable crush on a girl there who was both the prettiest and the smartest because she laughed at every line I had put down on paper. Unfortunately I lost her to a Marine who was twenty-eight and covered with battle ribbons from the epaulet on his left shoulder to the one on his right shoulder.

At seventeen, I found I could enlist in the Army's Specialized Training Reserve Program, which meant that you would be sent to a university, where you could train for active duty and get a year's worth of college education at government expense. I enlisted, was accepted and waited for my shipping orders. I was crazy about the term "shipping orders." I had never been out of New York City until then and I was hoping I'd be sent to the University of Arizona or Georgia Tech or Texas A&M. This could be my only chance to travel and see America before the war ended, and I would have to go back to being a messenger boy for Black and White Scotch. I was thrown a goodbye party by my parents and friends and the best gift I got was an ID bracelet. I wore it proudly and wisely, since it was possible I could get killed in the crowd following the football game between the University of Texas and Texas A&M. I envisioned being sent home in a slow-moving train, taking the same route that President Lincoln's body took shortly after his assassination. I would be buried in Arlington Cemetery with full honors. Maybe Susan Hayward would be there in a veil to cover her tears.

A few weeks after I turned seventeen, I received my shipping orders. With trembling, excited fingers, I tore open the official-looking document. It was not the University of Arizona or Georgia Tech or Texas A&M. I was being sent to New York University, which had an additional campus up in the Bronx. I went there on a trolley car, but I could have just as easily walked. Life is much more shattering than we could ever imagine.

AT NYU, we mostly marched and did gym exercises. The most difficult for me was climbing the thick hemp rope that hung from the ceiling twenty feet above the floor. I could get about five feet off the ground and that was about it. I would hang from there for about four or five minutes, making them think I was having a gall bladder attack but still bravely trying to make my way up to the top. It didn't work after a while because no one could have that many gall bladder attacks. Most of the other soldiers could get up there as fast as those Pacific natives who climb up palm trees to get coconuts. I asked the sergeant why this exercise was necessary. I assumed you would use it only if you were taken prisoner of war and wanted to escape by climbing over the wall. But what were the chances of there being a rope exactly where you wanted to escape? He failed to see my logic.

I didn't do well in the classroom either. We were taught only three subjects: trigonometry, physics and advanced science. All three were my very worst subjects. My luck was running bad. I was at the bottom of my class in studies and at the bottom of the rope in gym. I was, however, quite good at marching. As a matter of fact, since I was doing so badly in the first two, very often they would send me out to march alone. All around the campus. In snow or sleet.

There was another problem that soon came up. I had enlisted to go into officer candidate school once I was in the actual Air Force, and there I would be trained to be either a fighter pilot or the pilot of a bomber. No one asked if I could drive a car, which I couldn't, but I assumed someone would drive me out to the field and help get me into my plane. I was also found to be color-blind, unable to distinguish some colors from others, particularly blue and brown. This left a very good chance that I could easily bomb London instead of Berlin. I could sense that the Air Force would have to rethink their plans for me.

On July 4, 1945, I turned eighteen, and a week later I received my orders from the Air Force. I was to report to Grand Central Station on the morning of August 8, where I would be met, along with a hundred or so other young men, all from New York State, by three noncommissioned officers, and then taken by train to Fort Dix, New Jersey. There we were to receive our shots, uniforms and indoctrination into a life that I was completely unfit for. My parents, much to my embarrassment, accompanied me to Grand Central to say goodbye.

The war in Europe was already over, and Japan was just about to capitulate after the bombings of Hiroshima and Nagasaki. Nevertheless, our company sergeant shouted as we were about to board the train, "Say good-bye to Momma, we're off to Yokohama."

In a lot of ways, the Army was like a bad musical comedy.

ON MY SECOND DAY at Fort Dix, our arms were pounding with pain from the myriad of shots we had received from the medics, whose ineptitude at giving shots was so great that we could only assume they arrived as recruits just the day before we did. On that morning, we received our first day's duty. Wearing our fatigues, sort of a dark khaki jumpsuit that was issued already prestained to show you how it should be done, our job was to pick up every cigarette butt in the area, the area being most of New Jersey. We had to split them open with our fingers, roll up the paper and release the left-over tobacco to the winds, which eventually blew into Pennsylvania, making its way across country to Idaho. In Idaho, the tobacco was served to pigs that produced bacon that was already smoked. It was menial and embarrassing work and I was glad Lana Turner didn't drive by that day. The lowest point of the day was when a truckful of soldiers rode by, laughing their heads off at us. What made it so humiliating was that the truckful of soldiers were German prisoners of war. German laughter, a rare sound indeed, is infuriating when you're the recipient.

After a five-day railway trip from Fort Dix, New Jersey, to Biloxi, Mississippi, where we tried to sleep on hard-back seats, the floor, the baggage rack above or on the john after a two-hour wait to get in, we looked like seasoned veterans. For fuel, the engine of the train was fed a combination of coal, wood, paper, Army shoes and used tires from jeeps. The soot that emanated from the funnels covered the once beautiful green hills of Delaware, North Carolina, Georgia and the Gulf Coast with ten inches of black residue that didn't come off until the Korean War some five years later. It got into our hair, our eyes, ears, nostrils and mostly on our food. Everything looked like it was made by the cook who created blackened catfish. You kept chewing long after you finished your food. Our blackened faces made us look like camouflaged commandos just back from blowing up munition dumps. At every whistle-stop along the thousand or more mile trip, people appeared from nowhere, waving flags at us and throwing doughnuts, kisses and, in some cases, telephone numbers, to the brave young men who were giving their all for their country. And we hadn't even arrived at Biloxi yet.

It's not true that the equator is the hottest spot in the world. Biloxi, Mississippi, in August easily topped it by twenty degrees, all humidity. As I marched and crawled from the train to the camp two miles away, I also carried a duffel bag that was not only sweating, but which also seemed weighted with unused cannonballs from the Revolutionary War. I thought to myself, "I can't take this. I'll be dead in three days. I must talk to our sergeant and tell him that the Army would be better served if they sent me to Nantucket or to Maine in the early fall when the leaves were just turning. I would definitely not be able to do my best soldiering in this oven."

In the play *Biloxi Blues,* Eugene Morris Jerome, né Marvin Neil Simon, complained weakly as he trudged the dusty road with his buddies.

"Boy, it's hot . . . This is really hot . . . This is like Africa hot . . . Even Tarzan couldn't take this kind of hot."

For years afterward, these words were quoted by cab drivers in New York, football announcers in Southern Florida and gamblers who just stepped out of a casino in Las Vegas. It caught on everywhere. When traffic cops recognized me as they stood in the middle of traffic at 57th and Broadway, they'd smile and call out, "Hey, Neil, it's like Africa hot today, right?"

Once in San Diego, I was driving to the airport, deep in thought on the new play I was trying out at the Old Globe Theater, and I missed a stop sign. I was pulled over by a policeman.

"You know you just went through a stop sign there?"

"Did I? I'm sorry, I wasn't thinking. I guess I did."

"Let me see your driver's license." He looked it over carefully, then squinted at me. "Neil Simon? Are you Neil Simon?"

"Yes, officer."

"Africa hot? That Neil Simon?"

"That's right."

"Wait a minute," he said, then turned and called to another cop. "Charley! You know who this is? It's Africa hot."

Charley came over, smiled and shook my hand. "Not even Tarzan could take this kind of hot, heh?" he said, laughing. After two autographs signed, "Africa Hot . . . Neil Simon," I was set free with a polite warning to watch out for stop signs.

I've always worried about the translation of my plays into foreign languages. I write idiomatically. Also very New York. There is some humor that is almost impossible to explain to someone who just doesn't get it. I cannot explain why "Africa Hot" is funny, but it just is. The audience laughed at every performance of the play that I attended and every time I saw it on the screen. What Eugene means, obviously, is that "this is as hot as Africa." Not funny. Just a statement. "Even Tarzan couldn't take this kind of heat" is mildly amusing, but not as funny as "this kind of hot." What I was trying to convey was the state Eugene was in when he arrived in Biloxi on that steaming day, dragging two tons of duffel bag—that was how he was going to spend the next two months.

During times of great stress, your mind plays cruel tricks on you, and you realize that you don't have the mental capacity or physical strength to say things correctly. A man who's lost in the desert for a week and suddenly sees a caravan come along might drop to his knees, hold out his arms and ask pitifully through his cracked, parched lips, "Water . . . water." If he were in a restaurant, he would say, "Oh, waiter. May I have a glass of water, please?" Biloxi in August was not a restaurant. Saying fewer words, mangling the syntax and not giving a damn about the grammar would be the only way you could communicate. Thus, "this is like Africa hot," not only makes sense to Eugene, it is understood perfectly by the other dehydrated soldiers whose brains have turned to dry rot. So far I think I've been able to explain this to you in understandable English. But to put these expressions into Spanish, Swedish, Russian or French, there probably is no equivalent expression as "this is like Africa hot." They would inevitably go to the nearest translation, which would be, of course, "this is as hot as Africa." No laughs. No applause. No good reviews. No royalties.

I guess one would have the same concerns for Shakespeare. How did they translate all his magnificent plays and still have them rhyme in couplets? Their rhyme would have to be different from Shakespeare's English, and I doubt that he ever saw a penny in foreign royalties. Still, many of my plays have enjoyed great success in Europe although sometimes for different reasons. They lose the humor so they go more for the character and the story. I once saw *Plaza Suite* performed in Holland. Some of *Plaza Suite* consists of meaty, gritty dramatic scenes, but more than two thirds of it is meant to be funny. In the Dutch production that I sat through painfully, there was hardly a laugh all evening. Not even a hint of one. But as the final curtain fell, the audience rose to their feet and gave it a standing ovation. They didn't see the play I meant but saw it as being more serious, which Europeans generally prefer. Charlie Chaplin solved the international problem by never speaking a word. Unfortunately, I didn't know how to write silence.

HAVING GROWN UP in the safe confines of Washington Heights in upper Manhattan, I never noticed the word "bigotry" used nor even the act of bigotry, certainly not in the ugly way we've come to know it in the last few decades. There were neighborhood fights, to be sure, but mostly it was because you lived below 170th Street or on the wrong side of St. Nicholas Avenue. We fought for our territorial rights, not our color or creed. Even at that, there wasn't much fighting. There was a lot of wrestling to the ground and once in a while there was a punch thrown. None of us knew or even suspected that in a few more years, six million Jews and others would go to their deaths in gas chambers in Germany, or that blacks were being lynched in the South. By the time I joined the service, I knew there was mass murder going on, but I still hadn't seen much bigotry. At least until I came face-to-face with it when I was thrown together with a kind of people I never knew existed before I hit the Army. On my second day in Biloxi, I was passing the post exchange where the beer was sold, and I was tripped up by a couple of tipsy noncoms, who laughed and said, "Don't they teach you how to walk in New York, Jew boy?" Another flipped a lit cigarette at me and said, "Pick that up, Hymie. Don't think you Jews can come down here and mess up the beautiful state of Mississippi." These two men were our cooks and weighed about two hundred and sixty pounds each, most of it beer sweat, so I didn't need a lot of experience to know I'd better keep my mouth shut, continue walking and not look back.

The "colored boys" were segregated and the word "nigger" was still quite popular in this region. At eighteen, some boys hardly shaved, and the smoother your skin was, the more likely you'd be called "faggot" with an invitation to come into the latrine and "have some of this." I was so naive that the more my eyes were opened to a world I barely knew existed, the more my mouth was closed for fear of getting my teeth knocked out behind the barracks by an angry cook who hated anyone who could spell a word with more than five letters in it.

It was this story I wanted to tell in *Biloxi Blues,* not to open the minds of audiences in the 1980s, who knew it only too well, but to make the generation of eighteen-year-olds aware that we must always be on guard. I also wanted to tell of Eugene's rite of passage, of losing his virginity and then meeting the first girl he ever fell in love with at a dance in a Catholic girls school in Gulfport, Mississippi. This, plus the fear and poignancy of young men being thrust into a life much more harshly and speedily than they would have had they never left the comfort and safety of family and home, were to be the themes of my play.

FEAR AND LOATHING aside, I made a pretty poor soldier. At five A.M. we were thrust out of our semibearable cots, onto the dusty ground in front of our barracks. We were going on a ten-mile forced march. I never knew what that expression meant except that we were forced to do it. We were given ten brief minutes of instruction of how to pack our backpacks correctly and how to fold our mosquito netting, which would be the most important piece of equipment we'd be taking. This was followed by the phrase "swamp land," which put terror into my New York heart. I am not always a very good listener, especially to directions. In the external world, I am an explorer without a map. I was never taught how to write a play. I found my way through years of experimenting, making mistakes and painstakingly fixing them. I did not, however, have years to learn how to pack my gear or fold my netting before leaving for our forced march into Swamp City; I had only moments.

A mile into the march, under a blazing hot sun, my backpack simply fell apart, falling piece by piece onto the dusty road. There was no one willing or anxious to help me since they were all busy enough laughing their heads off. They made the German prisoners seem like my best friends. It was right out of an Abbott and Costello movie. Every time I bent down to pick up my small shovel, I would drop my canteen. When I picked up my canteen, my helmet fell off. It felt as if I were carrying three cartons of milk without the cartons. As we approached the end of the ten miles, I was not only exhausted, I was also missing half the equipment the Army gave me. Needless to say, I had to pay them for the loss. For what it cost me, I would have been better off taking a forced cab ride.

But there was good news ahead. I saw cabins in the distance. I would not need my shovel to dig a foxhole. Why the cabins were hotter than the blazing sun, I'll never know. There were bunks with wooden slats but no mattresses. That was no problem because we were told to double-fold our blankets across the slats and use our backpack as a pillow. Mine would be a very flat pillow, since my pack was almost empty and my blanket was five miles back, just off the dusty road, now probably the home of squirrels and field mice. I watched how my buddies carefully unfolded their mosquito netting and stretched it over the bunk, and then tucked in the sides. Even if I was smart enough to remember their instructions on how to put your mosquito netting into place, I was too tired to care. I collapsed onto my slats and threw the damn netting over my head, arms, body and feet. I soon fell asleep, being serenaded by the buzzing of a billion insects now gathering at the edge of the swamp, synchronizing their watches for the exact time they would attack.

I awoke in the morning to find soldiers looking at my face and saying, "Holy shit, what happened to you?" I was told that my face looked like a field of fresh strawberries. What it felt like was tiny little bubbles of hot lava. I also now had earlobes the size of a Ubangi tribesman. The mosquitoes went home that day with enough of my blood to start up their own blood bank in the woods.

Since the mosquito netting episode was noted on my record, the Air Force nixed the fighter pilot idea. Six weeks later, I was shipped off to Lowry Field in Denver, Colorado, just about the same time the swollen strawberries were shrinking. The war was now over and we young recruits had to fill the shoes of the departing veterans. Since they still had an Air

Force and planes to go with it, I was sent to gunnery school. I was put in a small darkened room, barely making out a screen set up just ahead of me. There were buttons to push, located on a stand just at my fingertips.

"An enemy plane will appear on the screen at any time. The moment you see him, you start to fire. Wait a second too long, and you and your crew are dead men . . . Are you ready?"

"Ready, sir."

I squinted at all four corners of the screen, waiting for the enemy plane to show up. My fingers were a millimeter away from the buttons.

"Here we go," said the officer. Before I could see anything and fire, the officer said, "You're dead, son," just as a tiny speck on the screen grew slightly larger and then promptly went out of sight. I prepared for the next one, squinting even harder.

"You're dead, son," he said without emotion, as the dot came out of another direction.

After five "you're dead, sons," the lights went up. "Let's forget about gunnery school, son. Maybe they can find some office work for you." I could imagine an entire battery of German prisoners writing home about this humiliation.

One morning I saw a notice on the bulletin board: "All personnel interested in Journalism, report to Capt. Burke at 0900 hours." What could this be? Was the Army looking to turn us into journalists to cover the war? And what war? That was over. Did they want us to cover the peace? Since I was inquisitive by nature, I showed up. I was also the only one to show up. Captain Burke waited until a quarter after nine and since there were no other comers, he called me into his office and said, "Well, Simon. Since no one else wants it, you are now the editor-in-chief of the *Rev-Meter*, the official Army Air Force newspaper. Good luck and good day."

I stepped out into the hallway and looked left and then right. I didn't know where the official Army Air Force newspaper was. I was finally given a small office and a typewriter and since I had no journalists working under me, I had to write my own stories and then edit them. I was a tough editor. I kept correcting my mistakes and cutting out the parts that bored me. I wanted to fire me but that didn't seem practical. Eventually, I started to cull items and stories from magazines and newspapers about anything aeronautical. After three months of this, I was so bored, I was hoping they would put me back on cigarette duty, where at least I could see tobacco flying off to more interesting places than my tiny office.

Finally, I was reprieved. I was told that almost all the draftees were now out of the armed forces and the government wanted to build up a new and more permanent regular army. Now there was another phrase that confused me. Wasn't the Army that fought the war a "regular army"? Or were they just like regular guys but nothing special? I was much too literal-minded for Army terminology. At any rate, my job was now shifted to recruitment to help build up this "regular" army. They wanted me to write a short radio program, heard only in the Denver area, to entice young men away from their homes, their girlfriends, dates, sex and good food, to join the "regular army." Can you just picture young men rushing home from basketball practice to hear this incredible new radio show that was on from 4:00 to 4:10 P.M., their cars pressed against the speaker since our program came out of a small station with just enough wattage to light a firefly for one glowlette? After a month, we were getting neither recruits nor an audience. I threw caution to the wind and suggested a revolutionary idea to Captain Burke.

"What if you gave us more time? Say fifteen minutes. And what if I made it funny? And in between the funny news items or Army humor, we could put in a plug for the benefits of joining the regular army, where you could end up with a college education given under the G.I. Bill of Rights and perhaps learn a new trade that would steer you into a new career."

To my enormous surprise, he said, "Fine. Let's try it."

Together with an announcer, a singer and a couple of G.I.'s who could get my humor across, we put on a show. Eventually the show was stretched to a half hour, but we were still heard only in the Denver area. Then we were sent out on the road, to Colorado Springs and to other Western towns with Marlboro Country type names. I was actually enjoying myself and people had started to listen to our little amateur show with down-home humor. Were we a success? Well, just look at the size of our armed forces today; count our nuclear submarines and Stealth bombers. However, before I could get into building our space program and float my idea of putting a man on the moon, I was discharged, after a year and a half of dedicated service to my country. When I arrived home in New York, I had no clothes that fit me, since I had grown taller and more muscular, but I did know what I wanted to do for the rest of my life. I wanted to write for the stage, for films, for television and I still wanted to find out what the "regular army" was and why did they call it a "forced march"?

BILOXI BLUES opened on March 28, 1985. I finally got my first rave from Frank Rich of the *New York Times.* And my last. The play also won the Tony Award. *Brighton Beach* had opened two years before at the Alvin Theater. *Biloxi Blues* opened at the same theater, but the name had now been changed.

A few months before, Jimmy Nederlander, the owner of the Alvin Theater and the second largest theater owner in America, called and asked if he could come to my New York apartment to talk to me. He wants me to do a musical or fix up a play that was coming into his theater, was all I could think of. When I heard what he had to say, I was completely bowled over.

"I've been thinking for a long time," he started, "and this is what I'd like to do with your permission. I want to change the name of the Alvin Theater to the Neil Simon Theater."

I looked at him blankly. Was he serious?

"Look, it's good business for me," he continued, since I wasn't able to form words just yet. He went on: "The Alvin Theater is a great theater but I never liked the name. It was named after two men who owned it before me. Alex somebody and Vinton Freedley. They put their two names together, Al and Vin, and they got Alvin and to me that sounds like one of the Chipmunks. To call it the Neil Simon Theater gives it a built-in atmosphere. It doesn't mean just comedy. It means the kind of entertainment that you've been bringing to New York for years. And with your permission, I would like to do it for your next play, *Biloxi Blues.*"

I started to think of all the plays and musicals I had seen at the Alvin since I was a boy: Moss Hart's *Lady in the Dark, The Great White Hope, A Tree Grows in Brooklyn* and *Mister Roberts*—the list went on and on.

This honor had come so suddenly, so out of the blue, that I grew suspicious. "Does this mean that I have to do all my plays in a Nederlander theater? Not that I mind because you have great theaters, but if this is a payoff, I would feel very uncomfortable accepting it. It would be a business deal rather than an honor."

"No strings attached," said Jimmy. "I just want to see your name on one of my theaters. What do you say, Neil? Can I do it?"

"I'll have to sleep on it, Jimmy," I said. "Wait right here. I'll go inside, take a ten-minute nap and come out with my answer . . . Are you kidding? OF COURSE YOU CAN."

The name of the theater was officially changed from the Alvin to the Neil Simon. On the day that the official ceremony was going to take place, with so many of my friends, actors, directors, etc., in attendance, I got into a cab, my heart beating like a Bob Fosse number.

I did not want the cabbie to stop in front of the theater at 52nd Street off Eighth Avenue. I told him I wanted to get off at 51st Street and Eighth Avenue. I wanted to walk up the block, then turn the corner onto 52nd Street, so I would see the sign for the first time. I was going to milk every drop of ego out of this. I turned the corner and saw it. You couldn't miss it if you tried. It wasn't big, it was enormous. It was at least twenty feet high, and at night, when it was lit up, you could probably see it from New Jersey. Maybe even from Fort Dix. I thought to myself, from tearing up cigarette butts to this is a long way. For a long time I actually had trouble saying it. If someone asked me where *Biloxi Blues* was playing, I thought I exceeded the bounds of humility by saying aloud, "It's at the Neil Simon Theater." Being proud was one thing, but self-aggrandizement is another.

But even today, as I drive in a cab down Broadway to see a play, as we pass 52nd Street, I turn my head to the right, just to see if it's still there.

THE ODD COUPLETTES
25

FOR YEARS I had received dozens upon dozens of letters from all over the country, asking me to allow an all-woman production of the play of *The Odd Couple*. Those making this request included numerous stars based in both Los Angeles and New York, who wanted to tour the production and then bring it to Broadway. None of the letters, however, made any mention of how they would do it. Did they intend to simply change the names of Oscar and Felix to Olive and Florence, and have them drink Diet Cokes instead of beer? It *could* be done, I thought, but not that way; I would have to rewrite it completely. I'd keep the exact same structure as the original, but make the characters women—real women, not women behaving as men as played by women.

Rather than take the risk and head straight for Broadway, I had a reading of the new version of the play in the game room at my brother Danny's apartment, where he often taught comedy to his always packed classes. Danny was considered to be the best teacher of comedy writing on the West and East Coasts, and eventually he traveled all over America and Europe giving his classes. His classes have spawned countless numbers of young men and women who are first-rate comedy writers, and who eventually filled the staffs of some of the best television comedies on the air. Heads of studios and networks even took his classes, predicated on the sensible theory that if they wanted their writers to write well, they'd be better off knowing what they're talking about themselves. There was only one person he did not allow to take his class: me.

He said he would feel self-conscious with me in the room, despite the fact that he was the only mentor I ever had. Actually there was one other to whom the embargo applied. Woody Allen was also not allowed in Danny's class, and for the same reason I wasn't. Danny had written with Woody Allen, and Woody was quoted as saying, "I learned more about comedy from Danny Simon than anyone else I know." So the moral is, if you made it big in this business because of Danny, you couldn't take his class.

Danny directed the read-through of *The Female Odd Couple,* doing an incredible job. It erased my misgivings about the project, and the new version finally ended up on Broadway starring Rita Moreno and Sally Struthers. *The Female Odd Couple* is now performed almost as frequently as the original. One of the scenes that benefited from the transformation was turning the English Pigeon Sisters into the Spanish Costazuela Brothers, formerly of Barcelona, where they worked for Iberian Airlines. The Brothers, Jesús and Manolo, are invited to dinner at Olive and Florence's apartment. The boys, a little shaky with their English but long on charm and manners, arrive with flowers and candy.

OLIVE

Well, come in, amigos.

MANOLO

Amigos. Very good. Jesús, you have
something to say?

JESÚS

Sí. With our deep felicitations, we have
brought you fresh flowers and fresh candy.

OLIVE

Oh, how sweet.

JESÚS

I hope you like the candies. They are no good.

OLIVE

They're no good?

JESÚS

Sí. The candy is no good.

MANOLO

Sí. Is very chewy.

OLIVE

You mean nougat?

MANOLO

Ah, yes. Nou-gat. Not no good. Nou-gat.

JESÚS

I'm sorry. We're still new at English.

OLIVE

But very thoughtful. I'll put these in water.

MANOLO

Just the flowers. Candy in water is no good.

JESÚS

I thought it was nou-gat.

OLIVE
(Holding the flowers)
Well, the flowers are certainly beautiful. I
feel like Miss America.

JESÚS
I feel the same. I miss Spain sometimes.

Comedy is not always profound, but laughter often makes it feel as if
it is.

THE GIRL FROM NEIMAN MARCUS
26

I HAD BEEN a bachelor for almost three and a half years, and I can't deny that the many attractive women I met during those years were more than a single man could ask for. Surprisingly, it also got tiresome. Each first date was like a first session with a new analyst. It was mostly about giving information about your past. I also found out that sex without love was not very satisfying. (Then again, love without sex can be a drag as well, as can love without love, which is when you're just saying "love" in order to get sex.)

The best years of my life had been the nineteen years with Joan, and then the eight and a half years with Marsha. After that I had to learn step by step how to be a bachelor. It had its benefits, to be sure, but freedom doesn't always bring happiness. On the other hand, the opposite of freedom (we're talking marriage here) implies obligations, responsibilities, accountabilities and burdens. But without a partner, what you miss most is sharing, giving, connection, kinship and commonality. What I missed the most was caring for someone so much that I couldn't wait until morning to see her serene, placid face, half asleep just inches away from mine, giving me a warm, quiet "Hi" to start the day. My problem was that I wanted all of the latter without again going through the excruciating pain of death or divorce, not to mention that endless feeling of anger, despair, loneliness and desolation. I know that I either had to take a chance one more time or be lucky enough to find a woman who would want all the things I desire in life, without the commitment of marriage. Since I had not met that woman in three and a half years, having to make that choice was not an issue. What I also feared greatly was that I would meet that woman, but shy away because of fear that I was not then, and possibly never would be again, able to enter into a relationship that didn't end disastrously.

It was with this new sense of cautiousness that I wandered into the Neiman Marcus department store in Beverly Hills on November 22, 1985. I was there to look for a Christmas gift for the young daughter of Ann Bell, who was no longer my companion, but had become my friend. I always made a point of shopping early to beat the holiday rush. I found the gift I wanted, had it wrapped and sent. I walked down the three flights of stairs without a clue of what I was going to do next. On the ground floor was the large, imposing perfume and cosmetic section. Why I was wandering through there was another mystery because there was no one I knew for whom I wanted to buy perfume or cosmetics. The gifts I bought for Ellen and Nancy were always more personal, and something I would search for with care I turned to leave and suddenly, behind the Anne Klein counter, I caught sight of a woman, a girl, a presence, an aura, a quality and an existence you couldn't help but see.

I always remembered what Mildred Newman, a doctor friend I knew and admired, once said to me. When you see someone for the very first time, you know more about them than you think you do. It doesn't mean you know specifics, but you do have a sense of what kind of person this is. It pleases you or it doesn't. You admire that person or you don't. That person gets your respect or doesn't. And all this happens in a flash of an eye, mind you.

The woman I saw in my eye in Neiman Marcus, just before my lid closed for the first time, was tall and fair, dressed conservatively, and she did nothing to present herself as beautiful because there was no need to. She was blessed with beauty. And while the appeal of her looks was enough to attract me, looking at her I realized I wanted something more: I wanted to know her. For now, though, I would settle for just speaking to her. She had that fresh clean look that made you think she'd be as lovely sitting atop a tractor as she would behind a counter in one of the most expensive stores in the world. I was simply drawn to her, as though someone had slipped roller skates on me unnoticed, I found myself moving closer and closer to her. She looked up and smiled, not necessarily at me, but it didn't matter. Her smile was warm as well as breathtaking. I had the feeling we had met before, but that was unlikely. You don't quickly forget a woman who makes you feel you're wearing roller skates in a department store.

"Can I help you?" she asked, not as a salesperson, because she really wasn't selling anything. As I later found out, she was doing inventory. She offered help because I looked lost.

I murmured something about "just looking" even though I never once glanced down at the counter.

She peered at me for a moment before she said, "You look familiar. Do I know you?"

"I don't know," I said. "My name is Neil Simon. I'm a writer." I knew it was a shameless plug I gave myself, but I hoped it might give me a slight advantage.

"Oh, God. I'm sorry. I should have known."

"Why should you have known?"

"Because I'm an actress. I just work here part-time. Yes, I've seen you on television a few times."

Later on she confessed I looked like an English professor at UCLA, although at the time I was wearing a beaten-up old Air Force jacket and an old scarf, not my idea of what professors at UCLA wore.

I suddenly ran out of conversation and thought that anything else I said would be brazen and pushy. I said, "Well, nice meeting you," turned and left the store with my valet parking ticket in my hand.

The parking attendant started walking toward me. In the brief few seconds it took him, this is what I thought to myself: "If I drive away now, I will never see her again . . . Ever . . . Go back in. Say something . . . Maybe she's not married but small chance of that . . . Find out. You haven't met anyone like her in years even though you don't know a thing about her. Trust your instincts. You said that last time about Marsha, twelve years ago, but can't you be forward and cautious at the same time?" All this while the parking attendant was still walking toward me. I waved him aside and walked back into Neiman Marcus.

"Hi, again," I said as I approached the counter. "I'm back."

"Did you forget anything?" she asked.

"Yes. I know this is crazy, but could I look at your fingers?"

"My fingers?"

"Please."

She seemed as much puzzled as amused by my request, but she put her ten fingers down on the counter. I looked at them.

"Not a wedding ring on them, I see," not believing I had that much nerve. I held up my hands. "Same here."

Where this surge of audaciousness, boldness and courage was coming from, I couldn't say. I was just tap-dancing as fast as I could, possibly even with roller skates on.

"Look, this is the first time I've ever done this in my life," I said. "I do not wander around department stores trying to meet someone . . . But I knew if I drove away just now, I'd never see you again. So I'll just plunge in . . . Do you have a lunch hour because I do and maybe we could have a bite together."

"I'm sorry. I don't have a lunch hour. And we're not supposed to see customers on the outside."

"What about if we ate here, in the chocolate department? That's not outside." Was that a mistake? I wondered. I was afraid she might think I was "on" all the time, and that's not how I was. "Does that mean you can't *ever* have dinner out sometime with someone you meet?"

She smiled and said, "Right."

I was dead. Stone dead. A tall man in a dark suit was walking the aisles, and he glanced over at us a few times. If he was a company man, which he was, was he angry with her or with me? Still, I made one last entreaty.

"Tomorrow night. Coffee, a drink, a Perrier. I'd settle for anything."

"I'm going to a Republican convention tomorrow with a friend," she said. Ah, there was hope. She didn't say no. She just said she had other plans.

She looked nervously at the man walking the aisles and she got busy doing her inventory. I pretended I was looking at merchandise. I whispered, "If I had your phone number, I could call you and you could turn me down then."

She tried to hold back the smile just beginning at the corners of her mouth and quickly wrote something on a Neiman card and handed it to me.

I picked it up as preciously as I would a diamond and slid it into my pocket. This time I walked out of the store, got into my car, drove off and wondered if tonight was too soon to call.

I waited a day to call her. Perhaps two. After all, if she was a Republican and I was a Democrat, there'd be trouble ahead.

I dialed her number as carefully as if I were opening a safe.

"Hello. It's me. The guy in the Army jacket from Neiman Marcus."

"Oh, hi. I wasn't expecting you to call so soon."

"You want to hang up? I could call back in ten minutes." I thought humor was safe by now.

"No, it's fine. I just walked in the door actually."

"Look, I hope you didn't get into any trouble the other day. Talking to me so long, I mean."

"I got fired."

"WHAT?" I was shocked. Devastated. Did I ruin her life? "Oh, my God, I'm so sorry. What can I do? Can I make it up to you? What if I called them? I can explain it was all my fault, which it was."

"No, it's okay, really. I was going to leave there soon anyway. I just took the job for a few days to make some extra money. Mostly I go out on auditions for commercials. That's what I just came back from."

"I have to make it up to you. Dinner isn't enough. I have to buy you a small restaurant. A diner or something."

She laughed. If I could have recorded it, I would have played it for a week.

"So is tomorrow okay or am I rushing it?"

"Tomorrow? Sure, tomorrow's fine."

"Morton's, seven o'clock? Do you know where it is?"

"Yes, I know. By the way, my name is Diane Lander . . . and I just wanted to say that I've never done this either. I'll see you tomorrow, okay?"

"Very okay," I said and we both hung up.

We sometimes remember moments like this with the dialogue a little more perfect than it actually was. To me, it was close enough to what I've recorded. If Diane remembers it otherwise, that's fine, but this is my memoir and I've put it down the way I would like to remember it.

I'M NEVER LATE. At seven o'clock I was sitting at a table in Morton's, sipping my vodka on the rocks. It was raining outside and I assumed the traffic would be heavy. I could see her through the window as she approached the restaurant, but she couldn't see me. Her hair was a little wet and windblown. I couldn't have asked for it to look any better. She came in and instead of asking for me, she made a beeline for the ladies' room. I was halfway through my vodka so I slowed it down. One was always enough for me. She came out of the ladies' room and her hair was brushed back and the smattering of raindrops on her face had vanished. She was shown to my table and sat breathlessly. She had, no doubt, put in a full day, but we greeted each other not as strangers, but as two people who had more than just a five-minute clandestine conversation over a counter in Neiman's. After all, we'd been through a lot together. I had managed to muster more nerve and aggressiveness than I ever had shown before, and she had gotten fired. We had a history and something to talk about beside the rain. I have very little memory of our conversation that poured out that night because there was so much of it to remember. We virtually closed up Morton's some four hours later. All I did remember was her telling me that she had a child, a year-and-a-half-old girl named Bryn, and that the father and Diane had already gone their separate ways. I accepted everything as good news. I don't know if it happened that night or some time later, but had I known what she was thinking as I approached her in Neiman's, I would have been far less nervous. She said that when she saw me, the first thing she said to herself was, "Oh, God, I'm in trouble." It meant two things: one was, she was attracted to me; the other was, "Oh, no. A celebrity. They're all slightly crazy."

I assume we ate dinner during that evening while we talked about everything. She finally looked at her watch and said she had to rush home. Baby-sitters cost money. I said something like, "When do I see you again?" It was just a few short days till Thanksgiving. She said, "Well, you could come to my house tomorrow for dinner if you don't mind watching me bake pies and amusing my daughter now and then." I accepted, conditions and all.

She lived in the Valley and she wrote out the address and the directions very explicitly. It didn't help. I drove past her house three times and circled back three times. She lived in an apartment in a two-story house, and when I saw outside a few unopened boxes still tied with cord, I knew she lived a somewhat transitory life. I rang the bell, waited, knocked on the door, waited and rang the bell again. When I saw how she was dressed for our second date, I knew *I* was the one who was in trouble. She was wearing an oversized sweatshirt covered with flour, baggy pants also covered with flour, and if I could see them, possibly sneakers. There wasn't an ounce of pretense in her, and baking Thanksgiving pies seemed to be just as important to her as our second date together. If the pies were as delicious as she looked to me, someone was in for a great holiday dinner. Everything about her was natural and easy and in the previous three and a half years I hadn't come close to meeting anyone like her.

Bryn had not yet made her appearance, busily absorbed in whatever it is that year-and-a-half-old children dream about in bed. In the kitchen, I marveled how Diane was handling both the dinner she was preparing for us plus the pumpkin pies, among others, that she was baking. She asked me to come into the kitchen to sit and keep her company. It was my first glimpse of the woman who would ultimately juggle being a single mom, a magazine writer, chairperson for every charitable function who clamored for her vitality and dedication and one of the hardest campaigners for the presidential election. It turned out she was a Democrat after all, and it was the date she had the night after we met at Neiman's who was the Republican. We crossed that river safely, I'm glad to say.

She asked me to read the baking instructions for one of the pies she was making, beginning to get flour on her face, making her already perfect nose all the more appealing. I read everything exactly as written until I said, "Two eggs beaten or thoroughly scolded."

She looked up puzzled and asked, "Does it really say that?"

"No," I answered, "just trying to lighten up the recipe."

She laughed and said, "But you didn't say it funny. You said it real."

I said, "The essential ingredient in humor. If the words are funny, you don't have to say them funny."

"You should be an actor," she said.

"No, thanks. I'm doing fine where I am."

Later on I made another comment on something, a pass at humor or a stab at irony, but it was clearly just a joke. It went by her, so I said, "I just did it again." After a while, she was finally able to separate fact from fun, and my dry humor began getting through to her. She was not used to any-one talking like that, especially in Jeffersonville, Indiana, where she was raised, a stone's throw from Louisville, across the Ohio River. She had no Southern accent except when she was on the phone with one of her three sisters and a brother, and she would suddenly turn into a country girl, which is why I think the tractor image of her became clear to me. When it came time to eat, she wouldn't let me help with the dinner dishes, but I was allowed to put the chairs at the table. I put one on each side. She said, "and the high chair goes in the middle."

It never occurred to me that Bryn would be eating with us. When a woman invites you to her home for dinner, you expect the atmosphere to lean at least a little toward the romantic. This one was purely domestic. Diane went into the bedroom and brought out a sleepy-eyed, blond-haired beauty, who rubbed her eyes and stared at me. She had Diane's face all right, and weren't they both lucky. Now with Bryn at the table, I expected dinner to be directed toward childhood behavior. "Don't throw your spoon, Bryn," or "Bryn, don't drink the water with your fingers." I was wrong. Bryn sat quietly, never making a sound, just watching me and Diane talk as if she understood what we were saying. She never once cried and never once made a demand. This experience was probably new to her and she was taking it in like a new television cartoon she didn't quite un-derstand.

When we were through, Diane brought the dishes into the kitchen, again rejecting my offer to help.

She left Bryn in my care. I tried my year-and-a-half children's conver-sation. "Hi, Bryn. My name is Neil. Do you have a doll? Can I see your doll? Would you like me to tell you a story?" As I was floundering, Bryn just stood staring at me, holding her bottle, and once in a while offering me a sip. Diane was in the kitchen fielding a couple of telephone calls, one from a friend and another from her agent about two auditions for com-mercials coming up the next day, and while doing all this, she probably also painted the kitchen an eggshell white just to keep her hands busy.

I put a cartoon on television for Bryn, but she'd have none of it. She was still standing there, staring me down, giving no indication if she ap-proved or otherwise. Finally, she made her move. She crossed the room, handed me her bottle, then proceeded to climb up my legs and into my lap, where she took her bottle again and seemingly settled in for the night. It was all so perfect, the suspicious paranoid in me thought that Diane had been rehearsing Bryn to do this all day.

Diane came out of the kitchen, shocked to see Bryn in my lap, and laughed loudly. "She almost never does that," she said. "I think I have competition." I didn't mind hearing that at all.

Bryn was finally put to bed, the pies were put out to cool, the dishes were put out to dry and Diane put on a new face in the bathroom, washing off the flour that I had enjoyed looking at.

"God! Why didn't you tell me I looked like that?" she said.

We were finally alone, talking and finding out who we both were, when a little figure appeared around the corner of the room, just wanting to listen.

"Go to bed, Bryn," Diane said sternly. "Neil and Mommie are talking."

Bryn ran quickly back to her bed, but not willingly. Four times during our conversation, Bryn appeared, each time just enough of her visible around that corner for us to know she was there. Each time she learned more about how to be discreet and yet be part of the activities. The last time, however, Bryn looked at me, pulling the zipper on her pajamas up and down slowly.

Diane laughed hysterically, although she was shocked. "It's not what you think," she said. "She's not a vamp. She just likes her zippers." Bryn finally retired from show business and went to sleep for the night.

All in all, it was a great evening, and I learned more about who Diane was than I would have learned on fifty dates with someone else.

Although I had plans to spend Thanksgiving with friends, Diane's invitation to spend it with her at her friend's house instead was not a difficult choice to make.

"I'm not making a pass at you," she said. "I just need someone to help me carry the pies." Which I ended up doing with pleasure. Her Indiana humor did not take second place to mine.

A BICOASTAL ROMANCE
27

OUR DATING continued, and our relationship grew steadily, despite the fact I was making that long, nightly trip out to the Valley, still driving past her house two or three times before I found it. In the ensuing weeks, we spoke to each other almost every day and I saw her as many nights as we both could manage. She was also not baking as many pies at this point. I was so glad she got fired from Neiman's because it was their loss and my gain. Each night I came to her house, Bryn crawled up my legs, nestled in and almost got me to drink from her bottle.

One day a call came from Diane to tell me she was moving again. The owner of the building where she was staying decided he was going to give the apartment to his mother, possibly because his mother would pay more rent than Diane could afford. Since Diane had neither a lease nor the money to get a lawyer to fight this outrage, she let it go and found herself another apartment. Perhaps that's why she rarely unpacked everything. The new apartment was in a nearby neighborhood, but I couldn't find that one either. Every place in California has names of things that grow, like Sycamore or Oak or Maple, all the way down to Creepy Vines and Crab Grass.

Diane was exceptionally self-sufficient, and had packed everything by the time I arrived to help. I did, however, help her unpack and move her worldly goods up the new, long flight of stairs. Diane was always surprised when someone did something nice for her, and I think what cemented our relationship was the sight of me carrying a number of heavy objects, including Bryn's tricycle, up the stairs. Diane is also a compulsive furniture mover, but she wouldn't let me help her. I watched as chairs crisscrossed the room, and the sofa was tried in fifteen different positions. Bryn and I helped with the more portable items, like Bryn's storybooks, which were unpacked one at a time. Within two hours it looked like a home, and Diane still found time to hang all her pictures (mostly family), albeit in temporary positions. She was capable of getting up in the middle of the night and rehanging them.

I almost always called her when I got home because that's when we had our most personal conversations. I might add that by now, our relationship had grown more intimate, and it had become increasingly difficult for me to leave at night and drive back to Bel Air. Being the good mother she was, Diane didn't want Bryn to wake up in the morning and see a man in the house, although by now Bryn had seen me so often, she must have thought I was a piece of furniture.

CHRISTMAS was approaching, and on that day Nancy would celebrate her seventeenth birthday. Long before I met Diane, I had promised Nancy I would take her someplace in Europe where we'd never been. We chose Gstaad in Switzerland, and were scheduled to arrive a day or two before Christmas and stay through New Year's Eve. I invited Diane and Bryn to come with us. She declined because she and Bryn always spent the Christmas holidays with her family in Indiana, and they especially wanted to be with Diane's mother, Valerie, or Gingee, as she was affectionately called by her grandchildren. When it was time for Nancy and me to leave for Switzerland, I asked Diane one more time to come with us. With some hesitation, she finally relented. She flew to Gstaad a few days after Christmas and stayed with me while Nancy had a room down the hall. It was a perfect holiday. We then decided to fly to London for a few days before going home. While we were in London, I was forced to deal with a subject I dreaded. Diane began to talk of marriage. Not pushing, not aggressively, but she made it clear it was something to think about in the future. I explained to her, for the very first time, my experiences after the death of Joan and the divorce from Marsha. As much as I cared for Diane, and I was clearly falling in love with her by now, I said that marriage wasn't a possibility for me. Couldn't we just go on living as we did?

"Not with a young baby, I can't," she said. "I have her future to think about, and a long affair leading nowhere is not what I want for either of us."

We returned to New York and Diane flew off to Indiana to pick up Bryn and then went back to California. I returned to my new apartment in New York on 70th Street and Park Avenue. I hadn't been so foolish as to think the subject of marriage would never come up, but I was steadfast in my resolve that marriage would end badly for us. I spoke to Diane a few nights later and it ended badly sooner than I thought. Diane broke off with me. I tried hard not to think of her and once more returned to the one place that was always a safe haven for me—the typewriter.

THE THIRD B.B. PLAY
28

SINCE I HAD no idea I would write a trilogy, I also had no idea that all these titles would be "B.B." plays. *Brighton Beach Memoirs* was chosen because it was more alliterative than "Far Rockaway Memoirs," a low-rent beach community close by to Brighton Beach, where most of the original story took place. I used *Biloxi Blues* because that's where I took my basic training that hot summer in 1945. The third play was to be about the final breakup of my family, the ultimate parting of my parents, with Danny and me moving to Manhattan to pursue our writing careers. I liked *Broadway Bound* because it was also part of the lexicon of the theater, meaning that a play that had passed its tryout stage somewhere in the hinterlands was now bound for Broadway. The symmetry of the titles happened by accident and coincidence; if I had only done one play instead of three, it still would have ended up with the same title.

Since the first two plays were extremely successful, the burden of making *Broadway Bound* equally successful lay heavily on my shoulders. Like any other chain, if one of the links were weak, the strength of the trilogy would be broken. Since I had a very clear picture in my mind of who the characters were and how they behaved, I became more confident and secure each day I worked on it.

It all started with one image in my mind: my mother waxing her dining room table. It was a metaphor of all she would be left in a life that still needed her love and attention. A scratch left on the table by any of us would be like a stab in the back. Her life was falling apart and she realized she couldn't live out her days without taking care of someone, but instead she decided to take care of some *thing*. I knew that basically I was writing a tragedy, and that the laughs that came often during the evening were all bittersweet. I created her aging Socialist father because he was needed as the go-between in an effort to save his daughter's marriage. He had the wisdom of experience, and although he knew his son-in-law had been unfaithful to his wife, he understood and accepted it by admitting he had done the same thing to his own wife in younger days. He also knew that throwing away a thirty-two-year-old marriage for an indiscretion was a foolish thing. He knew too that his daughter was stubborn and obstinate, and so he tried to get her to bend a little, to forgive and forget.

As for the mother (his daughter), she could have looked the other way, but her jealousy, anger and humiliation wouldn't permit it, so her husband leaves. Her father, now ailing, reluctantly moves to Florida to be with his wife—an unfortunate circumstance since neither one has any love left for the other. (Although his wife, unlike his daughter, would rather be with him no matter how cold the relationship, than not have him at all.) For him, it was against his Socialist beliefs to move where the rich and idle live—not exactly an honest statement, but like so many of us, we all have to rationalize the truth to fit our moods.

At the end of the play, the two young brothers leave to fulfill their hopes under the bright lights of Broadway. They take with them a blessing from their mother, and a batch of freshly baked cookies to "see them through their first lonely week in New York." As the curtain falls, the mother is seen waxing her beloved table, given to her years ago by her own grandmother. Eugene, the younger son (my alter ego), who is also the narrator of the evening says to the audience:

> EUGENE
> Contrary to popular belief, everything in life
> doesn't come to a clear-cut conclusion.
> Mom didn't do anything very exciting with
> the rest of her life except wax her

> grandmother's table and bask in the glory of
> her sons' success. But I never got the feeling
> that Mom felt she sacrificed herself for us.
> Whatever she gave, she found her own quiet
> pleasure in. I guess she was never
> comfortable with words like "I love you." A
> hard life can sometimes knock the sentiment
> out of you . . . But all in all, she considers
> herself a pretty lucky woman . . . After all,
> she did once dance with George Raft.

At the first reading of the play I discovered two flaws, not recogniz-able to anyone, except possibly Manny Azenberg, our producer. When people ask me, "How do you know there's a flaw in the play after only one reading?" the only answer I have is that I am following my instincts. I not only see and hear the play in that rehearsal room, but I can also visualize it on the stage on opening night in New York. What sounds bad in one place is sure to follow suit in the other. The first flaw was that I created an un-necessary character in the second act, a young girl who was in love with Eugene. In her one scene, Eugene is sick in bed with the flu and she comes to visit him at night in Brighton Beach. The two of them shared a similar problem; her parents were breaking up as well. It was an attempt on my part to say that in life, we are all, at some period, losers. The young actress, a very adept one, was reading her scene intelligently and honestly. The other actors sat in rapt attention—all except me, and then I soon noticed that Manny Azenberg was distracted as well. Usually he reads the script silently to himself as the play moves along. This time, however, he was turning the pages of this scene fairly quickly, looking to see where it ended. In a sense, he was saying quietly to himself, "How long does this thing go on?" I had reached that conclusion before he did. I took my pad, wrote something on it and passed it to Manny, who was sitting next to me. It said, "Don't worry. I can fix it." He smiled at me and nodded, then put his arm around my shoulder in appreciation. That note is now framed and sits in Manny's office just above his desk.

After the first reading that day, Manny, director Gene Saks and I walked slowly to the Chinese restaurant we usually frequented on the first day's reading.

Gene said, "What do you think about the scene with the girl? I think it needs something, don't you?"

Manny offered a suggestion how the scene might be more potent, more relevant to the play. My mind was elsewhere as they spoke, thinking ahead to what I would do. Then I turned to them and said, "Oh, don't worry. The girl is out of the play."

Gene said, "You mean the actress? I thought she was pretty good."

"No, not the actress. The part. We don't need that scene at all. It doesn't push the play forward. I have another idea of what should be there."

This was the second flaw, and cutting the play wouldn't do it. As I listened to the play in its entirety, I realized that the mother did not have a truly happy moment of her own. She had nothing to celebrate, nothing to look forward to, and we never got to see the joyful side of her. Was she always like this? I wondered, thinking of the audience's reaction to her. If they thought her a drab, self-pitying misanthrope, they would miss who she truly was. If indeed she was a cheerless woman, the audience would understand the husband's reason for leaving her. Did she ever love him? Did he ever love her? I had to find a scene in the play that revealed the mother *and* the father completely devoted to each other and aware of each other's special qualities. The problem was that I could not stop the play or break the continuity to show this scene, nor could I go to a flashback, thus breaking the tone and style of the play. It all came to me when I thought of the story that the mother constantly told and retold about the night she danced with George Raft. I would have to go to the past through the mother's memory, prodded on by her sympathetic son, Eugene.

When all seemed bleakest, Eugene encourages the mother to tell the story once again. As she does, she reminisces about her early life, about the gift her grandmother gave her, the dining room table. She tells about how her parents didn't like the idea of her going to a dance hall. She tells about how she met her husband, how she respected him and ultimately came to love him. She remembers him as he was and not as he is in the present. As she continues to tell the story, Eugene gets up, turns on the radio and we hear the soft clarinet sound of Benny Goodman and his band. He tries to coax the mother up to dance with him. At first she is reticent, embarrassed, afraid to go back to that place which was once so perfect. Eugene is persistent, and finally he takes her hand, leads her to the center of the room, and says, "Show me. Show me how you danced with George Raft." She slowly takes a step, holding Eugene tentatively. Then another step . . . and then they are dancing, her leading, teaching Eugene how to hold her, to turn her, and as we watch, we see her when she was sixteen, the dancing pride of the East Bronx. She is as graceful as she was then, as perfectly controlled in her movements as a young girl, and as happy in her reverie as she probably was on that night she became the talk of the neighborhood. We see the mother as a wonderful, hopeful and lovely young thing, some thirty-five years ago. As acted and danced by actress Linda Lavin, she was as brilliant as any actress I've ever worked with. When the dance stopped, the applause from the audience was thunderous. It seemed as if I must have had that scene in my mind from the outset, and had built a play around it. You never know how the mind works. Perhaps that scene was always embedded in my subconscious . . . and it took its sweet time before it revealed itself to me. *Broadway Bound* became a huge hit, and with my picture on the cover of *Time* magazine, it was called "The Best Play of the Decade."

As I wrote the play, I connected into my own life—the one I was going through while I wrote—and projected it to the future, thirty-five or forty years later. Would I be alone, throwing away my own happiness as my mother did? I called Diane in California. I told her how much I missed her and missed Bryn. She admitted she felt the same way but that nothing had really changed between us. I asked her to give it more time, to let the relationship grow instead of ending it without giving it the chance for me to feel secure in taking that major step she needed for herself. She decided to come to Washington, D.C., where we were still previewing *Broadway Bound*. When she arrived, and we embraced, I thought that all was well again, that we'd go on, as before, knowing in the future I would have to make that commitment. We didn't discuss it much, but shared (she for the first time) the nerve-wracking business of going through another opening. As the curtain went up on that first night, I knew that nothing was really settled between Diane and me, but with the fate of the play and my life both hanging in limbo, at least for the next two and a half hours, I just hung in there. I felt jittery and nervous, more than I had since my first play some twelve years before. I could hardly breathe and wanted to run out of the theater. I stayed pulled together long enough for the final curtain to come down. If enthusiastic audiences were any sign, we were a hit. More experienced by then, I knew nothing was a hit until the reviews came in. We all waited anxiously at a small party and I suddenly felt I had to sit down alone, away from the mingling guests. I began to get chest pains, which I attributed to nerves, but the pains persisted. Surely they would disappear once the reviews were read. Good or bad, nerves usually abate and either joy or anger takes over.

As the first review was read aloud, written by David Richards, the critic from the *Washington Post,* the most important paper in town, it became clear very quickly that he was enchanted by *Broadway Bound.* The review was so glowing with praise and affection that I felt overwhelmed. Still, I had fears. Did I write a good play and did I treat my parents fairly? I knew I'd been honest, but had I been fair? Since both were now gone, I didn't want to be haunted from the grave, thinking that I betrayed my parents, invading the privacy of their own inner turmoil. But by doing so, I think I made the play accessible to all. The audience could identify with their own parents, and in some cases, their very own experiences. Some could applaud, but you never knew what went on inside their own private thoughts. They might completely miss the fact that the people on stage reflected their own experiences, and instead, they would assume they were just watching the problems of other people.

Despite the fact that David Richards's review was probably the best I ever got from anyone, the pains in my chest did not abate. By now I had begun to worry. Diane came over and sat next to me, asking what's wrong, and I could hardly get the breath to tell her. She called Manny Azenberg aside and said, "I think we'd better get Neil to a hospital quickly." Senator Alan Simpson of Wyoming and his wife were there and instantly rushed all five of us to his car, then sped through Washington to the nearest hospital.

We reached the hospital and I got out of the car, helped carefully by Manny and Senator Simpson. As we reached the front door, a nurse asked what we wanted. Alan said, "I think our friend here may be having a heart attack."

"I'm sorry," the nurse said. "This is a woman's hospital only. We can't take any male patients."

Manny didn't want to say the word "death" in front of me, but stated that I could be in real trouble. The nurse wouldn't budge. It was so ludicrous, that through my pain, I started to laugh. We piled into the car and headed for the next hospital, hoping they wouldn't say, "Sorry. Catholics only."

A Wyoming native, Alan Simpson could drive a car as well as he probably rode a horse. Whatever hospital it was we got to next, I was taken in immediately, with IVs stuck in my arm, and every other gadget we're used to seeing on TV's *ER*. In the meantime, Diane, always cool and clear-thinking in times of trouble, called and woke up Ben Bradlee, then still the managing editor of the *Post,* whom we had met in East Hampton. Almost as quickly as he broke the Watergate story in his paper, he called his cardiologist, who arrived at the hospital within ten minutes. And this was about one in the morning.

Did I die? No, but it felt like it. It turned out it wasn't a heart attack, but a combination of not eating all day, nerves about the play and probably hoping Diane and I could stay together and that the word "marriage" would be outlawed in America. I was told by the doctor to go back to L.A., to rest and do nothing for a few weeks. I had to leave *Broadway Bound* just the way it was, and I never saw another performance of it in Washington. The play remained unchanged thereafter although, once I saw it at the first New York preview, I didn't think it needed changing. The further good news was that Diane and I were seeing each other again in Los Angeles.

I was back in New York for the opening and Diane and Bryn flew in a few days before, but they stayed in a hotel instead of with me. At the party following the opening, Diane assumed the role of hostess, which was perfectly fine with me because if there was one thing Diane could do, it was give a great party. She made all the arrangements for the food, a four-piece orchestra (who easily could have played a dirge if we were a flop) and the seating for all my friends and family. The party was held in an Italian restaurant in the East 60s. Diane greeted everyone with a smile, found them a place to sit and something to drink. I watched her only peripherally as I sat with Bob Fosse, Paddy Chayefsky and my brother, Danny, while waiting for just one review. That, of course, would be from Frank Rich. Paddy and Fosse were great supporters and told me not to worry. Danny was also enormously reassuring, but Danny always had a problem with his height, which never stopped him from winning the favors of more women than I thought possible. Danny's only complaint about the play had to do with Jason Alexander. Not that Jason wasn't fantastic in the play, portraying the role of my brother more than brilliantly, but he was upset because Jason was even shorter than Danny. As if we first looked for a short actor and then hoped he could act. It took a few minutes to convince Danny that we first look for a great actor and never pay attention to his height.

Diane seemed at home and left the worrying about the play to me while she got the orchestra to play a lively tune and picked out the first guest she could find to get up and dance with her, hoping that others would soon follow. I didn't want to discourage her from her gaiety even though I thought that this was the last thing that should be going on that night. *Broadway Bound* was an important play to me, and one so personal to write that even if the reviews were good, I didn't think a celebration was in order. Not to make any comparisons, but I couldn't imagine Eugene O'Neill sitting in a restaurant on the night that *Long Day's Journey into Night* opened, a play so searing he asked that it not be performed until twenty-five years after his death. In it he revealed that his mother was a morphine addict, his brother an incurable drunk and his father a tyrant and a deeply selfish man. When the reviews would come in, would O'Neill jump up and scream happily, "A hit! I've got a hit. I'll make millions from this."? I think not. That's why he preferred to be dead instead of at a party. Eventually, the *New York Times* review came in. There were a few respectful quotes from Mr. Rich, but again, as usual, there was a lecture on how a play should be written. He is a fine writer, I'll give him that, but fine writers don't always make good critics. Perhaps he was even a good critic, but since he received so little joy from and had so little respect for my work, I really don't have the inclination to give him the benefit of the doubt. My doubt, not his. Still, his review was important, and despite those reviews that soon filed into the restaurant that night, extolling the play's virtues, it was Mr.

Rich's review that pained me most. Time heals all that. As I write this many years later, it all means nothing to me. The good *or* the bad.

As we left the party later in the evening, not knowing I'd be on the cover of *Time* the following week, I was simply drained, and glad that Diane was with me. She was encouraging and warm as we drove back to my apartment. I was exhausted and started to undress slowly, exhausted from the experience. Taking off a shoe was an enormous effort. I looked at Diane, assuming she would soon climb into bed next to me and we would both sleep off the joy and the fears of that memorable night. But her coat was still on as she was saying good night.

Surprised, I said, "Where are you going?"

"Back to the hotel," she answered.

"Tonight? You won't even stay with me tonight?"

"I don't think it would be right," she said. "Nothing has changed."

If God tested Job's patience, He was now giving me my college entrance exams, and I hadn't even cracked open a book in preparation.

ONE GREAT STEP FOR MARRIAGE-KIND

29

I KEEP no journals, no diaries, no date books. Since I write so much in my plays and films, it would be as pointless as me taking a picture of me taking a picture of me. Consequently, although this is a memoir—meaning what I remember of my life—the chronological order of events may not be in the exact order of when the events actually happened. What I do remember correctly is what happened, where it happened and most importantly, why it happened. This distinction runs counter to what every person of my age was taught as a schoolkid, especially in early history lessons. Dates, dates and more dates: Columbus, 1492. Lindbergh's flight, 1927. The U.S. entry into the First World War, 1917 to 1918, and the easiest one to remember, the War of 1812. If you got those correct, you were two thirds of the way toward a good grade. Of course, you had to wait until adulthood before you found out *why* any of these things happened or were important, but at least you knew *when* they happened. Well, I'm not like that. I am not a scorekeeper. To a writer, it's the story that counts.

Diane and I finally got married quickly and quietly one morning at the City Hall in Los Angeles. Not a soul knew about it—not my daughters, not my brother, not Diane's family, no one. Except Bryn, and Bryn thought a wedding was a party and why were we going to a party at nine-thirty in the morning? she asked. I drove downtown, nervously and silently, barely sharing a word with Diane. We moved down the empty streets without a sound. Sort of like a romantic commando raid. Suddenly on Melrose Avenue, I pulled the car over to the curb, stopped, opened the door and disappeared out of Diane's sight. It didn't occur to me that Diane thought I was taking a quick powder, abandoning her with the motor still running. When I returned moments later, her face had gone completely white, almost to the point that it erased her makeup as well. I slid into my seat and put a bouquet of flowers in her hands, kissed her cheek and drove on. She was still so completely flustered that she looked at the flowers on her lap as if to say, "What are these for?" I soon learned that Diane is not someone you should sneak up on. If she opened her bathroom door at the same moment you were about to knock on it, her bathrobe went into cardiac arrest.

We arrived at City Hall about ten A.M. and took our seats on the benches in the old marble hall waiting room, along with dozens of other nervous and much younger couples, some of them holding hands, some laughing and some drinking coffee from a paper cup and sharing an Egg McMuffin. Most of them looked like the price of a one-day honeymoon trip would be a hardship.

When the official in charge boomed over the blaring speaker system, "Diane Lander and Neil Simon," not a head turned. No one there ever heard of me or even cared, which is partly why we chose City Hall. The marriage ceremony was brief and businesslike, and our witnesses were two female court employees. As soon as the "Judge"—if that's what he was, wearing a purple shirt and a green striped tie—said, "I now pronounce you man and wife," our unmoved witnesses offered their hurried congratulations, no doubt wondering how many more times they would have to do this before their lunch break.

Our wedding breakfast was actually a brunch. About three hundred people attended, but none of them knew us, looked at us or were even aware we were just married. We were in a huge Chinese restaurant just a few blocks from City Hall, and for this meal only dim sum was served. These wonderful, tasty Chinese dumplings came with about fifty different kinds of fillings and there wasn't a loser in their vast ovens. We were, as I recall, the only Caucasians in the building, and we felt as if we were in Shanghai without having to take the sixteen-hour flight. We each had about six or seven dumplings, which had enough calories and protein in them to get you halfway up Mount Everest. That, plus the four glasses each of Chinese wine, made it seem possible that with one more sip, I would get up and toast my bride in fluent Cantonese. We would have thrown rice at each other but this was the kind of rice that would stick to your face and eyelids. I may have been a reluctant groom but there was no doubt that I was in love with my two-hour-new wife.

Diane was wearing a brown linen suit and a silk scarf around her neck, which was mine, an art deco relic I found one day in SoHo in New York. I wore a sports jacket, a sleeveless sweater and a shirt with no tie, which for Los Angeles in the morning was very dressy. Now that I think of it, I realize I was making some sort of statement that I didn't want to make a big deal out of this ceremony. The truth is, I married Joan, Marsha and now Diane, all in municipal buildings. Still, I'm sure you'll agree that Diane was a knockout when you see the wedding picture as you drift through the pages of this book. The photo was taken hurriedly outside City Hall by a fast-talking photographer, who I'm sure sometimes used a pony in his work.

We drove home, told our housekeeper the good news; she smiled happily and kissed us both. The rest of the morning was spent on the phone calling family, friends and anyone who was in our separate phone books.

"Yes. We're very happy . . . Yes, we're surprised too . . . You'll never guess . . . Chinese dumplings . . . I swear . . . In a Chinese restaurant . . . Wait! Talk to Neil . . . Hello, who's this? . . . Oh, hi . . . Yeah. We did it . . . This morning . . . What's wrong with City Hall? . . . Wait! Talk to Diane . . . Mom! Your daughter's married . . . Oh, God, my mother's crying . . . Her dog is crying too . . . Who? . . . Who's this? . . . No, miss. We already subscribe to the *L.A. Times.* Will you please get off the phone?"

Bryn smiled and kissed us both when she returned from preschool. She was mostly overjoyed at the big, creamy cake that was being lifted out of the freezer . . . I never thought I'd be married three times . . . I was in a slight daze . . . No matter what you plan in life, it's the unexpected that always takes over . . . After all the phone calls ceased, the house became quiet . . . I looked at the ceiling . . . It was only about one-thirty in the afternoon . . . I wondered if I should go inside to my office and write for a few hours?

SEND IN THE FARCE
30

WHEN PEOPLE ASK where the idea for a play comes from, very often my answer is, "It depends on what state of mind I'm in." Having just finished a dark examination of my parents, of their broken promises and lost love, I wanted to erase those bitter thoughts from my mind and spend a year enjoying myself. A trip around the world would have been a good solution, but I had a different yearning. I wanted to laugh and to make audiences laugh. I chose to write a farce, not realizing that technically speaking, writing a good farce may be the hardest undertaking in a writer's career.

Oddly enough, in the 1930s and 1940s, the New York theaters were filled with good farces—plays like *Once in a Lifetime, Room Service, Three Men on a Horse* and *Arsenic and Old Lace*. They're still good enough to be revived in regional theaters all over the country, but perhaps a little naive for today's world. The irony is that, though these once classic farces are now considered old-fashioned, if you attempt a *new* farce for Broadway, you will inevitably be asked to measure up to the old farces I've just mentioned. "Catch-22," Joseph Heller calls it. Worse still you will also be compared to the classic farces of Molière and Feydeau, which are always considered in style, and if you're really looking for trouble, don't try anything that is brittle, wise and witty because they'll say "a cheap ripoff of Oscar Wilde's *The Importance of Being Earnest.*" Lesson One, don't mess with masterpieces.

I did not know a thing about the mechanics of farce until I got caught up in the endlessly intricate details of its machinery. For those foolhardy enough to test these white-water rapids, I'll pass on a few hints I learned along the way and also give you the names of a few doctors who attended me after the battle was over:

1. The play must move like greased lightning. Any kind of grease will do.

2. The story starts with a minor problem, complicated very soon by a slightly more complicated problem, and inevitably never ceases being caught up in ever increasing minor problems, which soon become catastrophic problems. In the end, all the problems are solved in one hilarious sentence. If you can do that, you should have been the one who invented the computer.

3. It must be funny. Then funnier. Then funniest. Only two people have gone beyond funniest, but they didn't live to tell the story.

4. The stakes must be high. Since almost all the characters are hiding something, if caught, it could be calamitous. Calamity always hovers two feet above everyone in a farce.

5. You cannot do a farce without swinging doors (which go in and out), closets to hide in and beds to crawl under. Very often someone hiding in a closet is joined by someone else hiding in the same closet. They may or may not see each other depending on how many fur coats separate them. A sure laugh is when the adulterer's wife in the play says, "I feel chilly. I think I'll get my fur coat." If the audience doesn't laugh at that, give them their money back. They don't belong in the theater.

6. This is not a steadfast rule, but farces, historically speaking, are about rich people and never about poor people. Poor people have enough trouble without getting caught in a farce. Rich people, on the other hand, deserve what's coming to them. Watching them squirm gets howls from the audience. If they don't laugh, send them home with the people who didn't laugh at the fur coat joke.

7. In many farces, characters often have infirmities or various disorders. These include people who lisp, stutter, are almost blind, have the gout, a tic, a whining nasal problem, are allergic to mattresses, which causes them to sneeze while hiding under beds, or—a device Shakespeare often used—two sets of twins, male and female, who cannot be told apart even by each other.

If you got all that, you may now write your farce. Good luck. You may never be heard from again.

EVEN AWARE of all these difficulties, I still undertook the writing of *Rumors*. We rehearsed and tried it out at the Old Globe Theater in San Diego. At the first reading, we knew we were funny. But not funny enough. We thought we had enough complications in the play until you realize that in a farce enough is never enough. At the final curtain, the audience must be as spent as the actors, who by now are on oxygen support. If the audience is only wheezing with laughter, you need rewrites or actors with stronger lungs.

I WAS pretty much spent myself because in the year and a half that Diane and I were married, I also did the film of *Brighton Beach Memoirs* and wrote the screenplay of *Biloxi Blues*. Diane was kept busy redoing the house on Chalon Road, the house I bought with Marsha, although it took some readjusting Diane, moving from a tiny apartment in the Valley to a more imposing home in the green hills of Bel Air. She was still unsure if she should unpack everything. In some way, I think Diane was inundated by my busy schedule, even though I was totally unaware that I had such a busy schedule.

There were constant parties and events to attend—film premieres, charity dinners, private parties and as much socializing as your clothes closet could keep up with. Diane had no trouble fitting in with any crowd, although privately, it may have taken a toll on her. Since I had been through all this for the past couple of decades, I was used to it even though I didn't necessarily enjoy it. Someone once said to me, "It must be very difficult for someone to be married to a celebrity," but in truth, I never considered myself one. I was neither flattered nor annoyed by giving autographs, and if possible, would try to walk away from a crowd rather than go through it. It didn't occur to me whether Diane thought she was just "tagging along with someone famous," or if she enjoyed the limelight herself. I thought we were together, no matter how many photographers were shouting on an opening night, "Hey, Neil! Neil! Look this way!" I was not with them. I was with her. But, if I put the shoe on the other foot, I suppose it would be a touchy situation.

Before I met Diane, I went out on a date with a very pretty and well-known TV newswoman from CNN. We walked into a restaurant, through the crowded tables until we were seated. My date seemed a little miffed. She said, "That's the first time I walked into a restaurant where everyone was looking at the man I was with instead of me." She didn't like the competition. It was our first and last date. It truly wouldn't have bothered me if she were the one they were all looking at. I am not insecure about my personal popularity. Unlike an actor or a famous athlete, whose physical presence is always right there in front of the public, it's my work that I'm known for and I never write in front of a crowd.

Meanwhile, back in San Diego, I was still rewriting *Rumors*. It was like a huge animal that needed constant feeding and there were times, many times, that I simply ran out of food.

There were so many plot points that needed clarifying, so many scenes that needed a new concept, so many lines that weren't as sharp as they could be and so many actors who had to be made happy for fear that someone else was getting bigger laughs than they were. "Neil, couldn't I get a better exit line here?" "Sure," I would say to myself. "Get on a plane, say goodbye and fly back to New York." I really needed help and the best person to turn to is almost always the director.

Gene Saks is a truly funny man and a wonderful director, and like many others in that job, was unable to tell me *how* to fix it. I depended on him to tell me *where* it needed fixing. Sometimes a director can just redirect a scene into working, but his and the actors' jobs would all be easier if I could get the script right all through the play.

Each night after the show, Gene and I would go to the restaurant in the hotel where we were staying and I'd have Gene quiz me. I was so busy with my own rewriting that Gene was more objective about the play as a whole and would point out where he thought our ship was sprouting holes and listing a few degrees into the water. I needed him to ask me questions. *Any* questions. I didn't need answers. I would eventually supply those myself. But I needed him to be the diagnostician, indicating to me where he saw symptoms in need of my doctoring, all this despite the fact the audience was howling with laughter through the play every night. It's why the theater is such a hard place to succeed in.

Perhaps we were more demanding than the audience, but we knew the critics in New York were more demanding than any audience alive. Our twelve-character cast were simply wonderful and too numerous to list all their names here, but I thought Christine Baranski was our standout and she went on to win the Best Supporting Actress Tony Award in New York. As for the play, the critics carped, praised, cheered, smeared, loved, loathed, liked and disliked it enormously. That's about all you could ask for. All in all, I was happy with what I did. I juggled twelve balls in the air at the same time and dropped only two or three along the way. We ran well over a year and the play runs on today almost everywhere, especially in schools where the teachers wisely take out all the F words.

Diane and I were now married a year and a half, and without my really noticing it, the marriage was quickly collapsing in front of my eyes. They say you never see the bullet that kills you.

ALONE AGAIN . . . AGAIN
31

IT ALWAYS amused me, in a grim sort of way, when a couple breaks up after some years of marriage, someone, anyone, even your closest friend, will inevitably say, "My God! What happened?" . . . As if it could be answered that easily, or even answered at all. To me, the answer probably lies in some ancient Chinese lesson for children about where the ocean comes from.

"A bird sits in a tree waiting for the rain to stop. The sun comes out and he flies off, as a single drop of water falls from his wing onto a shiny rock. The droplet slides from the rock into a tiny puddle and the puddle soon finds its way into a quiet pool, which flows into a lake that runs into a river, which eventually gathers force from the wind and finally blows into the great ocean which was born when a tiny droplet of water fell from a bird's wing." Go around that one a few hundred times and you'll know what it feels like to try to remember when your marriage first started to fall apart. Why does "I love you more than I thought it was possible to love" slide slowly but progressively into "It's over"?

In retrospect, it's fairly amazing, given our disparate backgrounds, histories, families, temperaments, attitudes and outlooks on life that Diane and I would fall in love. Yet fall in love we did, despite both the thousand things right between us, and the thousand things wrong. What does it take to throw the balance one way or the other? Nine hundred ninety-nine things right and one thousand and one things wrong? And what was the one thing wrong that started the slide? "Are you drinking from my coffee mug?" Could it be that fragile? The petty squabbles that most people endure during their first year of marriage are pretty universal, and as was the case with Diane and me, once a bond of trust is established, the squabbles disappear rather quickly.

As far as I was concerned, I was finally in a marriage that would last a lifetime. Yet, one day, Diane sat me down on our bedroom sofa and said to me, with tears in her eyes, that she had to go, to leave the marriage and to leave as soon as possible. Where did this come from, and why didn't I see it coming? There are some things in a marriage that one partner would never divulge to the other, or some things they will just touch on but make it clear it's nothing they need to share since it's well under control, while there are other things they are quite willing to discuss.

I thought we were pretty frank with each other, and I quite honestly saw nothing so dire that it would interfere with our happiness. With that in mind, there we were, with our marriage not only in trouble, it was virtually over. Before we were married, Diane asked me to promise that I would never write about her, whether fictionalized or in truth. She wanted her life, Bryn's life and our life together to be private and never public, whether good or bad, wanting and needing something so valuable as our marriage to be simply that: our marriage was not for public consumption. Given my history with using my family in many of my plays, I had no trouble in agreeing. In the first place, no one I ever wrote about, no one, ever came to me and said they were hurt by what I said. In many cases, I've taken the truth and fictionalized it to the point that if I did write about someone, they would never guess I was writing about them. In most cases, I write about the essence of someone, not the facts. No one has accused me of stealing their essence.

To even write about Diane in this book, I had to get her written permission. Somewhere in that wish for privacy is a thread that may or may not have led to the dissolution of our marriage. I don't think Diane left easily or without pain. I didn't want her to leave at all. Diane moved out to our beach house where she was staying for a while with her family, and I asked her to come back to meet me and talk, to discuss the possibilities of avoiding this breakup. Less was said than I thought there would be.

"Can we work this out?" I asked Diane, without really and truly knowing what it was we had to work out. Diane was cryptic about it and I knew that pushing her would get us nowhere. She looked up at the ceiling, seemingly for minutes on end, as if looking for an answer somewhere in the minuscule cracks that were forming in the paint overhead and in some similar crack in our relationship. She looked calm, not puzzled. By the look on her face, I was positive she was going to say, "Yes. I would like that very much." She didn't. She said, quite simply, "No. I can't. I have to leave."

There was nothing left to say. I shrugged my shoulders and said, "I'm sorry." There was no argument, no shouting, no anger, no tears. Just a simple, quiet loss. She got up, went to the door, got into her car and drove away. I sat there stunned, but quietly stunned. I said to myself, "I've been through a death and a divorce before, I guess I can get through this." We were only married a year and a half, and I think the lack of longevity in the marriage made it at least bearable to deal with. I was still sitting in the same chair a half hour later when the phone rang. It was Diane, calling from somewhere on the road to the beach. There was a plaintive sound in her voice when she said to me, "I just want you to know that I love you more today than I ever have before." End of phone call. End of marriage. It sounded like the title of some off-Broadway comedy. *I Love You More Than I Ever Have Before So Goodbye.* If I couldn't truly understand why she was leaving, how could I understand why, today of all days, could she love me more than she ever did before? What do you do when something like that happens and you still have the rest of the day to get through? Watch a ball game? Call someone for a game of tennis? I already shot the pool once and I was not angry enough to toss in a hand grenade on a beautiful afternoon.

I knew what she just said on the phone was sincere, which only made the question of why she was leaving more unanswerable. Maybe for Diane, it was "not yet time for happiness." This was my third loss of a wife and what I hoped would never happen again, happened again. I fought against getting married for a third time, instinctively knowing it would end disastrously. At least my instincts were intact, but being right about something like this offers very little consolation. I walked into the den, turned on the television and watched a baseball game. There is nothing worse than watching a ball game when your wife just left. I turned it off and walked into my office and sat down behind my desk, and answered some mail.

I NEVER THOUGHT I was one to philosophize about life, but today, a good deal older and perhaps a little wiser, but certainly more experienced in life, I think about this: If you can go through life without ever experiencing pain you probably haven't been born yet. And if you've gone through pain and think you know exactly why, you haven't examined all the options. And if you think you can avoid that pain the next time it confronts you, you haven't looked over your shoulder. And if you give up living and loving to avoid the pain, you don't appreciate the good things you once had.

Time went by without my seeing Diane, and no phone calls were exchanged between us. I knew she had moved back to the Valley, to a small house, rather than to one of the transitory apartments she used to hop to and from before I met her. We made a financial settlement and she was on her own. You always think you won't get over something, but you do. Life has made room for that to happen. I never got over Joan, but yearning for someone who is dead is a pointless exercise. I always think of her and I could still talk to her occasionally by candlelight in my darkened room, wondering if she hears me or not, and yet, as before, when I awoke the next morning, things seemed clearer for me. Eventually Diane would bring Bryn over to my house so that she and I could spend some time with each other. I truly missed Bryn, as much for her joyfulness and sweet personality as for her youthful wisdom. I looked forward to those Saturday afternoons and pizza lunches, which eventually grew into Disney movies and the Disney movies grew into a trip to the zoo, even though Dad got lost, flustered and bewildered until Bryn said, almost patronizingly, "Dad, why don't you drive up to that gas station and ask for directions?" She got me again.

I noticed at the zoo or at those Disney movies how many single fathers were escorting their son or daughter or both through the Saturday afternoons that were allotted to them. I was now one of them and that's one of the pains I never saw coming. There were days, when she was still small, that Bryn wanted to stay with me a little longer. When time is limited, it is so much more precious.

The house on Chalon was actually too big for one person to live in and I rarely went down the long hall to see the empty bedroom Bryn used to sleep in. Gradually, I let the house put its arms around me and comfort me. I loved the paintings on the walls that I had started buying with Joan, and then continued with Marsha; a few had been bought with Diane. I went to Paris alone once and a few times with Ann Bell, the girl I always seemed to turn to. I enjoyed buying these paintings in obscure shops around Paris and finding, through the eyes of Ray Stark, who taught me about art in our various trips to museums and galleries all over the country, that I did indeed have an eye for quality. I didn't buy masters because they were simply too expensive and I thought, even if I could afford a Renoir or a Matisse or a Picasso, I wasn't interested in owning them. The discovery of someone new and young, or even old and overlooked, was a much pleasanter experience for me.

The days were never a problem for me. Writing and some tennis allowed me to avoid loneliness. What I had to get through were the hours of the night, and the sound of nothingness that echoed silently throughout the house.

I was back to dating again and those timeworn expressions from friends who were always pitching new prospects. "Very attractive . . . lots of fun . . . extremely intelligent . . . loves the theater . . . a former model . . . her father owns the left side of Wall Street . . ." Followed by, "Just have a drink with her, what can you lose?"

I was hesitant. I already had my three strikes and you're out. I didn't think there were any more home runs for me. Maybe I'd had enough times at bat. No one ever introduced me to the three women in my life. I met Joan, Marsha and Diane on my own, and I knew if there was ever anyone again, that's how it would have to happen.

During this time, I found no one I wanted to risk my future for, nor anyone who had measured up to the women I loved most.

Instead what I found was the play I was waiting all my life to write.

LOUIE THE GANGSTER
32

MY FATHER had a sister who was married to an accountant, as the story was told to me when I was about ten or twelve years old. Perhaps I was eleven but everything that far back is sketchily remembered. Actually, the story wasn't told to me personally, because grown-ups don't usually tell eleven-year-old boys the innermost secrets of their lives. This is what I overheard as the family talked in hushed tones in the living room while I pretended to read a comic book in the adjoining room. My aunt's husband, the accountant, worked for a firm in the garment district on Seventh Avenue in New York. It seems the firm also had some connections with the underworld, gangsters, the Mafia or whatever nefarious group one wants to label the organization my unsuspecting uncle worked for. Whether he knew of the underworld connections, or naively thought he was just keeping the books of an upstanding dress manufacturing company, no one knows. What ultimately happened was that my uncle mysteriously disappeared. He left home, went to work one morning and was never seen or heard from again. The consensus was that he was done in by the mob for probably knowing a little too much about their finances. Since I don't remember ever meeting him, he became sort of a romantic figure in the mind of this imaginative adolescent. From a small neighborhood where the biggest crime I could remember was the boy who stole two books from the library, a real-life murder in my very own family was chilling stuff. For my aunt and her children, my cousins, it was a terrible tragedy and a great loss.

Now we fast-forward to 1989 and I am sitting in my office in Los Angeles, searching the blank ceiling or the trees outside my window for an idea for a play. Remembering parts of this story loaded with color and mystery, I began to jot these notes down on my pad.

I envisioned my father (my fictional father) having to go somewhere down South to earn some money to repay what he borrowed from the not-so-friendly loan sharks to pay for my mother's hospital expenses as she lay dying from cancer. Having no place to leave me, a boy of thirteen, he goes to his mother, a tyrannical aging German Jewish woman of eighty, who walks with a cane, a limp and a permanent scowl. He pleads with her to take on his only son for about eight months. The father has to beg and shed tears before this selfish tyrant will do any one of her children a favor. She finally relents, but assures my father that if I am noisy, dirty or break anything, I will be out on the street. Occasionally living with her is her other son, a small-time crook who often comes by to lay low in Mom's apartment above the candy store she owns in Yonkers, New York.

All this takes place in the early 1940s, during the Second World War. Louie, the name I gave this petty hood, befriends me and teaches me how to cheat at cards, how to steal something from the five-and-ten-cent store and how to smoke my first cigarette. Uncle Louie was my fictional hero, a much safer and less dangerous version of a Mafia warlord. Those were the first characters and sketchy outline for a story that I put down in my spiral notebook on that first day. I called it, "Louis the Gangster." Was it a comedy? A farce? A drama or a tragedy? I hadn't gotten that far yet. Let it rattle around in your brain for a few days first, I wisely advised myself.

RARELY when a play comes to me do I know how I will develop it. I never know who all the characters are nor how many there will be. It comes out drop by drop, as I let them sink into my thoughts, picking out what I can use and discarding anything and anyone who is less than of major importance. On the first day I start to write, I will put down almost anything, just trying to get the first introductory scene on paper, whether it's good or not. I am introducing myself to the characters and them to me. Amenities over, they begin to speak. I envision the father sitting in his mother's bedroom, the door closed behind him, talking in a quiet, plaintive way, pleading with her to take in his son. I also know we will never hear this scene because in the stage plan I have in my mind, the interior of her bedroom is not visible. This leaves the young boy, Jay, sitting by himself in the living room, not even knowing his life is being discussed a few feet away from him. But how do we know what his thoughts are? What fears he has? No problem. I give Jay a younger brother, Arty. Now they can discuss at length how much they fear the grandmother and hope that Pop will come out soon so they can all leave. We've not only established the brothers and their plight, we know a great deal about Grandma Kurnitz long before she makes an appearance.

Would Eddie, the boys' father, be Grandma Kurnitz's only child? Hardly. She was brought up in the era of large families. I arbitrarily pick the number of her children as six. Is her husband alive? I pictured him as a hardworking German immigrant, who might have tempered Grandma's cold and unemotional dispositions. Still I couldn't see him in the play. I decided that he died shortly after the family arrived in America and moved to Yonkers, where they opened the candy store. It was a job that needed no skills. If they migrated in the 1920s or 1930s, the rate of death among newborns and small children would be high. I killed off a son and a daughter, Aaron and Rose. These enormous losses are the bedrock of the grandmother's anger toward the world, and shape her philosophy for raising children. Survival is everything. Joy, happiness, love, charity—these are only for the rich. Survive at all costs.

If Eddie is successful in convincing his mother to take his sons in, it would be a disaster for all of them. The boys needed a confidant, someone who would be a buffer between them and their grandmother. I invented Aunt Bella. About thirty-six or thirty-seven, and still living with her mother, working in the candy store from early morning till closing time; even giving the mother back rubs and leg rubs to ease her pain. There would have to be something wrong with Bella, frightened as a child. In the first draft, I wrote Bella as a sweet, shy and nervous woman, but loving to her two nephews. It wasn't enough. With a mother whose only concern is that her children survive, without love, without warmth, without affection, they would have to become a dysfunctional family. In the next draft, Aunt Bella changed. She was almost retarded, but not in a clinical way. Her growth as a human being was stunted. She became a fifteen-year-old child in the body of a thirty-eight-year-old woman, with all the desires and needs of a mature woman, but with the inability to understand these desires. With Arty and Jay now moving in, we see Bella happier than she's ever been before, even though Jay, fourteen, and Arty, about twelve, seem more grown-up than she is.

Who then are the other surviving, dysfunctional children? There is Eddie, of course—weak, still frightened of his mother, and seemingly unable to get over the death of his wife. Then there is Gert, Bella's sister, who is married and lives with her husband, but scarred like her siblings. When Gert cried as a child, the mother pounded her cane onto the floor and shouted, "STOP DOT CRYING! BE HAPPY YOU'RE ALIVE!" Gert stopped her crying immediately, but only by stifling her own breath, thereby being unable to speak a full sentence without gasping for air. It's not a surprise when Gert later tells Arty and Jay that she doesn't do that all the time. It's mostly when she comes to visit her mother.

Louis the gangster, or Uncle Louie to the boys, began in my mind as the uncle who disappeared gangland style, but soon gave way to being just a petty crook, the only one strong enough to stand up to his mother. He may stand up to her, but he can never win a battle, whether with her or with life. He's a survivor, but he's also a loser.

With my characters all now in place, I began to write the play, going back to the first page. As the story began to reveal itself, I found myself identifying most with Aunt Bella. She is the one I loved, the heroine of what became *Lost in Yonkers*. Late in the play, she fights a pitched battle with her mother, wanting permission from her to marry a boy—a boy of forty—because like Bella, he too cannot function in a normal world. Perhaps the two of them together can make a go of it. Bella pleads with her mother to say yes, to let her marry this boy, to let her be his wife and eventually a mother to her own babies—babies she will love and cherish and not let them grow up to be weak and twisted like her own brothers and sisters. The mother, of course, denies her this right by saying nothing and leaving the room without a word, and Bella cries out to her family, "Help me. Someone put their arms around me . . . please."

Bella never quite wins her freedom, but when she says to her mother in a later scene, referring to her dead brother and sister, "Maybe Aaron and Rose were the lucky ones," she has finally wounded her mother. Bella leaves the room while the mother, alone in her chair, wants to scream in anguish, and has to put a handkerchief in her mouth to keep the world from hearing her final punishment.

GENE SAKS again was picked to direct the play. Gene did such a brilliant job with the Brighton Beach Trilogy, and then again with *Lost in Yonkers,* because he knew the very fiber of these people. He grew up with all of them and probably understood the characters in these plays as well as I did. Maybe better.

The first time I saw Kevin Spacey was in a revival of Eugene O'Neill's greatest play, *Long Day's Journey into Night.* It starred Jack Lemmon, and Kevin played the role of the older, wayward son, an incurable alcoholic, played in the original production by Jason Robards, Jr. Kevin took my breath away, as he still does in everything he touches. He was my first and only choice for Uncle Louie. I breathed a sigh of gratitude and relief when Kevin said yes to us.

Casting the role of Aunt Bella, I imagined, would be the hardest. Since I was living in California again, it was decided by Jay Binder, our casting agent, and probably the most important casting agent on Broadway today, that I see some preliminary people in Los Angeles by myself, and if I found anyone I thought was a possible contender, to send her into New York to be seen by Gene and Manny Azenberg. The first actress to walk through the door of my office (and the first time I would hear spoken any of the words I had written) was Mercedes Reuhl. I had seen her in smaller roles in a few films and knew she was talented. But could she be Bella?

With a young man seated on the sofa next to her to read the lines of the other characters, Mercedes took a few moments to look through the first scene again, then looked up at me and said, "May I ask a question? Just how far-out is Bella?"

I said, "She's not retarded, if that's what you mean. I think the mother kept her as a child through the force of her will."

I was about to say more, when Mercedes nodded her head and said, "Okay. I get it. Let's see what happens." And she began to read.

Within a few minutes I felt so moved that there were tears coming into my eyes. I knew in an instant that she was perfect. There was no point in seeing anyone else, even though I did have to go through the motions. I remembered Herbert Ross not wanting to take Quinn Cummings until he had seen forty other young girls, but of course we ended up with Quinn Cummings. We quickly flew Mercedes into New York to read for Gene and Manny. She was signed immediately. As Marsha Mason so wisely said to me years before, "You don't pick them. They pick themselves."

The grandmother would be the most difficult role to perform. She could easily come off as a hateful character, and the part called for an actress of great depth who could show us why this woman behaved as she did, without ever being sentimental about it. Any number of actresses were submitted, but the one name that came up the most was Irene Worth, pronounced Irenee. She was born in the States but appeared so often in London, acquiring an English accent along the way, she was thought of as British. We sent her the script. She read it and accepted. No problem. Except for us. Gene wondered if she could do a convincing German accent. The only way to find out was for Gene, Manny and myself to fly to London and meet with the Great Lady herself.

We met her for lunch at the Inn on the Park Hotel in London. In her perfect English, she said she thought it was a very fine play and was looking forward to doing it. Since she already accepted the part, she thought it very extravagant of us to fly all the way over just to have lunch with her. None of us knew how to bring up the issue of the German accent without insulting her.

Gene jumped in first. "Are you comfortable playing a German Jew?" Gene asked.

"Yes, darling. I'm an actress. May I have some more Chablis, please?"

We all looked at each other. We'd better be more direct.

"Have you ever played a German before?" Manny asked.

"I've played everything, darling. Am I the only one having dessert?"

Finally, Gene made the big push. He laughed first, to soften her up, and then said, "Is there any special dialect you would do? That you could show us so we'd know which one to pick?"

She looked at us with a cold, chilling stare.

"If you're asking me to audition for you, you've come a long way for nothing. I haven't auditioned in forty-two years."

"No, of course not," Gene rushed in trying to save the day. "I wasn't thinking of an audition," he begged off.

"Then let's drop the subject . . . Waiter, may I see the dessert cart, please?"

We had lost. We were never going to hear the accent. The waiter wheeled over the large dessert cart and placed it before her to peruse. She looked from one dessert to the other and then said, in a perfect German accent, "Should I haff ze strudel, or perhaps ze apple tart? Nein. I sink ze chocolate tart looks best, yah? Danke schoen."

She never looked at us or smiled. She was smarter than all of us. We had our Grandma Kurnitz.

ON THE NIGHT of the Tony Awards, I thought our biggest competition was John Guare's *Six Degrees of Separation,* a wonderful play that Frank Rich called "his masterpiece." He had given us only a middling review. The Tony Awards show began, and pretty soon the awards began to mount up.

"Best Supporting Actor in a Play . . . Kevin Spacey."

"Best Supporting Actress in a Play . . . Mercedes Reuhl."

"Best Actress in a Play . . . Irene Worth."

"Best Play . . . Neil Simon's *Lost in Yonkers.*"

Almost a clean sweep except for Gene Saks, who I thought was a shoo-in. Perhaps he didn't get it that year because he had already won for two plays in the Brighton Beach Trilogy.

ON APRIL 9, 1991, I received a telegram from Michael Sovern of Columbia University. It was a short, understated, single sentence.

"You were awarded Pulitzer Prize for Drama today. Congratulations."

I won something I never dreamed would come to me. I called my brother and said, "Danny, I just won the Pulitzer Prize."

"Wait a second," he said. "I have to stop the water in my tub." A few seconds later he was back. "So what happened today?"

The little things of everyday life sometimes temper the magical things. And that's how it should be.

JEFF
33

FLASHBACK:

I thought perhaps what eventually happened in writing *Lost in Yonkers* found its seed in the dark and calamitous years that preceded it. Not just to me, but to my family, to my eldest daughter, Ellen, in particular.

In 1984, Ellen, divorced from John Leland and living with her son, Andrew, in Nyack, New York, went to her best friend's wedding. Sitting at the same table as Ellen was a young man with a vibrant personality, attractive and intelligent, with a maturity beyond his twenty-six years. Jeff Bishop could not take his eyes off Ellen, who was sitting across from him at the large round table filled with guests. He soon rearranged the seating, which put him in the chair next to Ellen. Ellen has a smile and a personality that light up a room, and Jeff was now sitting in the glow of that light.

He had graduated from Princeton University and was now going for his Ph.D. in astrophysics at the University of Chicago. I can readily say that no one in my family had ever majored in astrophysics, nor, I'm sure, even knew exactly what it was. Ellen, in those days, was far more reticent to talk to me about her personal life, since she was so determined to become her own person. As time went on, Ellen relaxed her concerns and as she became surer of herself, began to include me in most matters that concerned her. The cycle of the child clinging to her parents, then moving away as she took on her own life and personality, eventually came full circle to a point where she can now include me in most of the important events that happen to her. I like it better this way.

She appeared one day at my new apartment on 70th Street and Park Avenue (that was a move made somewhere in this story that has no date nor time that I can recall) with Jeff Bishop, following a whirlwind romance that blossomed as Ellen was making almost weekly visits to Chicago. I was living alone at the time and enjoying the first apartment I ever owned with a terrace; it was on the twentieth floor, and had a view from New Jersey to the East River. There were, once again, women in my life, but not *a* woman and certainly not *the* woman.

I was, however, delighted to see that Ellen had found *the* man in her life. Jeff never flaunted his intelligence or his academic success. All he ever talked about was Ellen. All he ever looked at was Ellen. No matter how much he lived his intellectual life in the mysteries of the universe, nothing shined and glittered more to him than the dark-haired girl he was sitting next to on the sofa, both beaming at me, anxious to tell me their secret. The inept Inspector Clouseau could have figured this one out. They had come to tell me they were getting married. I feigned surprise, but Ellen didn't want a feign from me. She wanted a YIPPEE AYE YAY OKAY from me, which I did in my own quiet, subdued sort of way. I hugged them both, delighted and overjoyed with their happiness.

They married, Jeff graduated, Andrew was growing up and I was ecstatic, except for the news that they would soon be moving to Toronto, Canada, where Jeff received a postdoctoral fellowship at the Canadian Institute for Theoretical Astrophysics. I now had the comfort of knowing that if ever I had a problem with theoretical astrophysics, I knew exactly to whom I should turn. By 1987, they missed being home and Jeff applied for and received an associate professorship at Columbia University in the heart of New York City. They moved back to the house in Nyack and I kept wondering if Joan had a bird's-eye view from the same heavens that Jeff explored, and could see how happy her daughter and grandson, Andrew, were.

Jeff began to cough quite a bit and since he didn't smoke, the symptoms were worrisome. After examination, the diagnostic results came back. Jeff had cystic fibrosis. The news was staggering and devastating. I called a doctor friend and asked what the prognosis was. He said, in a very solemn tone, that if you had the disease as a child, you wouldn't live much past twenty. Since Jeff was an adult, the news was somewhat reassuring. There was no telling how long a life he would have. With proper care and exercise, his life expectancy could be anything. He could live to forty, fifty, even sixty and possibly longer.

Much has been learned about the disease since that time, and great progress has been made in fighting cystic fibrosis, but all that knowledge was not available then as it is today. Each morning Jeff would run a few miles on the roads of Nyack to help open his lungs to ensure better breathing and better health. Ellen always prepared breakfast for him while he was gone, waiting for his return. One morning he seemed later than usual, and Jeff was very prompt about everything. When he was a half hour late, a worried Ellen decided to get in her car and look for him, in the event he was having some difficulty. Eventually she saw a few cars parked at the rim of a hill along with two police cars. She stopped and asked if anyone had seen her husband, describing the running outfit he was wearing. The officer eyed her slowly and said, "Yes. He was in an accident. They took him to the hospital." Ellen's reaction was, "Just like Jeff. He's probably lying there with a broken leg." Since the policeman didn't show too much concern, Ellen didn't either. She drove to the hospital and asked a nurse standing near the desk where she could find her husband, Jeff Bishop. The nurse took Ellen aside, sat her down on a bench, then got a paper bag and told Ellen to start breathing into the bag.

"Tell me what happened," Ellen asked.

"First breathe into the bag," the nurse repeated.

As Ellen took a few breaths, the nurse said, "He didn't make it. He was hit by a car. He died instantly."

The room began to spin for Ellen, and she couldn't quite grasp what the nurse was telling her. Dead? No, that's not possible.

I was three thousand miles away and there was nothing I could do for her. I heard the news about five-thirty in the morning. Ellen's friend and next-door neighbor, Claudette, called to tell me what happened. In one short, somber, declarative sentence, she said to me, "Jeff was killed a half hour ago." I never heard what else she said because a sound emanated out of my body that never occurred before. It was a long, plaintive cry of

"Nooooooo." It seemed to go on forever. The only time in my life I experienced grief so deep and so quickly was when the doctor in New York told me on a back staircase that Joan only had about a year and a half to live. But Ellen didn't have another year and a half with Jeff. Ellen was never going to say goodbye to Jeff. It was over in an instant, and the blow she felt must have been as sudden and as devastating as the one that killed Jeff in a single moment. I got on a plane as quickly as I could. All I could think of was that she was too young to lose her mother and then her husband, too young to go through such losses just as she was experiencing the happiest days of her life. The only comfort I had was to know that by now, her son, Andrew, and her sister, Nancy, would be by her side, holding her hands. I realized then that we not only grieve for our own losses, but we grieve for the loss that our loved ones have to endure themselves.

MAYBE THIS TIME
WE'LL GET IT RIGHT
34

THE NEW YORK winters were getting harder for me to take, so I was back in California, living in the house on Chalon Road. The work poured out, day after day, while I filled out the other hours with tennis and dates, generally unsatisfying. Not the tennis. The dates. If there were a prize for the Worst Bachelor of the Year, I would win it.

But why did I pursue another marriage at all? I wondered why I thought that marriage was preferable to staying single. God knows my parents weren't very good at marriage, nor was my brother, Danny, whose marriage ended years before. The truth was, it wasn't the idea of marriage that really appealed to me; it was simply the idea of meeting the right person. That was what I hoped for. But I knew I couldn't have met anyone righter than Joan, and perhaps there was my problem. I talked to her again one night in my meditative position. "Joan," I said softly. "I think dying was a big mistake. Got any ideas?"

I felt I had been born on the day I met her, and while I hadn't died on the day she did, I definitely had been crippled, and have hobbled my way through the rest of life. Of course, that's not an accurate statement; it's a very dramatic and theatrical statement. I get that way sometimes. I had a wonderful marriage to Marsha, if you leave out the divorce part, and a wonderful marriage to Diane, if you leave out the "No, I have to go" part. Was I an ideal husband? I doubt it. But I was a first-rate father because neither Ellen nor Nancy ever said to me, "I want out. I'm getting a lawyer." If I was blessed with anything in my life, it was my daughters, and now their children and their husbands.

If you can follow my time lapses, we have reached 1990 and Diane and I were apart for almost a year and a half. I no longer thought of her very much, but since that statement is not definitive, it must have meant that I thought of her occasionally. Dating became more meaningless to me and I hated it when I found myself repeating phrases to another new face in another new restaurant. Why was it so important to me to be with one woman and why was I so caught up in the past, thinking I could never find someone to compare with Joan? Comparisons such as these are hazardous and should never be made. They cause you to miss the "Someone New" person's virtues. You can't see the forest for the memories. For example, after Marsha and I broke up, I couldn't find anyone who had *her* virtues. Still I kept on dating, often blind dating, a form of social behavior that has, for the most part, absolutely *no* virtues.

Each new date was a repetition of the previous date. I'd ring the bell and a surly twelve-year-old girl would open the door. I'd say, "Hi. I'm—" and she'd say quickly, "I know, she's upstairs getting dressed," then walk back to her television set, leaving me in the doorway. To be generous, one has to consider how many times the twelve-year-old girl would open the door to another loser. As I entered the house, certain telltale signs warned me this would be a one-time-only date. The sight of two cats prowling around the living room was enough to give me my walking papers. Cats, birds, fishbowls and hamsters not in their cage were indications for me that the small talk I made at dinner would be so small it would be inaudible. Dogs, on the other hand, can win me over handily. If I found the right dog, I wouldn't care if my date ever descended the stairs. Many times, in fact, I wished I had taken the dog for a walk instead of my date to a restaurant. If I sound misogynistic, I don't mean to be. I knew how many times the woman opened the door, saw me there, and recognized two hours of her life being thrown down the drain. She most certainly must have hated blind dates as much as most of us do. And she must have thought to herself as she sat across the table from me, "My God, is he going to talk about his dead wife all night long?" She had a point.

PBS HAD (and possibly still may have) a series of one-hour profiles of people in the arts who had achieved, in their estimation, a singular reputation in their own field. The program was the *American Masters* series, and I was fortunate to be chosen as the subject of a one-hour documentary on my work. It took them from three to four months to put the program together, because the details of one's career and life were carefully documented in the course of that one hour. Producer Mannya Starr and her husband, producer-director Amram Starr did an impeccable job, my favorite footage being a visit they arranged for and filmed of me in Far Rockaway, now a tumbledown beach resort. When I was young, my family and I spent a few summers there, in a boxlike cottage that housed my family and my aunt's family, eight people in all, none comfortably. It was the memory of those summers at this place that turned out to be the origin for the three plays in the Brighton Beach Trilogy. When the documentary was completed, there was a screening for a few hundred people in Los Angeles, to which I invited my friends and family and ex-family. Marsha showed up and I was very pleased to see her. When it was over, there was a cocktail party in the lobby of the theater, in an area that extended out onto a patio. I made the rounds, chatting with almost all the guests, and then I stepped out on to the patio to get some relief from the smoke. L.A. had not yet cracked down on smoking in certain areas. I was talking to a few of my friends when I spotted a woman who looked vaguely familiar coming up the stairs. I was about to turn away when the woman called out to me: "Hi, Neil."

I looked at her again. She was portly, and had a very pretty face, and I still did not recognize her. Politely, I said hello, ready to walk on, when she smiled. It was a smile I definitely had seen before, and I stood there trying to make out who she was.

"It's Diane," she said.

"Diane?" I asked, taken aback for a moment. "Diane, hi. I didn't know you would be here." I also didn't know she had put on at least thirty pounds. It became immediately apparent that in the year and a half since we had been divorced, she had gone through some major personal changes. I could see the struggle reflected clearly in her eyes. Still, extra weight and all, I was glad to see her, recognizing immediately that whatever spell she cast on me that first day at Neiman Marcus was still working its magic on me. Some people have it, some don't. Despite the fact her face was now puffy, Diane was still beautiful to me.

She told me she hadn't been invited, but had heard about the screening and just wanted to come by and say hello. We talked a little about Bryn and about what Diane had been doing for the past eighteen months. She had been going to a school—a college, if you will—that both taught and had its students participate in their own psychotherapy, one playing the analyst to the patient and then reversing the roles. It's clear as I talked to Diane that the effort had taken its toll. This was a different Diane than the one I had known. She was far more subdued than when I first met and fell in love with her, yet whatever attracted me a year and a half before was still there—the embers miraculously were still glowing. It was a dimmer light to be sure, but nevertheless, the glow was unmistakable. All the twelve-year-old girls who scowled at me as they opened the door, all the dates that descended their stairs, all the dinners in all the restaurants, and all the meaningless small talk I engaged in, had vanished in this one moment of seeing her again, and I realized I was not quite through with Diane just yet. Still, I did not see myself getting married again.

It was with some caution that I later visited her in her small rented house in the Valley. I knocked on the door, which was opened by Bryn, who stood looking up at me with a smiling face. Then suddenly a tiny red-haired poodle started to bark at me, first running whirlwind circles around me and then excitedly running from one end of the house to the other, surely breaking every existing record for covering that distance. Her name was Annabelle, and she'd been given to Bryn by Diane on the previous Christmas. Mabel Zeno, Bryn's nanny, was still with them, only her duties had probably tripled by then. Mabel Zeno is one of the good people in this world, and Bryn benefited enormously by having this loving woman watch over her.

If you've ever been through it, walking into the house of someone you once loved, lived with and was married to is a humbling experience.

No matter how sophisticated you might be, you don't know where to sit, what to say or how to say it. There is also a peculiar feeling of familiarity, yet of not knowing which rooms you are allowed to enter. I realized immediately that all the closeness I had felt during our marriage no longer applied here, and I wondered if Diane felt as uneasy as I did.

Bryn had grown in the year and a half and, if possible, was even more beautiful than I remembered her. It is not only easy to love Bryn, it's impossible not to. She was certainly not yet twelve, but of all the girls who opened the door for me in her mother's house, she was the only one who greeted me with a smile and a kiss. Diane may have gone through some dark days, but she was blessed in having the best child, the best nanny and the cutest dog in the neighborhood. She also seemed comfortable where she was living, away from the glitz and brashness of Hollywood.

We got into my car and drove to an Italian restaurant not far from where Diane lived. When you're nervous, you tend to read the menu eight times before you realize these are the names of food that they have to serve you. You also tend to push your food around the plate a lot, even making designs in your spaghetti before you understand that you're supposed to eat it as opposed to making art out of it. The closeness between us was gone, glowing embers or not, and we were virtually starting from the beginning again. Still, one had to make conversation, and I wasn't afforded the chance to ask or answer questions like, "And what is it you do?" A vodka for me and a glass of wine for her thankfully lowered the pressure we both must have felt, and suddenly Diane laughed her winning laugh, almost always getting the mumbled nuances of my humor, which I was aware of using as a device for avoiding the hurts of the past.

The evening went okay—not great, not bad. Actually, maybe it even went better than okay. We were polite when I got her back to the house, and a kiss on her cheek was all I could offer or all she was ready to accept. I told her I would call her again and I made the thirty-five-minute drive over the hills to my house in Bel Air, thinking to myself, "Slowly. Go slowly with this, Neil." Still, over the next few dates, I did notice that she was beginning to lose some weight and was laughing more easily and readily as we tried all the restaurants in her neighborhood. I think what I was hoping for was for Diane to greet me at the door, dressed in her bulky pie-making outfit, and ask me to help her read the recipe while she baked. The embers were glowing more brightly now with each new visit.

AS THE memory bank in my mind occasionally breaks down, it's hard for me to remember exactly how long it was before the time came when I drove to Diane's house with something burning in my pocket. I do know I was more nervous than I could ever remember being before. Was I about to walk into another situation, one which would lead into another mangled marriage? There was nothing to indicate that history would *not* repeat itself. Yet there I was, about to put myself in harm's way again. And was Diane worried about the same future for herself? I rang the doorbell and in my nervous mind, the bell sounded as loud as all the bells that rang throughout the country on the day World War II ended. Diane did not seem a bit nervous, however, but rather cheerful. She and I kissed Bryn good night and Mabel Zeno smiled from the kitchen and called out, "You two have a good time tonight," as if the past year and a half had never happened. We got in the car, shut the doors but I didn't start the engine.

Diane looked at me, concerned for the first time. "What's wrong?" she asked.

"I don't know when to do it," I said.

"Do what?"

I reached into my pocket and took out a small box. "Do this," I said, as I handed her the box with the familiar name of Tiffany on the top. She kept looking at the box. "It's better when you open it," I advised her.

She did, and her eyes opened wide, and the music I thought I heard was coming from inside her head. She took out the diamond ring and put it on her finger.

"Oh, God. It's incredible. Don't start the car. I have to show Bryn and Zeno." She ran inside, with me trailing behind.

"Is it real?" Bryn said.

"Yes," I answered. "But I just rented it for the evening."

"Do I smell another wedding?" Zeno asked with a laugh.

"Well, either that or my brain is on fire," I thought nervously. All I can remember as we walked around the area after dinner was that we held hands and we kissed a lot. Another Chapter Two to my life.

THE WEDDING took place in the large foyer—or gallery, if you prefer—in the Chalon house. It was also the largest room in the house. It was the first time that Diane's family and mine were all under the same roof together, although each group tended to stay on their own side—not out of animosity, but simply because they didn't know each other. If anyone felt the difference, it was me. We had such disparate backgrounds. Diane's family was Catholic, mine was Jewish. Diane's family were Midwest, mine strictly East Coast.

It's not the differences that cause problems in a marriage, because when they come up, with a little understanding, you can ride out the storm. It's the lack of common responses and attitudes that sometimes can make people feel like total strangers to each other. It's when he or she feels so right, and so sure that the other is dead wrong. I once said something to Diane that hurt her feelings, although that wasn't intended. I hadn't realized she would be so sensitive to my remark, so I apologized and hoped we could move on.

"No," she said. "Once something is said, it can never be taken back."

I looked at her, bewildered. I didn't know what culture or religion or tribe that rule came from, but it was so unforgiving, it made me feel that I was damned for life. And I also didn't know that twenty years later I still would be begging her to forgive what I once said in a casual conversation.

"Isn't there such a thing as forgiveness?" I asked her.

"Of course. I forgive you. But what you said can never be taken back."

I said, "What if I went to a doctor and had a laser beam remove it from my tongue?" Sarcastic humor doesn't always work.

I didn't know if she heard this unforgiving dictum in a sermon at church, or from some girlfriend she grew up with who heard her parents say it. I do know that when the chance came to retaliate, I jumped at it.

"Diane, what time is it?" I asked.

She looked at her watch. "It's five after six . . . No. I'm sorry. It's five after seven."

"No," I said. "It's too late. It's five after six. You said it, and it can never be taken back."

Marriage is not always for adults. It sometimes brings out the child in us. Geography also plays an important role in marriage. We fall victims to our own folklore, imprisoned by our separate cultures. Stray too far, and problems arise. Sometimes the wise decision is to marry "the girl next door." The problem is, it's not always the girl next door that we fall in love with.

A PLAY FOR NANCY
35

I WROTE the play *Jake's Women* to do the impossible. Years after Joan's death, my daughter Nancy expressed to me a wish she had for a long time. Nancy was ten when Joan died, her sister Ellen was fifteen. Nancy told me she always wished she could have had the five extra years that Ellen had with her mother. As time passed, Nancy was willing to settle for just one day with Joan. She wanted Joan to meet the man she had fallen in love with and married, David Florimbi, knowing that Joan would have overwhelmingly approved of her choice. Most especially, Nancy wanted Joan to see her granddaughter, Sofia, who in so many ways resembled Joan's dark-haired, olive-skinned beauty. Of course, no one was able to grant Nancy's wish, but I wanted to give it a try.

Jake's Women is not, in a true sense, an autobiographical play, because almost seventy percent of the play takes place in Jake's mind, in his ever active imagination. Are your thoughts autobiography? Webster says, a little skimpily, it's the biography of a person narrated by himself. Biography, they go on to say, is the written history of a person's life. Are thoughts part of your life or does it become actual life only when those thoughts are put into words or deeds? Webster says, "I'm not in that business. Try a philosopher." I decided to make up my own definition. *Jake's Women* is a thoughto-graphical play. It's "auto" because it's my thoughts. It's also a fictional nonfiction play, since Jake is fiction and I am Jake, I being nonfictional.

Look how complicated it gets, and I haven't even put down a word of the play. Actually the audience doesn't care much about these scholarly excursions. Only critics do. That aside, I decided to write about Jake/Neil, surrounded by the most important women in "his" life, since it's women from whom I've drawn my greatest strength.

The magic that writing plays gives you is the ability to make anyone you want to appear on a stage for all to see—and then to disappear just as quickly. You can see your daughter at twelve, and in a flash, she reappears at twenty-one. You can make your analyst say anything you want to hear, and you can summon your wife from the dead, so that you can relive all the joys you both shared when you were young. When Jake needs advice from his sister, he can pull her out of a movie theater and make her appear in his living room. Even though his thoughts are in his imagination, he still gives them a life of their own. When his sister is summoned, she looks in the mirror and is furious with Jake for dressing her so gaudily. She thinks she looks like Bette Midler in mid-concert. He apologizes: "I'm sorry. I didn't have time to go shopping for you." He can and does talk to his second wife in the present (not in his imagination), and in the past (as he remembered it), or in his mind (as he wished she would behave). He is a controlling human being, this Jake, but that's why he became a writer. Writers are given this privilege. Bad writers abuse it.

But Jake plays the "summoning game" too often, ultimately making it difficult for him to know when he's functioning in reality or operating in an imagining mode. As the play and Jake's life move on, the imagined women start to appear even when Jake hasn't summoned them, just as Mr. Hyde begins to appear long after Dr. Jekyll regrets ever giving him a life. These women start to take over Jake's life, and in the process reprimand him for the bad choices he sometimes makes. It's only Jake's daughter, Molly, and Julie, his deceased wife, whose appearances always please Jake.

In the play, I reversed Nancy's wish. It's his dead wife, Julie, who appears and asks Jake to let her see Molly, to talk to her, to be filled in on Molly's life that Julie never lived long enough to see. Under duress, Jake agrees, and Julie returns to Jake's room on her birthday. The gift she asked for is to see Molly the way she is today, all grown up, a college senior. Julie waits in the shadows of the room as Jake conjures Molly to appear at the door. Molly is slightly worried (playing out the game that Jake is inventing) because she was just taking a college exam and if her Dad pulled her out of class to be in his room, it must be something important.

"Are you all right, Dad? Are you sick?" she asks.

He shakes his head no, glancing back into the shadows, wondering how to effect this reunion without Molly backing away fearfully, maybe even running out of the room. But of course, she can't run because Jake controls the situation, although in his mind he is turning this reunion over to the mother and her daughter. Before Molly appears, Julie asks Jake to please leave when Molly arrives. She wants to be alone with her daughter.

Jake says, "I can't leave the room. You can't talk to each other without my thinking of it."

"Sure you can," says Julie. "You're smart. You'll figure a way how to do it."

Jake knows he can't think of something, then walk out of the room and leave his thoughts behind to continue a life without him. But this is not time for logic. Imagination can move mountains. He plunges ahead.

"Molly," says Jake. "There's someone here to see you."

Julie steps out of the shadows and Molly sees her. She is confused at first, even a little frightened. She takes a step back.

JULIE

Jake, she's having trouble with it. She doesn't
understand. Help her to accept it, Jake.

JAKE

I'm sorry. I didn't think it out. Let me start
over . . .

MOLLY

NO! . . . It's all right . . . Now I understand.
Now it's fine . . . Hello, Mom.

JULIE

Would you like to sit down with me?
Would that be all right?

MOLLY

Yes. Of course . . . I have a million things to
ask you.

And Jake steps back into the shadows as he watches the impossible come
true. He sees Molly getting her wish. He sees Julie getting her wish. And I
saw Nancy getting her wish. Mother and daughter talk, filling in the days
they never shared. They talk about school, about the boy that Molly is seeing. They talk about the past, the trips they took together when Molly was
small and Julie was there for her. They talk about the best day they ever
had together and soon they're laughing and reminiscing as if nothing ever
happened.

Jake watches all this but never interferes. He lets them play the moment out on their own, but he turns to the audience, to include them:

JAKE

(To audience)

Am I the only one who's ever done this? I
don't think so. There's not one of you who
hasn't thought, at three o'clock in the
morning staring up at a ceiling, of what it
would be like to talk to your father who
died five or twenty years ago. Would he
look the same? Would you still be his little
girl? . . . Or the boy you loved in college
who married someone else. What would
your life be if he proposed to you instead
. . . You've played that scene out. We *all* do
it . . . My problem is I never *stop* doing it.

We all know Andy Warhol's prediction that eventually we'll all have our fifteen minutes of fame. Would you trade that for fifteen minutes with someone who's passed on, someone that you loved dearly? I would. Well, that's not exactly fair—I've had my forty years of fame. And about seeing someone you loved who is now gone? I still do it all the time. With enough imagination, everything is within our grasp.

As the scene in the play between Julie and Molly progresses, Molly starts to talk about the mother leaving one day, and never coming back. She tells how lonely she was, how much she missed her mother as she grew up. Sensing that this conversation is going too far, going to places Jake hoped would never come up, he tries to stop it. But Molly gets angry with him.

MOLLY
(To Jake)
I didn't ask to play this game. You brought
me here. You brought Mom here. You
bring us together after eleven years and you
give us ten lousy minutes together. What is
that? Why do you do it? It's so cruel. What
is it you wanted to see?

JAKE
I wanted to see you both happy again.

MOLLY
By doing the impossible?

JAKE
Not so impossible, I saw you both laughing
again, together again. It made me happy to
see that.

But soon he realizes you can't live life only in your imagination; he realizes that writing is only a part of his life, and that it's time for him to get back into the world he so often avoids. He created this reunion between mother and daughter, but Jake is the one who has benefited most.

Thanks to Alan Alda's brilliant and demanding performance of Jake, the play had a successful run on Broadway and then again in Los Angeles. What mattered most to me was Nancy's reaction to it, especially to the reunion scene. It was only a play, and what went on in Nancy's mind when she saw it, I couldn't exactly say. But I treasured the night she first saw the play and came to me afterward with tears in her eyes, and I embraced her, knowing I couldn't really do the impossible, but only Nancy knows how possible the impossible can sometimes be.

BRYN LANDER SIMON
36

SINCE THERE WERE no obstacles in the way, I decided to adopt Bryn. I adored her and my only fear was that if this marriage to Diane were as short-lived as our first one, it would not be fair to either Bryn or myself. I wanted to be a permanent father in a permanent marriage. There was every indication that Diane and I were here to stay as a couple, so we applied for the proper papers. Having done that, we were all interviewed in our house by a warm and friendly gentleman from the California state adoption system, whose job it was to see that this was something that all three of us wanted.

There are some professions that must be more satisfying than others, and I would think that the person responsible for bringing families together would be happier than someone whose job it is to separate them. Does a divorce lawyer like what he does? I don't know. I've known one or two who seem to be extremely decent people, but I've also seen some who are like sharks who smell blood in the water. They are out to get the best judgment for their clients, but in doing so, they sometimes push a husband or a wife to such extreme measures, advising their clients to make enormous demands on the other, that what could have been a friendly divorce—the mother of all oxymorons—instead turns into a wound so deep, painful and everlasting that they become enemies forevermore. It's in that instance, and only in that instance, that I agree with Diane's earlier statement about how once something is said, it can never be taken back. Divorce, and the act of breaking up what once was a relationship, is painful enough in itself, so one would hope that two people who once loved each other enough to take marriage vows might try to be fair and reasonable in the dispensation of money and property. Or am I being too naive? Yet I've seen lawyers for both parties reach into their bag of expertise and come up with demands that neither the wife nor the husband had ever dreamed of. For some lawyers, it's just a way of drawing the process out as long as they can, earning themselves bigger fees; for others, it's all about triumphing over their opponent, thereby inheriting a reputation of being a dangerous gunslinger, and thus increasing the demand for them as a divorce lawyer— and thus increasing their fees as well. As I said, there are some lawyers like that, but certainly not all.

Adoption, however, unlike divorce, is a joyous occasion. Diane tried to explain to young Bryn that I was soon going to adopt her and she would forevermore be my daughter, and I her father. Bryn nodded and smiled in agreement, although it's hard to know if someone seven or eight years old really understands the rules and legal interpretations conceived by adults.

Once again Diane and I drove down the familiar road to the County Courthouse, but this time it was for a marriage of another kind. This time I wore a tie and this time Diane was not nervous about me jumping out of a car on Melrose Avenue. Bryn sat silently in the back seat, lost in her thoughts, showing no emotion one way or the other. We were now about ten minutes away from the courthouse, when Bryn broke her silence. Out of nowhere she said, "Will I still be able to see you both?"

Diane and I looked at each other, puzzled, not quite understanding the question.

"What do you mean, Bryn?" Diane asked.

"After I'm adopted, will I still be able to see you both?"

Diane and I were about to break into tears. Bryn thought she was being put *up* for adoption, that she would have new parents, and she was wondering if she would still be able to see us. The innocence and poignancy of her question was so overwhelming, so heartbreaking and touching, that it haunts me to this day. If that's what she thought, why wasn't she sitting in that back seat screaming and wailing? Was she so terrified or so confused about how life was dictated by adults, that if something like that could really happen to her, she would just have to accept it?

Diane almost broke down when she explained to Bryn that she was going to be my legal daughter, even though I wasn't her biological father. I think that went over Bryn's head too, but by this time she was so relieved, even euphoric, that she wasn't leaving us or that we were not abandoning her, she simply smiled and said, "Oh. I get it. That's a lot better."

The courtroom was filled with anxious men, women and children. Some in the same position as we were, while others were childless couples who were ecstatic that they were now able to adopt a child, fulfilling all of their dreams. The judge was a warm, gentle man who obviously loved his position as one who makes families instead of breaking them. He spoke slowly to Bryn, as he did to the children who went before us, informing her that becoming the daughter of her new parent was not a temporary thing. He explained that a mother or father could get a divorce, but a child or parent could *never* divorce each other. Bryn would be my daughter for life; I would be her father for life.

Every parent and child who walked out of the courtroom that day was either crying tears of happiness or smiling joyfully. Bryn Lander became Bryn Lander Simon, and I just had my third daughter. This time we did not go to Chinatown for dim sum. Instead we went to Bryn's favorite restaurant where she ate sparingly until she got the huge dessert that she obviously had been thinking of all the way from the County Courthouse.

GOODBYE, *GOODBYE GIRL*
37

ALTHOUGH I was enormously pleased with the film of *The Goodbye Girl,* I had great doubts it would make a good Broadway musical. The idea originated with David Zippel, the lyricist of the very funny musical *City of Angels* (not to be confused with the Nicholas Cage movie). I thought the story was too small in scope to be opened up for the kind of outsize musicals that seem to work today, basically because it was a story of just three people. True, there had been successful small musicals, some that had only *two* characters, among them *I Do, I Do* and even *They're Playing Our Song,* which I wrote with Marvin Hamlisch and Carole Bayer Sager. Strangely, a two-character musical makes sense, but adding just one more character makes it seem unwieldy. Four wheels on a car is fine, five wheels and you might go off in all directions. But David Zippel and Marvin Hamlisch doggedly pursued the idea, and finally convinced me they could write a full score for a cast of about twenty-four people. I didn't know where the twenty-four people would come from, unless they planned on using the audience in the first two rows. Still, Manny Azenberg was very keen on the idea, as was director Gene Saks. Manny tested the waters with the theater party people and they were enormously optimistic. I decided to take a stab at writing the book, expanding the scope by adding other characters, some of whom already appeared in the film, but in smaller parts. I now made them *bigger* parts.

I already had learned that other people's enthusiasm should never affect what is doubtful in your own mind. Making larger parts out of smaller parts does not automatically make them *better* parts. Still, I wrote what I thought was a funny script, and once people read a funny script for a musical, they see the magical but usually elusive words in the sky, "LONG RUN."

The script enticed actors Martin Short and Bernadette Peters, and once their names were released to the press, the show suddenly became the hottest item coming to Broadway in the fall. Marvin and David Zippel wrote the first seven or eight songs for the show, and those who heard them suddenly were taking money out of the bank to invest in the show. Manny, who could budget a show down to its final twenty-five cents, told us the show should come in for close to five million dollars. For the very first time in my career, we did a backers' audition, complemented by two or three first-rate singers (who were not necessarily going to be in the show), and it was decided that I should read scenes from the show, assuring them that Martin Short had nothing to worry about.

A backers' audition is very often a *Reader's Digest* version of the final work. You hear only the best work, and what eventually will run two hours and fourteen minutes on the stage, runs only about fifty minutes at the reading. Would you buy a house if you only saw the living room and the kitchen? If you would, then you'd probably put money into our musical. Nevertheless, the audition was a resounding success. Everything seemed to work. They loved the songs, howled at the book, and by the time the theater party people and other independent ticket agents jammed Manny's phone lines, we had a nine million dollar advance sale. Nine million dollars is a very, very large sum to have as an advance. I was now beginning to assume I was initially wrong, that my fears about the show being too small were unfounded, even though I was aware that I knew a lot more about a play's chances than I did of a musical's. When you read the script of a play and you're knowledgeable, you get a pretty accurate feeling as to whether it will work or not. Knowing if it works does not necessarily mean it will be a hit, of course. It just means that it works, that it has something to say and that it says it well, that it might have a life for years to come, but not necessarily on Broadway. I haven't a clue if a musical is going to work *and* be successful until I see it, and then I have to see it with an audience. And then I have to see it with the critics. And then I have to read the reviews. And then I have to see how much money they took in on the first week. And after all that, I still don't know.

But things were looking good. We signed Graciela Daniele as our choreographer and Santo Loquasto as our scenic designer. And suddenly we were into rehearsals. In the rehearsals you get more misinformation. If there are twenty or twenty-four dancers, singers and actors watching scenes, they tend to laugh. Big laughs. Dancers are notorious optimists about the shows they are in, simply because they want the shows to be a hit. Laughter at rehearsals is about as reliable as a fortune-teller with a cracked crystal ball.

I will say this, however: Martin Short was wonderful from the first reading of the script straight through our out-of-town tryout to opening night. He was, many said, less acerbic than Richard Dreyfuss in the film, warmer and more likeable. Richard Dreyfuss, however, won the Academy Award as Best Actor playing the same part, the youngest actor ever to win that award. Should that have told us something? If it did, we weren't listening. Bernadette Peters was the darling of Broadway audiences as well as the critics, but Marsha was a better actress and was nominated for the Academy's Best Actress Award in the same part. Did that mean anything to us? Not yet. The young girl in our musical who played Lucy, the third most important role in the show, was simply darling; she was also pretty and could sing rings around anyone her own age. Quinn Cummings had none of those attributes, but she almost stole the movie from Richard and Marsha. Was anyone listening? No, because we were too busy rehearsing. And we had a nine million dollar advance sale which was more than the movie ever had, although the film brought in about 50 million dollars, which, in today's equivalent money, would be more like a hundred and fifty million. We kept on rehearsing.

As well as rehearsals went, something still didn't seem quite right, but I couldn't put a finger on it, which usually means that the trouble is so big that a finger wouldn't cover it.

The set, by Santo Loquasto, who did a brilliant job for us with his design for *Lost in Yonkers,* came in a little late, but we could look at drawings and blueprints. I can't read a road map, much less blueprints. Director Gene Saks nodded to Santo that he thought it was good, but Gene did not display the exuberance that he usually does. When we finally saw the set, it was up on the stage of the Shubert Theater in Chicago, where we were to have the world premiere. When I saw the set, I was confused. I knew I didn't like it, but I was still confused, because I respected Santo's work so much, and if *he* liked it, I was probably wrong.

I'm not sure Santo actually did like it. It was a difficult challenge. He had to put five rooms on the stage, all at the same time, and our three principals had to walk from room to room without ever leaving the stage. What he came up with was something that looked like a merry-go-round, and in fact, worked like a merry-go-round. All the rooms were on a circular set and could turn in either direction. It could turn clockwise or counterclockwise. It was ingenious. Ingenious and bizarre. If you were in the kitchen and wanted to walk into the living room, the set would turn and you would walk in place as the living room would turn to meet you. Sometimes, however, if you had a character in the living room who you wanted to talk to someone in the kitchen, yet have both be seen at the same time, the set would turn clockwise, then quickly counterclockwise, stopping somewhere in the middle while the actors held on to something stable to keep them from flying out into the audience. No one saw the set at the backers' audition.

But the set was only one of our problems. We had a huge opening number where Lucy took two of her girlfriends to an ice cream parlor, where sixteen other people were either eating ice cream or playing waiters and waitresses. This number had totally nothing to do with the rest of the show. This was also not seen at the backers' audition. It was, however, seen by the critics in Chicago, who promptly said, "What is that god-awful number doing at the top of the show? Or the bottom of the show, for that matter?" It took weeks to rehearse and stage, and it went out as fast as a candle in a hurricane. And so the show suddenly opened with Bernadette and Lucy coming home to their cozy little merry-go-round, which not only confused the audience, it caused some of them to feel the effects of vertigo.

Despite the lackluster reviews in Chicago, the audiences responded enthusiastically, to which authors generally go into denial and say, "What the hell do critics know?" But Richard Christianson is a first-rate critic, one who went all-out in his wonderful review of *Lost in Yonkers.* Am I now going to say, "What does he know?" I did not. I knew we were in trouble, despite the fact that Martin Short was getting every laugh that was possible to get. Bernadette, however, accustomed to getting laughs as well, suddenly realized that her role was not a comic role. Marsha didn't get very many laughs in the film, but she was the backbone, the spine of the movie. Being the most empathetic character in the film, we rooted for her and Richard to get together at the end, since Paula, Marsha's character, got nothing from any other man in her life. Giving her jokes would have turned the piece into a sitcom. But there were rumblings of Bernadette being unhappy, and even more rumblings from her agents that she might want to quit the show. I liked Bernadette a lot and it was fun to work with her. If we lost her, we might as well have taken a huge ad in the *New York Times* saying, "Bernadette leaving show. Goodbye, *Goodbye Girl."* I gave in and started writing funny lines for her. She got the laughs, but we paid the price. The show was losing its heart. We didn't feel for the characters, we just laughed at what they said. I use the editorial "we" because I wasn't laughing at anything. I felt we were sailing on a ship designed by the architect of the *Titanic.* We didn't have enough lifeboats either.

Still, other problems arose. As I've said before, when I do a musical, if I have any problems, it's usually with the lyricist, and it's happened twice. If a song isn't working, the composer is usually facile enough to come up with a lively tune. Lyric writing is an arduous task, as even Stephen Sondheim will tell you, and it's hard to find anyone better than he. Stephen will work forever until he gets what he is looking for. Other lyricists, with the best of intentions, might look to put the blame on someone like the singer, the orchestration, the acoustics in the theater or the audience. I've already mentioned that I think David Zippel is a talented writer, but we hit an impasse with two lines he wrote in a song for Martin Short. They were comedy lines, and comedy lines usually have one obligation—they have to get a laugh. They don't have to bring the house down or get their own mention in the critic's review, but *some* people simply have to laugh. These two lines never got the laugh. David's answer to me was that the orchestra was playing it a tad too slow. I gave him the benefit of the doubt. That night the orchestra played it a tad faster. Still no laugh. David said, "No. Now it's a tad too fast." The next night the orchestra tadded it down. The audience was not amused. I said, "David, you could time it with twelve stopwatches, this line is never going to get a laugh. It needs to be a better line." David and I were still patient with each other, but Martin Short was the one who had to go out on stage at night and sing the laughless line. "Maybe I could just mouth the words and bring the sound of the trumpets up," Martin suggested to me one night. I said, "No. Because if there's a lip reader out there, it still wouldn't get a laugh."

To make matters worse, Marvin Hamlisch, always a hard worker, had to fulfill contracts he made before accepting the show, and so he left every now and then to do a concert. Suddenly the nows were coming up more often than the thens. Tempers were beginning to flare and egos were slamming doors everywhere. Late one afternoon, there was a meeting in Marvin's hotel room to discuss all our problems. I didn't think the room was large enough to house all our problems. Once again I begged David to change the lines in his lyric. I was changing mine every day because there were a lot of mine that weren't working any better than his. But I never said "it was because the audience was a tad too dumb."

I finally said to David, and quite sincerely, "David, you're too good a lyricist not to be able to fix it. Just write another line."

David said, "Don't patronize me."

The room got silent but I pushed on. "Jesus, David, why fight it? You write truly funny lyrics. Just give us another line."

David said, "Don't stroke me."

The silence in the room was deafening. Everyone else just looked down at the floor. I then said, as a matter of practicality, "Well then, why don't you go fuck yourself because I've run out of suggestions."

Manny covered his smile with his hand, while Marvin Hamlisch packed a bag to do a concert in Pittsburgh. Gene said we were getting nowhere, which most of us already noticed. Later that day, Manny called a meeting in the theater for the entire creative staff. We all met in the empty theater.

"We're falling apart here, guys. We're not fixing the show. We don't have a captain. We need a captain to steer the ship. So who's the captain?"

Silence until Gene said, "Neil is. Neil is the captain."

I said, "Whoa! Wait a minute. In a musical, at most I'm a second lieutenant. Maybe a chief petty officer, but never the captain. I've been in this business my whole life and I still don't know how they make the curtain go up and down. You need words, I'll give you words. You need a story, I'll give you a story. But I'm never the captain. That's a tad too much responsibility for me."

David Zippel laughed and I said, "If you just thought of something funny, David, we could use it in the place where we're not getting the laugh." I smiled and shrugged, hoping to diffuse the tension. I didn't. The meeting was over and Marvin was off to Cincinnati for another concert. Steven Spielberg, a good friend of Martin Short's, was in Chicago and came in to see the show with his wife. Spielberg loved it, but it's hard to tell friendship from sincere compliments. At least he was very convincing in his praise, and if I'm not mistaken, Spielberg came back to New York to see our opening. Still, we knew we had major fixing to do. Graziella Danielli left the show of her own accord and I was sorry to see her go.

If one of the creative staff was supposed to be the captain, Manny Azenberg, as the producer, was definitely the general. It was up to him to make a very difficult decision. If a musical is in trouble, more times than not it's the director who takes the brunt of the blame. I didn't think Gene knew how to fix it any more than I did, but neither did Zippel or Hamlisch. But we all couldn't get replaced. Manny decided to bring in Michael Kidd (*Guys and Dolls, Seven Brides for Seven Brothers,* etc.), but Gene stayed with the show, so now we had a captain, but the rest of us were common seamen. Gene got very angry with me for not standing up for him. I got angry with him for assuming I should be the captain. David Zippel offered to take over the direction, but he was a tad too late since Michael Kidd was there. Marvin did another concert and I kept writing jokes for Bernadette. Michael Kidd did his best in the little time we had, but no one's best was doing us any good at this point. My only solace was that my instincts were right from the beginning. *The Goodbye Girl* did not make suitable material for a big Broadway musical.

We opened in New York to thunderous applause from the audience, while the critics went home and wrote, "No, thank you. We'll find our entertainment elsewhere."

Gene and I eventually started talking to each other again, and later I was happy to see his terrific direction of Christopher Plummer in the wonderful *Barrymore*. Gene was in his milieu again. *The Goodbye Girl* did good business for a while, but once Bernadette left, and then Martin, who could have kept the show running if he stayed, that was that. We ran six months and the nine million dollar advance turned into a five million dollar loss. David Zippel is now writing animated films for Disney and I hear they like his work enormously. Marvin will always do concerts and I will always be fond of Marvin. Martin Short came back to Broadway for one week to do an encore production of *Promises, Promises*. He was spectacular. He also did a revival of *Little Me* at the Roundabout Theater. He was brilliant once more.

From this experience and other experiences I either took part in or observed, I conclude that the fate of a show is not decided by who stars in it or by who's directing or who's writing it. More often than not, a show that is questionable is destined to fail on the day that someone who has the power to make it happen says, "Hey! I think this would make a great show. Let's do it."

MRS. SIMON GOES TO WASHINGTON
38

BRYN WAS GROWING another quarter inch every night or so it seemed to those of us who stopped growing years ago. Ellen and Nancy each gave birth to a girl, about a year apart. Sofia for Nancy and David, Nikki for Ellen and Michael, Ellen's third husband. I didn't get to see my grandson, Andrew, much because he was either in school, reinventing the computer or riding his bike across and over the foot of the Rocky Mountains.

Diane was on the board of almost every charity in town and with good reason. She could raise more money than anyone else. Diane could charm a worm out of the beak of the first bird up in the morning, and was usually designated the one to go after studio heads for a donation, or perhaps to go even higher up—like to the wives of studio heads.

One morning the phone at Chalon Road rang. Diane answered it and suddenly her excitement decibels went up a few points. She called out, "Neil, for you."

"Who is it?" I asked, annoyed to be pulled away from the sports pages of the *New York Times*. It's a sure bet that if you read the batting averages of baseball players every morning when you're ten years old, you'll still be doing it when you're sixty-five.

"Bill Clinton."

"Who's Bill Clinton?" I asked. He sounded familiar, but my concentration was still on how the Yankees were doing.

"The governor of Arkansas," she said. "He's running for president, dummy."

I hoped he didn't hear her say dummy to me, because I knew it would probably hurt my chances to be picked as his running mate. Diane once said to me, in all seriousness I think, that I would make a great president. "I could never run," I said to her. "I always have a play in rehearsal in November."

I went to the phone.

"Ha, Neil. Bill Clinton here. Just callin' to say hello and get acquainted 'cause Hillary and I are comin' out to Los Angeles to get you and your friends behind our campaign."

I assumed Hillary was his wife because I think the Hillary who climbed Mount Everest was either dead or probably had already climbed enough mountains in his time. Clinton sounded very friendly, very down-home, but his "down-home" wasn't the "down-home" that I was from. No one ever called New York City "down-home." Still, he was very sincere, and I pictured Hillary standing next to him with a fistful of quarters to keep our phone conversation going. I worked on a few presidential campaigns in my time, but accomplished nothing you'd notice that much. I got Joan to vote for Kennedy, but I think she was ahead of me on that one. I suddenly remembered reading a speech that Clinton made at Georgetown University and I thought it was a first-rate talk and told him so.

"Well, I'm glad you liked it, Neil. I think I have some other interesting new ideas you ought to hear that could move this country in a whole new direction."

I also remembered that in an interview on television he was using the phrase "A New Covenant," and I wanted to tell him, "I'd think twice about that New Covenant pitch, Bill. People on the East Coast think a covenant is an old Pilgrim expression used in Salem during that witch hullabaloo a few hundred years back." I chose not to say it, although his speechwriters eventually chose to cut it.

I did eventually become an avid Clinton backer, but he was calling the wrong Simon. If Diane could raise money for Big Sisters, the Neil Bogart Memorial Labs that do cancer research and most of the hospitals in L.A., wait till he sees what she could do for a presidential candidate who spoke with the same accent as her brother and three sisters. Within a few weeks of our meeting, the Clintons were on a first-name basis with Diane, while I stood on the line, eating my hot buttered corn, waiting to have my picture taken with the affable candidate. It may have been my name and my contributions they wanted, but they got ten times more work from Diane in all the time she put in for him and the Democratic party. And this from a girl who came from Indiana, a state with a Republican governor.

Diane was in Little Rock, Arkansas, on election night, whooping it up as the results came in declaring that we had a new president and a new first lady. Diane had caught political fever, and in gratitude for her efforts, we were invited to the inauguration in Washington. Being invited to the inauguration by the president is a great honor, but don't picture yourself sitting on a podium, three rows behind the Supreme Court, with your feet warmed by heavy blankets to keep out the freezing January winds. No, sir. You'll be standing for five hours among thousands of other honored guests, stamping your feet and blowing on each other's hands, a crowd of people getting frostbite, a group of disciples who would eventually lose the tips of their collected noses. I voted for him but I wasn't going to get hypothermia over it. Every president I ever watched getting inaugurated on the bitter-cold podium didn't wear a hat while he was being sworn in, and that's another reason I decided not to run for office. What I did was wander over to the Folger Library, a beautiful and stately building that housed manuscripts of Shakespeare, and from where you can watch the inauguration in a lovely paneled room that was fashioned after the original Globe Theatre in Shakespeare's time, while drinking brisk tea or brisker vodka, and eating a small plate of smoked salmon sandwiches. As I said, I voted for him, but I still have the tip of my nose.

That night, we went to the President's Ball, and I heard more yahooing and country music than I'd ever like to hear in one night again. But when the president and the first lady entered and the gigantic room went wild, I knew I was experiencing a piece of history firsthand. The chill up my spine that I didn't get in the frosty crowds that afternoon was tingling now in the excitement of that incredible moment. Diane was like a little girl, and the tears ran down her cheeks as the Clintons held hands and raised them above the crowd. The explosion of victory, cheers, tears and utter joy was an experience I'll never forget. With all the problems the president ran into in his second term in office, for which I lost a lot of respect for him, I will always think of him as one hell of a president.

A few years later at Christmastime, the Clintons invited us to Washington for the lighting of the tree ceremony on the lawn. In addition, we were to be their overnight guests, sleeping in the Lincoln Bedroom. Okay, now this was big-time. Even Lincoln would be thrilled to sleep in the Lincoln Bedroom. We were told that most dignitaries preferred the room right opposite, which I believe was considered the Churchill Bedroom. I would have said yes to the Churchill Bedroom at 10 Downing Street, but this was Washington and it was the Lincoln Bedroom for me. On the lawn and in the White House I felt like a mere outsider because Diane knew the names of everyone on the staff, and they greeted her as one of their own. I wanted to wear a small pin saying, "I wrote *The Odd Couple*," so I wouldn't get lost in the shuffle.

I was interviewed by the National Press Club a few days later and they asked me my impressions of being on the lawn for the tree lighting.

I said, "Well, I saw a very interesting thing. Just before President Clinton was going to light the tree, Newt Gingrich asked the president, in a show of solidarity, if he would let Mr. Gingrich light the tree. Graciously, the president agreed. I was standing right near him and as the speaker of the House was about to do the honors, I said, 'Excuse me, Mr. Gingrich, but I don't think you're supposed to light the tree with a match.' " That was my contribution to the Democratic campaign.

A few days later, we were picked up by a Secret Service man in his Secret Service car in front of the Willard Hotel. Lincoln also once slept at the Willard Hotel, but he was not president as yet, so they changed the sheets the next day and the room lost its historic importance. When you know you're going to sleep in the White House, you spend days deciding which pair of pajamas to wear, worried that you might possibly wander around on the second floor about midnight and suddenly run into the president, who is wearing the exact same pajamas. I believe that would be a breach of etiquette on my part and I would be asked to sleep in the Herbert Hoover Bedroom instead, a tiny, garreted room which now houses documents about Prohibition. True, pajamas are a dumb thing to think about, but at a time such as this, you think about a lot of dumb things. For example, I knew we were invited to sleep in the Lincoln Bedroom, but I don't think they meant that you should actually sleep in his bed. There was a nice rocking chair in there and I thought of curling up in that with a bathrobe over me and try to get in a few catnaps. If a Secret Service man were to suddenly walk in to check things out, I could sit up and say, "I'm up, I'm up. I wasn't sleeping on the bed."

You're told that if there's anything you'd like to eat during the night, to just press the button next to your bed, tell them what you want and it will be brought up. You can't avoid the fear of pressing a button in the White House because of the odd chance that you may have just wiped Russia off the map. Can you imagine calling downstairs at two in the morning, waking up a Marine captain by mistake and telling him you'd like a corned beef sandwich on rye and to please trim the fat? What do you do if the bulb in your lamp starts to flicker? Is this a signal to go immediately to the underground safe zone in Montana? You just can't help thinking things like that.

What actually happened was a lot more prosaic. I fell asleep about eleven P.M., while Diane paced in her expensive new robe out in the hall for the *entire* night, too nervous to sleep. She walked gingerly down the corridor and there in his office, sitting at his desk was the president, working into the wee hours. He stopped and chatted with Diane and eventually Hillary came out and they all talked together for a while. I could hear them but what could I do? Stick my head out the door and yell, "Hey, knock it off down there. Some people have to work in the morning, you know."

We were served breakfast in Lincoln's office right next to his bedroom. They brought juice and eggs and toast and coffee, but once again, I wasn't sure we were supposed to eat it. Maybe it was the ritual breakfast that Lincoln had every morning and we were just supposed to look at it. Then they would take it away and bring us something that came in a little brown bag that said "White House," something to eat in the Secret Service car as we drove away. We left early in the morning, and I thought the president would consider me rude if we didn't say goodbye and thank him for putting us up for the night. But the president was in an emergency cabinet meeting and Diane stopped me from slipping a thank-you note under the door of the Cabinet Room.

As we drove away, we were exhausted from the strain, especially Diane, who hadn't slept a wink. Then I thought, should we have made up the bed before leaving although it was only slightly wrinkled? I decided not to ask Diane because she would have gone back and made up the bed. All in all, it was a hectic night.

ANDREW MEETS DAVID MAMET
39

MY GRANDSON, Andrew, lived with his mother, Ellen, in Santa Fe, New Mexico, and spent most of his school holidays with his Dad, John Leland, who lived in San Francisco. As a result, I didn't have the opportunity to see my only grandson as much as I'd like. Andrew had just turned thirteen, and at a family Thanksgiving dinner I suddenly had an overwhelming desire to go off on a vacation, just me and Andrew, a couple of guys on the loose. I asked Ellen if I could take him to London for a week as soon as his summer vacation started. By the time I finished my question, Andrew was already half packed, and in late June, we both flew to London on the Concorde. If you're going to give your grandson a thrill, go all the way. He sat in the cabin flying at supersonic speed, not talking very much because he was busy flying the plane.

He was a little shy with me at first because we had never actually spent much prime time together. I got a lot of "Yeah"s and "No"s to most of my questions about school and his life. However, once we unpacked at the Four Seasons Hotel facing Hyde Park, he began to take over the trip. Ellen warned me how sloppy he could be, and despite the long talk she gave him about how "Papa likes things neat," Andrew's clothes started to pop up in the strangest places, but rarely in the drawers. He did make an effort, and his winning smile was hard to argue with. After all, we were just "a couple of guys on the loose."

Even at thirteen, Andrew had a wonderful sense of ironic humor, amazingly sophisticated for someone so young, but the normal pesky thirteen-year-old part of him decided to see how far it could push me. He started to taunt me, annoy me, bother me and pester me. Because he was my grandson, the more he did it, the more I enjoyed it, and as long as he saw me laughing, he knew he was safe. There was no way, even if I really felt it, I could let myself get really angry at him. A jar of jelly beans in the mini-bar was about fifteen dollars. He started to tear off the wrapper and I said, "Andrew, that costs fifteen dollars. If you really want it, fine. But if you're only going to eat a few of them, no deal. This is not 'Let's Spoil Andrew Week.' " He opened the jelly beans, of course, and soon grew tired of them, but each morning I'd put them in front of him and say, "Here's your breakfast." He'd laugh, and now he knew the rules—which didn't mean it stopped him from breaking them.

At night, when he was ready for bed, which was two minutes after BBC Television went off the air, I'd say, "Andrew, I like to have breakfast in the dining room about eight o'clock in the morning. If you want to sleep in, tell me now and I'll tiptoe out so I don't wake you." He elected for sleeping in. At a quarter to eight in the morning, I dressed quietly and started to tiptoe past the Sleeping Giant. His eyes opened for a moment. I whispered, "I'm going down. If you want to go, I'll wait for you." He mumbled, "No," and turned over on his side. I walked across the room, and had opened the door as quietly as I could, when Andrew called out, "Wait, Papa. I'm coming with you." He dressed in three minutes, wearing almost everything he did the day before, and started after me, his hair standing straight up. Needless to say, he ate very little breakfast: two sips of juice, half a bagel, and a small piece of fruit, pulling out the stem like the wings off a fly. He looked at me and smiled, knowing I didn't approve. And still I laughed. This ritual was repeated every day for the seven days we were there. He announced he was sleeping in, and just as he heard the doorknob turn, I'd hear, "Wait, Papa. I'm coming." He finally changed his clothes more regularly, but his hair was still standing at attention. His breakfast choices didn't vary much. If he ordered bacon, they would put down four strips on his plate. He ate only one strip and made cholesterol designs with the rest.

We were up and out early every morning. I got tickets in advance to

visit the House of Lords at Parliament. Andrew sat in rapt attention, involved with everything going on. We went to the Old Bailey, the pic-
turesque courthouses of London, and he sat enthralled with the various
trials we attended, where the judges and barristers still wear their periwigs
and black cloaks. We went to Madame Tussaud's Wax Museum, to
Hatchard's, my favorite English bookstore, to Fortnum and Mason for
lunch, to the Tower of London, and on and on, every day.

As the days went on, Andrew began to feel his oats, and started taking
over, picking out a restaurant where he wanted to have lunch.

I said, "Andrew, I know this place. It's the pits."

"No, no, Papa," he said. "I've got a feeling about this. It's going to be
great."

We went in and sat down to an inedible meal. All I did was glare at
him as I pushed my food away. He found this funny. Not funny—hysterical. Once outside, I rubbed my stomach and said, "God, what was that
soup? I think they dipped a ladle into the Thames River." Andrew doubled
up with laughter. "If I die of food poisoning," I said, "you walk home
across the Atlantic." Tears of laughter ran down his face.

When I finally stopped talking about the bad meal, he said, "Papa, can
we go back there for lunch tomorrow?"

I took a swipe at him and missed. He found that excruciatingly funny.
For some reason, I fell in with it. Making him laugh was as joyous to me as
hearing an opening night audience screaming with laughter. "Andrew," I
said, "we're staying in tonight. I'm calling that restaurant and having them
send over dinner." He rolled his eyes, rubbed his stomach and said,
"Mmmm, yummy. I'd love that."

I took another swipe at him and he ducked, laughed and said, "Ooh,
beating your grandson in public. I may have to press charges against you."

He never knew when to stop and I never wanted him to stop. There
we were, two thirteen-year-old kids on the street, and I wondered if anyone could guess which one was the grandfather.

On and on we trekked, from the War Museum to the Tate Gallery.
"That was great, wasn't it?" I said as we left the Tate.

He looked at me and said, "Yeah, but not as good as that restaurant."
This time he ducked without my even swinging at him.

Finally, I said, "Andrew, truce, please. No more. Try to get something out of this trip."

He nodded in compliance. "You're right. That was a great gallery. I really loved that gallery. Let's go back tonight because I want to remember that gallery all my life," and then I got the big smile. Ellen told me he did the same thing at home, the same thing with his friends, the same thing in school in Santa Fe. I guess it explained why his grades went up and down, but also why he was the most popular boy in school and girls a foot taller and two years older wanted to be his girlfriend. I thought, "The only thing better than having Andrew as a grandson was if I could have been a little more like him when I was thirteen." Actually, I wasn't all that different but I'd never have the nerve to behave so brazenly with my grandfather, who never would have gotten the jokes anyway.

If your grandfather was a playwright, chances are you'd go to the theater every night, which was exactly what we did. Andrew adored Tom Stoppard's *Arcadia,* a brilliant play that challenged an audience's imagination and intelligence. Andrew was deeply engrossed in it, and at the intermission it was clear that he observed some nuances in the play that even I missed. It was the serious side of Andrew, the one that seemed more like a college student than a teenager, and I loved that side of him as well.

We saw *The Woman in Black,* the perfect mystery for someone with Andrew's imagination, and he never moved in his seat. When something interested him, his concentration was enormous.

Another play sounded like a good change of pace, and I thought it might be fun. From the title, I assumed it was a nice British farce, but it turned out to be a *not* so nice British SEX farce, with very little clothes, very little wit and very little reason for a thirteen-year-old to be seeing this with his grandfather. Andrew didn't hear much of it, because I kept apologizing all during the performance and bribed him not to tell his mother what I had done. He was amused that I was in trouble.

The next night I made sure we saw something much weightier, and during the intermission I met a friend who was doing the color commentary for HBO's televising of the Wimbledon matches. He set us up the next day with terrific seats on Court One. The match went five sets, a first-class thriller that lasted almost four hours. It turned out to be one of the best matches of that year's tournament. There wasn't a day in that week that didn't present a high spot for us.

The following afternoon we went to St. Paul's Cathedral, and suddenly the Huckleberry Finn side of Andrew showed itself. He climbed to the very top of the great dome, while Papa sat in a pew, grateful for the twenty-minute respite. Andrew called out to me from the top of the dome, but you didn't have to shout to be heard. The acoustics made it possible for Andrew to call in a modulated voice, "Papa," but the voice echoed and bounced around the cathedral, repeating itself all the way down to my seat. "PAPA . . . PAPA . . . PAPA . . . papa . . . papa . . ." When he came down, he wanted to go up again. "Not today," I said. "Come back one day with your own grandson."

On our final night in London, we went to see *Cryptogram,* a play by David Mamet. Andrew had never seen a David Mamet play, while I had seen pretty much all of them. Mamet is clearly one of America's top playwrights, and he has his own style. When you see his work for the first time, you have to adjust to the unique cadences of his speeches, which he uses in most of his plays. They are always intelligent, unique and powerful. He writes short, staccato sentences, some of which are never finished before the other character interrupts or finishes the other's thought. It's a rapid-fire chess game with the chess pieces coming at you fast and furiously from any point on the board. When it is done correctly, as in the brilliant *Glengarry Glen Ross,* the effect is magical. It becomes seamless, and although you think you are missing words or speeches, in effect, you miss nothing. He glues you to your seat, daring you to move or to take a breath.

Whatever attributes *Cryptogram* had, I think the English actors had trouble dancing to Mamet's music, and in a Mamet play, when the actors miss the beat, it sounds like they are forgetting their lines. (The same play was done much better the following season in New York.) But Andrew never heard actors read Mamet's dialogue before, and he was so taken with the style that once outside the theater, he turned into a character in a David Mamet play, written by Andrew, even before I suspected what he was doing.

I said to him, "Did you like the—"

"Yes," he answered. "I found it very—"

"Unusual," I said, falling in with him. "But what did you think of the—"

"Exactly," he answered. "What did *anyone* think of it? And what does thinking of it mean?"

I found a taxi and we headed back to the hotel for our last night in London. By now my mind was on other things besides the Mamet play, but once Andrew takes hold, he does not let go easily.

"We have to get up very early in the—" I started to say.

"What?" he asked me. "We have to what?"

"I was saying we have an early plane to—"

"To catch? Is that what you're saying? To catch a plane?"

"Yes, David. Can we put the play aside for a moment?"

"A moment? Why a moment? Why not an hour? Why not eternity?" he went on.

By now the cab driver was glancing at us through the rearview mirror.

I tried to continue. "I had a great time with you, Andrew. I thought the—"

"The cathedral? Is that what you're thinking? Don't think of the cathedral. Hear me out—"

I heard him out in the elevator, in our room in our beds and while I turned the lights out. I was soon asleep as Andrew continued speaking broken and interrupted sentences. In the morning we had our last breakfast and drove out to the airport. Andrew was silent, probably thinking of all he had seen and done during the last week. They announced our flight to New York and we got on the end of the line waiting to board with the other passengers. A tall, elegant woman stood in front of us, immersed in her morning London newspaper. I turned to Andrew and said, "It was really great fun, wasn't it?"

"What? Wasn't what? Fun, is that what you said?"

He was back in a Mamet play, so I indulged him. "The trip. The trip to London. I thought it was—"

"Fun. Oh, I see what you mean. Yes. But why did we—?"

"Did we what?" I answered.

"I don't know. Does anyone know?"

"Does anyone know what?"

The woman in front of us turned, listening to us, a very slight trace of a smile on her face. Andrew continued.

"Does anyone know what they mean? What does 'mean' mean?"

"Exactly my—"

"Point? No. I never mentioned points."

The elegant woman surprised us when she said, "I assume you've just seen the David Mamet play?"

Andrew looked as if he got caught with his hand in the cookie jar.

"Yes," I said. "Last night. Have you seen it?"

"Many times," she said, smilingly. "I produced it."

Andrew suddenly looked up at the ceiling and I jumped in to save the day. "Oh. Congratulations. We loved it. We loved the play. This is my grandson. Didn't we love the play, Andrew?"

All he did was nod. Where was he when I needed him?

She thanked me, then moved on as we began to board the plane. Andrew was uncommonly quiet for quite some time.

We were both tired and slept for a good deal of the trip. Once in New York, I took him to another airline that he was going to take to Santa Fe, to be met there by Ellen.

I put my arms around him and gave him a hug. "I just want to thank you for one of the best weeks in my life, Andrew."

He nodded, shyly. "Thanks, Papa. It was great."

As he started for the plane, I called out, "Andrew. Don't eat the food on the plane. I ordered you something special from that restaurant in London you loved so much."

He nodded, smiled and then flew back home. I remember someone once saying to me, "If you have an instinct to do something good, don't dwell on it. Just do it." I always think of that when I remember asking Ellen if I could take Andrew for a week to London. And thirteen was just the right age to get him. I lived vicariously through him all that week, and I was grateful that by taking him on a journey, he took me on a journey into his world. I loved every minute of it.

THE DAY I WAS PICKETED
40

MANNY AZENBERG and I had been mulling over the possibility of doing my next play off-Broadway. The financial figures no longer made doing a play *on* Broadway a viable option. It cost a million six hundred thousand dollars to mount a play on Broadway a few short years ago, while that same play could be done *off*-Broadway for less than a third of that sum, somewhere under five hundred thousand. True, if we were a hit off-Broadway, the profits would be infinitely smaller, but the chances of having a long run with a play *on* Broadway seemed near to impossible. Musicals were fast taking over all the available theaters, and even getting a play *on* took a major star or a successful run in London prior to New York. We opted for going off-Broadway.

Like *Plaza Suite* and *California Suite,* both highly successful as plays and then films, *London Suite* was comprised of four one-act plays, all taking place in the same hotel, this time, obviously, in London. In doing *London Suite,* I think I was prompted in wanting to complete another trilogy. We had a good start by reprising the best play from *California Suite,* the story of Sidney and Diana Nichols, a bisexual antique dealer married to a major British actress. Maggie Smith had won the Oscar for playing Diana in the film version.

In the new play, it is sixteen years later. The couple have parted, divorced, Diana has moved to California, and is now starring in a hit TV series, while Sidney has moved to the Greek island of Mykonos, this time following his true instincts by living with a younger man, a painter-sculptor from Switzerland. Sidney and Diana have a reunion in a posh hotel in London, where he has come, hat in hand, to borrow money in order to care for his sick and dying lover in Greece. Diana eventually discovers the lie, that it is Sidney who is dying and the money he wants is to leave his cherished companion with some security for the future. Diana, who still yearns for Sidney, no matter what his sexual preference, gets him back by promising to take care of Sidney through to the end, if he comes back to California with her. He agrees on the condition that his penniless Swiss mate can come with them. Diana, who has just been shocked to learn that her own secretary, Grace, is gay as well, accedes to Sidney's wish.

> DIANA
> Of course. We'll all be together. You, me,
> Max and Grace. Can't you see *that* story in
> *People* magazine? "TV star takes in dying
> gay ex-husband, his male Swiss sculptor
> lover and her devoted female secretary who
> turns out to be a cowboy."

> SIDNEY
> And we'll go on those daytime talk shows.
> And people will call in from Omaha and
> Memphis and ask questions like, "I know
> you people are all disgusting but your life
> seems so interesting, doesn't it?"

Sidney seems to relax as he knows that Max, his Swiss friend, will be taken care of, and that Diana will be there for Sidney during his last days. He says, with his typical black humor, referring to his cancer:

> SIDNEY
> . . . Aren't we lucky that something like
> this came along?

We first tried out the play at the Seattle Repertory Theater, run by the gifted director Dan Sullivan. *London Suite* was a huge hit in Seattle, garnering excellent reviews and breaking a few attendance records at the same time. We were all ecstatic and wondered if we were making a mistake by bypassing Broadway. But we stuck to our guns and moved east to the Union Square Theater on 17th Street.

It was an odd building for a theater, principally because it was never built for that purpose. It was originally Tammany Hall, a wonderful place for political rallies or meetings of various trade unions. It had a high domed ceiling which was lovely to look at, but unfortunately sent most of the actors' words aloft, where they stayed, suspended in air next to a few pigeons who had flown in on a pass. This caused pockets of silence in many areas of the auditorium, principally where the audience was sitting. Still, it had a nice ambience and I was glad to be there, despite an unsettling feeling that somehow in the middle of the night, truckers had moved me, my family and all our furniture to a dark corner in Pittsburgh. Where were the milling crowds gathering in front of all the theaters on 44th and 45th Streets? Neil Simon was off-Broadway but the Neil Simon Theater was *on* Broadway. I found myself going to the Union Square Theater at night and dressing *down*. An expensive Ralph Lauren camel's hair coat looked out of place here.

On the night of our first preview, the crowds began to gather, waiting for the theater to open its doors to the public to view Neil Simon's first off-Broadway play. There was electricity in the air, but the wattage couldn't compete with what was so bright on the Great White Way. Suddenly reporters and photographers turned their attention to two men walking with placards. As I got closer, I saw they were pickets from the Stage Hands Union. Their signs read, NEIL SIMON UNFAIR TO STAGE HANDS UNION. HE BELONGS ON BROADWAY. At first I thought they were strikers picketing on behalf of the young writers who were trying to get *into* an off-Broadway theater. It was quite the opposite. They were strikers for the Broadway Stage Hands Union, protesting that I was hurting their income by doing my play off-Broadway.

Imitation is not the highest form of flattery. Protestors from the Broadway Stage Hands Union complaining that I was depriving them of my talent by working for *less* money off-Broadway was more than flattery. It was downright reverence, shown in the most absurd way. The crowd outside mildly booed the strikers, who, I must admit, smiled and shrugged. I crossed to them and said, in my most amiable manner, "Are you seriously picketing me because you think it's wrong for me to abandon Broadway?" They shrugged and said, "Sorry, Neil. It's our job. We're told to do it. You know?" "Sure," I said. "No problem. Good publicity for my play." Two nights later they were gone.

The off-Broadway audience who came to our previews didn't look much different than a Broadway audience, but these days very few people dress for the theater. The reaction to the plays was unclear. The audience laughed, but not as much as in Seattle. They applauded, but not as much as in Seattle. They stood at the end of the play, but not as high as in Seattle. In sports, we have what is called "home court advantage," that is to say, the Mets should win more ball games at Shea Stadium than they will at their opponent's stadium. In the Union Square Theater, I somehow felt I had lost my home court advantage. No boos, no cheering for other authors, but something was missing. The reviews, as usual, were mixed, and Vincent Canby of the *New York Times* said the play "was somewhere in the middle of my oeuvre."

If we had done the play on Broadway, we would have lost about a million dollars. Having done it downtown, running five or six months, we paid off a good deal of our investment, and today with *London Suite* released to playhouses around the country and abroad, we are now in profit. Our risks had been diminished but so had the excitement. Still, I knew I'd better get used to it. As far as I was concerned, a play on Broadway is something an audience goes to on the night the musicians forgot to show up.

AS DIANE and I were moving into the seventh year of our second marriage, the ebb and flow of our relationship was beginning to ebb more than flow. This is the sort of private information that Diane wanted to avoid making public by virtue of her wishes in our prenuptial agreement. I agree with her. The difficulty in adhering to that restriction while being honest in one's memoirs creates a thorny issue for the writer. Having taken you so far down the road with my life, I now have to put up a detour sign and skirt the cracks and crevices that were confronting Diane and me more and more. It is neither my wish nor intention to relate my side of the issues at hand and only conjecture what was going on in Diane's mind. I will say this, however: in a marriage that is beginning to stumble, the difficult part to go through is not just the disagreements and disappointments. What causes the real pain is the matter of residual love that still exists. The good times were so very, very good—but where did they go to, when did they leave and why did they disappear? The hurt is so much sharper when a cry of deep anger comes *at* you and *from* you, and the person on the receiving end is someone you once deeply loved. I couldn't bear another item in a gossip column that said I was divorcing again. I had never left anyone before. Joan died, Marsha left for reasons of her own and Diane left the first time to confront major issues in her own life that didn't seem related to our marriage, as odd as that may sound. I still remember the day she left seven years prior, when she said, "I love you more today than I ever have before." Aside from Joan, I asked myself, "Is it me? Is it because I'm a writer? Is it because I'm a *successful* writer? Is it my own fame that diminished *them?*" There were no answers left on my desk that morning.

I decided to stick this one out, even if I slipped into oblivion in the soft armchair I sat in each night after dinner, while the arms of the chair warmly engulfed me and finally swallowed me whole until I disappeared, thus avoiding the shame of still another divorce.

PROPOSALS was my thirtieth play. A magic number for me, not that it held any real personal significance. Somehow I just didn't want my obituary to read, "Neil Simon, writer of twenty-nine plays, etc., etc., . . ." As I look for the right rhythm and music in my dialogue, twenty-nine seemed to lack both rhythm *and* music. It was flat. The image in my mind was that my fingers were reaching for the tip of the high wall that surrounds the playwrights' Valhalla, and if I weakened and could climb no higher than twenty-nine, the rest of the obituary would read, ". . . who fell short by one play of attaining the heights that all playwrights dream of." Nowhere did I ever read that thirty was the number that all playwrights dream of. It's something you make up in your mind, as I did when I was ten or eleven years old, sick with the flu and fever, wrapped in my father's heavy bathrobe, looking out my bedroom window and counting cars: "If I see ten trucks by the time I count to one hundred, I will have a wonderful life." When I had counted eight trucks and was coming up fast on "ninety-one, ninety-two, ninety-three . . . ," I stretched those last remaining numbers by speaking as if my tongue were paralyzed. No matter how long it took, you just didn't say one hundred until you had seen that tenth truck, then you'd let out a whoop and a holler and cry, "Yes! I made it. I'm going to have a wonderful life." I may have cheated a little, but the truth is, yes, I did have a wonderful life.

I had worked on and off for almost five years to complete *Proposals*. Every time I got stuck, I'd move on to something else, and when finished, I'd return to *Proposals*. It was a play I would simply never let get away from me. I knew it would be the last play I'd ever write about Joan as I remembered her, as she was when I first met her, when I knew immediately that this was the girl I wanted to spend the rest of my life with. This, however, was not strictly a play about Joan, or about me, either—it was more than that. It was about a time and a world that no longer exists, that was not necessarily better than this time and world, but it did have values, principles and qualities that seemed to have gotten lost today, and that should not be forgotten.

I cannot be objective as to whether *Proposals* was as good as I wanted it to be. But as we moved from city to city, audiences in Los Angeles, then Phoenix, then New Haven received the play progressively better and better. By the time we reached the Kennedy Center in Washington, D.C., the play exploded with our best reviews and immediately became the biggest hit I ever had in that city. In our four-week run there, there was not an empty seat. Not even for me.

The play then moved on to New York, and once again I was on Broadway, where I thought *Proposals* belonged. It was, if not in structure, but in intent, a sort of *Midsummer Night's Dream*. Ten characters, all in various states of love—new love, old love, unrequited love, lost love and the love that lasts beyond the grave. It is all seen through the eyes of Clemma, Josie's black nanny, as Clemma steps out of the past, having died long ago, only to come back to revisit the summer house where she worked and helped raise Josie when she was a child. The bond between Josie and Clemma dominates the play. The part of Clemma was played by L. Scott Caldwell, a former Tony winner in August Wilson's *Joe Turner's Come and Gone,* and she was consistently praised in our play as being "humorous, loving and touching, whose presence commands our complete attention and respect."

In the review by Ben Brantley of the *New York Times,* the heading above the review in large, bold type read, "A Black Woman Walking Down a Country Road? This is Neil Simon?" I know that in most cases the reviewer does not necessarily write the headline, although I never knew why. In any case, what the headline was saying to me was, "Why is Neil Simon veering into new territory? He's never written about blacks before. Shouldn't that be left in the hands of more qualified ethnic writers like August Wilson?" The quotes are mine. I was confused, to say the least.

We opened in November, and as we neared the Christmas holidays, most theaters drop in attendance, since most people are out shopping. Musicals, however, succeed in the face of hurricanes, fires and earthquakes. *The Lion King* and *Ragtime* were selling out, as was *Chicago* and all the old standbys like *Phantom, Les Misérables,* and *Cats,* whose nine lives will exist past nine thousand performances. A mixed review or even a bad review from the *Times* has not always stopped one of my plays from going on to a successful run. But now I was up against something much bigger. Without all the critics' approval (and we did have the cheers from many), the audiences would now walk right past our theater to the nearest musical, if they could get in. *Scarlet Pimpernel,* which did not receive much better reviews than we did, still did business. *Proposals* lasted two short months on Broadway. Since we had no star names to help us woo the audiences in, we didn't stand a chance.

It was a bleak season all around for Manny Azenberg and myself. He produced *Side Show,* a wonderful and courageous new musical—courageous because the story was about Siamese twin sisters. The reviews for that show from the *Times* critics, both Mr. Brantley and Vincent Canby, were glorious. They praised the show for all the right reasons, and even Frank Rich, the former reviewer of the *Times* and now a writer of editorials, was seen at the play on many nights and it was no secret that he championed the musical. But the audiences never came. The reason, or one of the reasons being, to quote someone on the street, "I don't want to see two women stuck together, no matter how brilliant it is." Ten, or even five years ago, the physical closeness of two sisters would not be an issue. Good is good and *Side Show* was good—and more. The audiences today are not necessarily tougher. Quite the opposite: they are easier for a more accessible theater. They say, "Don't test me. I just want to be entertained." There's nothing wrong with that, but it certainly limits the parameters of good theater. *Side Show* closed soon after *Proposals.* It was the worst beating Manny and I ever took in one season, and a great personal and financial loss to us both. I was saddened by the closing of *Proposals,* but not despondent. I have had too much success to cry foul. But I was confused. I do believe there will be an afterlife for both my play and Manny's musical.

I was uplifted, to say the least, almost three weeks after the closing of *Proposals* when Jack Klugman and Tony Randall revived my play *The Sunshine Boys* for Tony's National Actors' Theater. The reviews were unanimously joyous. Vincent Canby went so far as to say, "It's his [Simon's] *War and Peace,* his *Long Day's Journey into Night."* Amazing quotes that made me read them a dozen times before I allowed myself to believe them. So I was a flop on Broadway and a smash on Broadway within a period of less than a month. I thought to myself, "Ah, I see what they want. From now on I will only write twenty-five-year-old revivals."

IN MAY of 1998, I filed for divorce.

I knew I had been unhappy and depressed for over a year. I had stopped playing tennis, I had less and less desire to see friends in California, and work was no longer the joy or escape that it once was. During the pre-Broadway tour of *Proposals,* I was beginning to get agonizing pains in my stomach, bouts of diarrhea, sleepless nights and days that dragged on pointlessly. My daily routine was so confining, I thought I was living in the only prison cell in Bel Air. I had no outlets, no places to go that seemed inviting to me, and no one in particular that I wanted to see. I was making fewer and fewer visits to Santa Barbara to see my daughters and their families, I only called my brother, Danny, occasionally and saw him even less, and my trips to New York, always a safe haven for me, now grew tiresome, and after just three days, I wanted to return to my cell on Chalon Road.

I was looking and feeling older, and on my seventieth birthday, Diane had thrown a huge party for me at the house; it looked like anyone and everyone in the Los Angeles telephone book had been invited. More is not always better. I saw a few close friends and my family, of course, but they were in the minority. I was so spiritless that I hardly recognized many of the faces that smiled at me and wished me the best, all the while I was feeling my worst, and the two vodkas I had made it almost impossible for me to remember a name. "Hey, how are you?" was the best I could do at putting names and faces together. If it were up to me, I would have gone into my room, closed the door, gotten into bed and pulled a few yards of grass over me and put up a headstone that said, "SHH. He's Dying."

My doctor, Rob Huizinga, knew I was depressed for some time, and though he was one of the busiest doctors in L.A., he asked me to come by his office late one day. I sat with him and we talked for over an hour. An hour for him was equal to about fifteen normal patient visits, but he knew unless I could break through my depression, it could easily lead to illness. What he eventually suggested was that I break my routine, look for other outlets, change my life in whatever way I could. He had been treating me for many years and keeping me in very good shape and he knew me better than I knew myself. I trusted him and I knew his advice was sound, but once I got home, try as I might, I couldn't break the habits of a lifetime. I went to my office at the same time each day, but now I had little desire to write. I'd fall asleep after a few hours, and when I awoke, I was too tired to think clearly. I had little appetite for food and little desire to phone a friend. I was trapped inside my own loneliness and despair, and there wasn't a soul I knew who had a key to unlock my chains.

I knew my marriage to Diane had fallen apart, despite the fact we still managed to go out to a movie or a Lakers game or see some friends. Diane was working as a feature writer for *Live* magazine and more times than not came home late so that Bryn ate dinner first, since she had her homework to do, I ate next because Diane would say, "Don't wait for me," and when

she got home she ate in the den as I sat four feet away watching a basketball game without any investment of interest in who won or lost.

There was only one dependable ray of hope: our dog, Annabelle. She
greeted me warmly when I came home each night (as she did both Bryn
and Diane), and she ran for her ball. Dogs are not interested in your depression. They love you and assume you love them (which you do, of course),
and she'd look at me, wagging her tail as if to say, "If you'll throw the ball
to me, I'll run and chase it, catch it in my mouth, bring it back and drop it
at your feet and then we'll do it again. And then you won't be depressed, I
promise you." Dogs are the best doctors in the world and you don't need
an appointment. Just open your front door and she'll drop everything for
you. After a while, though, even Annabelle couldn't help. She could run
down a ball, but she couldn't chase away my blues. The sad fact is, if you
don't play with your dog, they can easily get depressed as well. Solving her
problem was easy—you throw the ball. I couldn't even find mine.

The stomach pains persisted and I was urged to see Dr. Gary Gitnick,
head of Digestive Diseases at UCLA Hospital, one of the best in the country. After a brief examination and a long heart-to-heart talk (Dr. Gitnick
calls you at home or in your office every few months just to ask you how
you're doing), he prescribed a number of procedures which we started almost immediately. First there was a colonoscopy, which came up negative.
Then an upper GI examination, which also came up negative. Next an examination by a cardiologist—no problem there. Finally, he ordered a test
for lactose intolerance, the inability to digest foods which contained lactose, or dairy products, e.g., milk, cheese, chocolate. Bingo! We nailed that
one. I had a moderate case of it, but moderate or not, it doesn't go away
unless you adhere strictly to the rules. No problem for me because discipline is a competitive game I play with myself and I almost always win. It
comes with forty-five years of writing and meeting deadlines. Slowly the
pains in the pit of my stomach receded, but it gave me a low punch in case
my mouth ever got too close to a cookie.

Still the depression persisted. I couldn't read more than three pages of
a book before I had to read them again, and still I didn't understand what
I'd read. I couldn't sit through an entire movie alone, or watch a ball game

on TV without changing the station every three minutes, hoping to find a better game. I wouldn't know a better game if it hit me in the groin. Plus, since my diet had been cut by more than half, the food I ate was as bland as my life.

I was referred to a therapist, a doctor who dealt primarily with patients suffering from moods and depression. If I had my choice, I would have taken moods because moods sounded as if you got breaks once in a while. Depression is your day and night job. One of the first questions he asked was did I ever feel suicidal. I said, yes, many times, but that didn't seem like much fun either. There was humor in my answer but despair in my subtext. I was not ready to die yet, but I also was not ready to live. Oscar Hammerstein beat me to that thought in the lyric for "Ol' Man River": "I'm tired of livin' but fear'd a dyin' ." That may have been true, but at least that guy was singing.

After a few sessions, the doctor explained that obviously I was depressed, but not in such an acute way that drastic measures needed to be taken immediately. Still, it's not something you want lingering around as you drive your car on the freeway at night. He told me that basically there were three ways of dealing with the state of depression I was in, which has since been called "Simon's Syndrome," meaning, "Sad enough to be sad, but not happy enough to be happy." Number one, he said, would be analysis. Well, since we figured out that I had more analysis than Freud's first patient, we could skip that. The second was medication. I am not keen on mood manipulators because I would rather be in the mood I'm in, than the mood he's going to *put* me in. Mine was miserable, but at least it was mine. Still, I decided to give it a try. He gave me a low dose of Wellbutrin, which sounded like a name Disney gave it, like a chummy old German bear with glasses who chuckles while he eats honey, and his name is Dr. Wellbutrin. But it was a better name I suppose than something called "Uplift" or "Stop Whining." Americans seem to like for their drugs to have names similar to their illness, like Halcion, to prevent you from taking the wrong pill. For example, you would *never* take something called "The Big Sleep" by mistake.

To be honest, the Wellbutrin helped. It does not give you a high, otherwise it would outsell Viagra, but it does level your feelings off but with

very little pleasure attached. For example, it's a little like kissing an absolutely gorgeous girl but you both have gauze on your lips. I thought perhaps a better name for the drug would be "Standoff," because that's what it
was. No one won, no one lost. I now started to call my depression "Sub-
marine" because you couldn't see it but you knew it was there lurking just
underneath the surface.

The third alternative to my coming back to a meaningful existence
was to change my environment. "You mean move?" I asked. "Why? I love
my house."

"No," he said. "Not your house. Your life."

Pretty much the same thing that Dr. Huizinga had said. But how do I
change my life? Stop writing? No. Bad idea, he said. Work you love, and
being productive is always healthy. But there are other things to life. I
looked at him, honestly without a clue as to what that other thing could
be. Take a year off and go to some South Sea island? A year in Bora Bora?
I would sooner rethink that suicide thing. He smiled at what I said. I still
had the ability to make someone laugh, but totally none to do the same for
myself.

After seven weeks, he took me off the antidepressant. "You don't really need it anymore."

I said, "So can we upgrade me from depressed to just merely totally
miserable?" In another seven weeks I could look forward to going from
being bored to death with my life, to watching reruns of *I Love Lucy* for a
year.

I could actually be amusing in the doctor's office, but once out on the
street, I felt hopeless. What a state to be in. Is this what the Catholics call
"limbo?" Diane and I continued to live our lives as if nothing had changed,
mainly because nothing *had* changed. But we were both unhappy with
each other, and somebody had to make a first move. What I had to wrestle
with was my inability to leave someone, to be the first to say goodbye, since
I was on the receiving end of goodbye so often in my life. I saw my father
leave my mother time and time again, and I saw the deep anguish it caused
her. From that time in my childhood, I never wanted to be the cause of
someone else's unhappiness by leaving them. But the problem was, by staying, I wasn't able to make them happy either. Again, a standoff. Joan left

when she died, but there was no betrayal there—just tragedy. Everyone lost by Joan's dying, but I think that by never breaking up in our marriage, it's possible that my two daughters, Ellen and Nancy, are stronger for it. Marriage was something they believed in, even if it failed once for Ellen.

So there I was, in a stalemate with myself. My life was not getting any better, our marriage was drifting toward the rapids, and yet the chess pieces stood motionless on the chessboard, waiting for someone to make a move. I went into the guest room to sleep one night, knowing that the battle that was raging inside of me would surely wake Diane and another nocturnal husband-and-wife fight would do no one any good—not that there was any guarantee that Diane was sleeping that night either.

It had been a long time since I had turned to Joan for an answer, not that I ever truly believed that she would hear my plea and send down a message giving me clearance to take off. I was in a half sleep and suddenly sat up and looked at the clock. It was just after two in the morning. The message—no matter where it came from, most likely from the year of unfulfillment that had been building up like a stockpile of nuclear fission—came in a voice that was clear and unequivocal. I had to leave. I had to change my life, to find myself or get hopelessly lost in the entanglement of my own neurosis. The words were short and simple: "Get out, Neil." If I didn't, I would only make myself and Diane unhappier than we already were.

Telling Diane early the next morning as she went to wake Bryn up for school may not have been timely, but I was afraid if I did not say the words, I might back off. It was the hardest thing I ever did in my life, yet I knew, difficult as it was, it was the right thing. I could see the pain in Diane's face, and she turned and walked away without saying a word, which was a lot more devastating to me than if she stood there and argued with me. But how different was it when Marsha did it or Diane did it the first time? Of course the circumstances are always different, and either of them could argue, "Yes, but you don't know what I was going through." Granted. Nobody knows at a time like that. There is, of course, always much, much more to the story of why two people break up, and even if we could find the words or the answers, it is certainly nothing that either one of us would want to share with anyone but ourselves.

I moved out of the house and into a hotel, and found that I had just traded one lonely place for another. Room service doesn't make it less lonely. I knew it was important for me to keep contact with Bryn, because the child in me identified with the child in her. Except that Bryn was smarter and more grown-up than I could even imagine. I called her and faxed her. We met and had lunch. She was cold at first, perhaps even angry, and certainly she was confused. But she was always polite and respectful. At fourteen, girls or boys do not usually communicate their inner feelings to their parents all that much, maybe even in something so dire as a divorce. It was not the first time she had seen it, since it is as much a topic of conversation at school with friends as grades, boys and Leonardo DiCaprio, not that I mean to denigrate her feelings. They had to be powerful, even though they were not always articulated. I knew she loved her mother. I could only hope she loved me. I love her very much and I am so proud to see the headway she is making during these difficult years, divorce or not. She is a beautiful, sweet and highly intelligent girl with a unique sense of humor, and I know from experience that humor is the ability to see the world from a very objective viewpoint. I found that she was unwilling to talk about the breakup, so I learned to steer clear of that issue.

Eventually, the ghastly business of divorce dominates your life. If you're lucky, you find a lawyer who is sensitive to the issues and feelings of both parties, thereby facilitating an early settlement. No matter what, both parties feel they found the right lawyer. Why not? They're on your side. I don't believe it's possible to go through a divorce without experiencing various degrees of pain, anger, relief, sadness and in some odd moment during the hostilities, something that strikes you funny simply because in one brief second, you find it all so ludicrous.

You'll notice that ministers, priests and rabbis rarely perform divorces. Since they are emissaries of God, they are interested in joining couples in the sacred business of matrimony, and one expression you'll never hear in a divorce court is, "You may now kiss your ex-wife."

Our divorce turned out to be contentious and a battle royal ensued. No matter how much each party trusts his or her lawyer, that lawyer very often has to bring news to his client that makes the client want to punch in every wall in the Chrysler Building.

Of course friends of each party invariably side with the one to whom they feel closer, offering advice like, "Go for everything you can get from him," or, "I wouldn't give her a nickel." Bad advice. This is like throwing ten redwood trees on a blazing fire. Mind you, in many cases, you never hear things directly from your adversary. Once I got a note from a woman lawyer from the opposite camp saying, "We can keep you in court for the rest of your life." I don't care if you're the greatest brain surgeon in the world, that threat scares the life out of you. There is also no saying that Diane had anything to do with that statement. Some lawyers just take charge and send these nuclear bombs on their own.

Our battle went on for six months and then suddenly, almost without warning, the two lawyers spoke to each other on the phone (for the jillionth time) and then called their respective clients to say, "It's all over. We have a settlement." Suddenly all becomes quiet. All is still. What do battlefields sound like on the day *after* the war stops? There *is* no sound. You get the picture in your mind of troops silently dragging themselves back through the deep, noiseless snow, headed home, to family and a warm meal. It's as though the fight never took place, as if the hurtful words, uttered with such anger, were never spoken at all. A few days after the dust had settled, Diane and I spoke to each other on the phone to arrange a lunch between me and Bryn. Diane said, "Hi, honey." I asked, "How are you?" The exchange felt warm and friendly although our lives were now changed forever.

Eventually, you begin to lick your wounds. In my case, during the angry faxes that flew into each other's camp like deadly missiles, a boxed painting I had bought arrived at my apartment in New York where I was staying, far from the field of battle. In anger, I fought to get the painting out of its box. I gave it one terrific yank and suddenly heard something tear. It was my rotator cuff. It took six months to fully heal. The same amount of time it took to complete the settlement. The inner hurt and sadness, the deeper wounds, however, will take much, much longer to heal.

TAKE IT FROM THE TOP

AS I WRITE THIS, a year has passed since Diane and I separated and eventually divorced. My torn rotator cuff has healed, but the end of an eight-year marriage still gives you aches and pains, whether it's rainy weather or not. If there was true love in the marriage, and there would have to be for two people to stick it out so long—at least a trace of it will linger, continually finding a way, somehow or somewhere, to remind you. For both of us, I hope there eventually will be friendship. I have achieved that with Marsha, and recently we worked together again, when she went to London, reunited with Richard Dreyfuss (since *The Goodbye Girl*) in a play I wrote thirty years ago, *The Prisoner of Second Avenue*. It was great fun watching Marsha saying my words on a stage, and saying them brilliantly. Time does not necessarily heal everything, but it does give you a chance to forget the anger and make you remember why you loved in the first place.

For Diane, I hope for a life that will make her happy. She always did find a way for herself. For Bryn, I hope she still has faith that a good relationship and/or marriage is always possible for her, if that's what she wants. Although it's not possible for me to see Bryn as much as we did when we lived under the same roof, as her father and someone who cherishes her, I hope we will always be close. For myself, I've already found the stirrings of a new way of living. At the age of seventy-one and in relatively good health, I'm still vigorous and excited about life. I'm not all that keen about plunging into old age, but I feel if I keep on working and being with exciting people, I may never notice that it came knocking on my door.

And I am writing again. I recently finished a new play called *The Dinner Party*. What is the subject? Divorce. No surprise there. It's not anything about Diane and myself, or even about Marsha and me. What I've tried to do was to follow three couples who were divorced two or three years ago, and I attempted to see what would happen if they were all to meet unexpectedly in very unusual circumstances. There's also another play I've started, one that takes place in South America. I can't explain it yet since it's making up its mind in its own good time to reveal itself to me. I said in my previous book, *Rewrites,* that I didn't know how to *stop* writing. I think now I actually *do* know how to stop, but the thing is, I don't choose to. It's an old friend, and it continues to travel with me wherever I go.

I still love the mechanics of it. I still feel an intense desire to put pen to paper, to put words to use, to put ideas into stories and to wed new stories into even newer forms. At this point I have no need or concern as to where my plays appear. Broadway would be fine, but so would a small regional theater in Louisville or San Diego. To paraphrase someone else's line, if you write them, they will come. That is, if you write them well. There will always be an audience somewhere who yearn for the excitement of discovering a new play or a new play playwright. That I might even be that new playwright.

For me, I hope there will be additional satisfactions besides my work. I hope to finally find more time for my family, for my friends, old and new, to enjoy a world of places I planned on seeing but put off because I had a play opening in a place not nearly so attractive. I need to become aware of ideas to which I've paid no heed before; to see for the first time that which I have so often turned my back; to pay attention to what someone asks of me instead of using "I'm working" as an excuse to explain that I don't have the time. I hope for all this and more. I feel now that while I have fewer years to live, I have more time in which to live them. I don't necessarily think of marriage again, but as for love and companionship, the door remains open. I've learned that you can't have everything but I've also learned that the simple truth is, you don't *need* everything.

In closing, I would just repeat a philosophy that the woman analyst in *Jake's Women* leaves with Jake as she slowly fades out of his imagination.

"Remember, Jake," she says. "You always have options . . . options . . . . . . options . . . . options."

INDEX

Abbott and Costello, 219

Abraham, F. Murray, 26–27

Academy Awards, 26, 101, 104–5,
    109, 139, 202, 203, 312
    Marsha Mason's nominations for,
        73–75, 141, 148, 165, 293
    Simon's nominations for, 74, 104,
        141

Actors and Actresses (Simon), 159–60,
    180, 190

Actors Equity, 197

Actors Fund, 197

Ahmanson Theater, 104, 114–15,
    152, 193

Air Force, 211

Alda, Alan, 287

Alexander, Jason, 247

Allen, Fred, 87

Allen, Gracie, 61, 202

Allen, Woody, 141, 225

Alvin Theater, 193, 222–23

Amadeus, 26

Ambassador Theater, 43, 55

American Conservatory Theater, 31,
    86

American Masters series, 276

And Then There Were None (Christie),
    129

Annabelle (dog), 277, 321

Annie Hall, 141

anti-Semitism, 217

Antoon, A. J., 21, 22, 29–31, 44, 46,
    47, 50, 57

Arcadia (Stoppard), 308

Armstrong, Neil, 123

Army Air Force, 211
    bigotry and segregation in, 217–18
    Simon's service in, 208, 210,
        213–22, 240
    Simon's writing and editing jobs
        in, 220–21

Arnaz, Lucie, 152

Arthur, Jean, 125

Astaire, Fred, 158

Auberjonois, Rene, 21

Audrey Rose, 96, 104, 108

Austen, Jane, 42

Avian, Bob, 98

Azenberg, Emanuel "Manny," 55
    Simon's plays produced by, 21, 22,
        29–31, 44–45, 57, 59, 173, 192,
        193, 242–46, 266–68, 291–92,
        296–97, 312, 318–19

Bacall, Lauren, 127

Ball, Lucille, 89, 122–24

Bancroft, Anne, 20, 34, 36, 127

Baranski, Christine, 256

Barefoot in the Park (film), 21, 38

Barefoot in the Park (Simon), 21, 38,
        84, 152, 164, 190, 191

Barnes, Clive, 199

BBC Television, 306

Beatty, Warren, 38, 127

Beckett, Samuel, 20, 142

Bel Air Country Club, 188

Bell, Ann, 229, 261

Belushi, John, 139

Benjamin, Richard, 84–85

Bennett, Michael, 66–67, 68, 97–100

Benny, Jack, 59–61, 80, 85, 207

Beverly Hills Hotel, 33–36, 97, 163

Bible, 64–65

Big Sisters, 300

Biloxi, Miss., 210, 214–19

Biloxi Blues (film), 254

Biloxi Blues (Simon), 215–16, 240
    New York opening of, 222–23
    rites of passage themes in, 218

Binder, Jay, 266

Birch, Pat, 152

Bishop, Jeff, 270–73

Bishop, Kelly, 99

Black and White Scotch, 211, 212

Bloomingdale's, 17, 74, 90

Blume in Love, 28–29, 30, 57, 73,
        77

Bogart, Humphrey, 13, 125, 127–28,
        150

Bogart Slept Here, 97, 108–12, 137

Bornstein, Jack, 54–55

Bradlee, Ben, 246

Brantley, Ben, 318

Brennan, Eileen, 130

Brice, Fanny, 37, 38

Brighton Beach Memoirs (film), 254

Brighton Beach Memoirs (Simon),
        191–200, 240
    autobiographical content of,
        193–95, 240
    Depression era themes of,
        191–92
    direction of, 193, 195–96
    ensemble cast of, 193, 195–96
    financial backing of, 192–93
    New York Critics Circle Award
        for, 199
    New York opening and run of,
        197–200, 222
    out-of-town tryouts and previews
        of, 193, 197

reviews of, 197–98, 199
set design of, 193
Brighton Beach Trilogy, 199, 210,
    266, 268, 276
    see also Biloxi Blues; Brighton Beach
    Memoirs; Broadway Bound
Broadway Bound (Simon), 171,
    240–48
    autobiographical content of,
        240–44
    cast of, 244, 247
    New York opening of, 246–48
    previews of, 244–46
    reviews of, 245, 247–48
Broadway Stage Hands Union,
    314–15
Broderick, Matthew, 193
Brooks, Mel, 87
Burke, Captain, 220–21
Burns, George, 61, 201–4, 207
    Academy Award of, 104–5, 202,
        203
    Mamie Simon and, 202–4
    one-liners of, 84, 85
    in Sunshine Boys, 80–85, 104–5,
        201–2
Burstyn, Ellen, 75

Caan, James, 72, 77
Caesar, Sid, 87, 210
Cage, Nicholas, 291
Cagney, James, 125
Caine, Michael, 187
Caldwell, L. Scott, 318

California Suite (film), 312
California Suite (Simon), 75, 97, 108,
    113, 187, 190
    central one-act play of, 100–104,
        312
    direction of, 193
    Los Angeles opening of, 104,
        114–15
    reviews of, 115
Calley, John, 111
Camus, Albert, 128
Canadian Institute for Theoretical
    Astrophysics, 271
Canby, Vincent, 315, 318, 319
Cantor, Eddie, 207
Capitol Theater, 60
Capote, Truman, 121, 122,
    132–33
Carrey, Jim, 164
Carson, Johnny, 122
Casablanca, 127, 150
Catch-22, 108
Cats (Lloyd Weber), 318
CBS, 69
Century City Hospital, 36–37
Chaplin, Charlie, 160, 217
Chapter Two (film), 148
Chapter Two (Simon), 142–49, 171,
    190
    autobiographical content in,
        143–48
    success of, 149
Chase, Chevy, 159
Chayefsky, Paddy, 247
Cheap Detective, The, 150

Chekhov, Anton, 20, 21, 31, 56–57, 59, 142

Chicago (Kander and Ebb), 318

Chicago, University of, 270

Chips (dog), 107

Chorus Line, A (Hamlisch and Kleban), 66, 97–100

Christianson, Richard, 294–95

Christie, Agatha, 129, 130

Cinderella Liberty, 72–73, 76, 77

City of Angels (Coleman and Zippel), 291

Clinton, Bill, 299–304

Clinton, Hillary Rodham, 300–302, 303

Close Encounters of the Third Kind, 112

CNN, 255

Coco, James, 130, 164, 165

Columbia Pictures, 127, 137, 139, 159, 163

Columbia University, 122, 269

Come Blow Your Horn (Simon), 38, 193, 198

Communists, 128

Connelly, Marc, 99

Connery, Micheline, 186, 188

Connery, Sean, 186–89

Constitution, U.S., 65

Coward, Noël, 31, 133, 150

Creative Artists Agency, 128

Crosby, Bing, 38–39

Cruise, Tom, 132

Cryptogram (Mamet), 309–11

Cummings, Quinn, 117–18, 137, 267, 293

Curtis, Tony, 153–57

Cyrano de Bergerac (Rostand), 31

Dalton School, 177

Daniele, Graciela, 293, 297

Dante, Nicholas, 98–100

De Niro, Robert, 108–11

De Niro, Robert, Sr., 111

Depression, Great, 187, 192

Destination Tokyo, 211

DeWitt Clinton High School, 210

Diamond, Neil, 122

DiCaprio, Leonardo, 325

DiMaggio, Joe, 128

Dinner Party, The (Simon), 328

Doll's House, A (Ibsen), 31

Dramatists Guild, 99, 100, 199

Dreamgirls (Krieger and Eyen), 66

Dreyfuss, Richard, 112, 327
    Academy Award of, 141, 293
    in *Goodbye Girl,* 115–16, 118, 137, 139, 141, 293, 295

Duffy (dog), 129, 184, 185, 186

ER, 246

Eugene O'Neill Theater, 67–68

Evans, Robert, 125

Exorcist, The, 75

Falk, Peter, 130, 135, 136

Fein, Irving, 80

Female Odd Couple, The (Simon), 224–27

Feydeau, Georges-Léon-Jules-Marie, 252

Florence, 76–78, 85, 97, 139

Florimbi, David, 282, 299

Florimbi, Nancy Elizabeth Simon (daughter), 177–79, 183, 185, 229, 273

  character in *Jake's Women* based on, 282–87

  childhood and adolescence of, 13–16, 21, 23, 24, 25, 32, 38, 41–43, 46–48, 51, 53, 55, 58, 72, 74–75, 76, 86, 88, 104, 106–7, 129, 141, 191, 238–39, 282

  education of, 96, 104, 122, 141, 177, 179, 184

  Ellen Simon and, 15–16, 41–43, 47, 48, 74, 141, 273

  marriage and motherhood of, 275, 282, 299, 324

  Simon's relationship with, 238–39, 275, 282, 287, 319

Florimbi, Sofia (granddaughter), 282, 299

Flying Tigers, 211

Flynn, Errol, 13

Folger Library, 301

Fonda, Henry, 125

Fonda, Jane, 75

Fonda, Shirley, 125

Fools (Simon), 161–63, 190

Fort Dix, N.J., 213–14, 223

Fortnum and Mason, 307

Fosse, Bob, 51, 177, 223, 247

Fosse, Nicole, 51

Frank, Mel, 20, 34, 36

Freedley, Vinton, 222

Freud, Sigmund, 322

Front Page, The (Hecht and MacArthur), 151

Funny Girl, 37, 38

Funny Lady, 38

Gardenia, Vincent, 66

Garfield, John, 211

Garland, Judy, 211

Gelbart, Larry, 87

Georgetown University, 300

Gerber, Roy, 87

Germany, Nazi, 217

Gersten, Bernard, 192–93

Giacometti, Alberto, 127

G.I. Bill of Rights, 221

Gingerbread Lady, The (Simon), 69, 134, 150, 151, 163–65

Gingrich, Newt, 302

Gitnick, Gary, 321

Glengarry Glen Ross (Mamet), 309

Globe Theatre (London), 301

God's Favorite (Simon), 63–71, 97

  casting and direction of, 66, 67–68

  humor and religion combined in, 63–66, 68–69

  out-of-town tryouts of, 67–70

  60 Minutes feature on, 69–70

Goldfinger, 187

Goodbye Girl, The (film) 113–18, 137–41, 291
  Academy Award nominations for, 141, 293
  casting of, 112, 115–18, 127, 137
  direction of, 115–18, 137, 141
  financial and critical success of, 139–41, 293
  performances of Marsha Mason and Richard Dreyfuss in, 112, 115–18, 137–39, 141, 293, 295, 327
  Simon's screenplay for, 50–51, 112, 137, 141
Goodbye Girl, The (Hamlisch and Zippel), 291–98
  advance sales of, 292, 293, 298
  cast and creative staff of, 292–97
  fatal problems with, 293–97
  New York opening and short run of, 297–98
  reviews of, 294–95, 297
Good Doctor, The (Simon), 20–23, 55–59
  casting of, 21–23, 25–32
  direction of, 21, 57
  Marsha Mason as five characters in, 56–58, 61, 72
  New York opening and run of, 57–59, 61
  rehearsals and out-of-town tryouts of, 43–48, 50, 51, 55–57, 72
  reviews of, 59
  writing and rewriting of, 45, 56, 59

Goodman, Benny, 60, 244
Graduate, The, 97, 108
Grant, Cary, 125–26, 133, 211
Grant, Lee, 104, 153
Grapes of Wrath, The, 125
Gstaad, 238
Guare, John, 268
Guinness, Alec, 130–34, 136

Hackett, Joan, 164, 165
Hamlisch, Marvin, 98, 150–51, 291–92, 296–98
Hammerstein, Oscar, 322
Hanks, Tom, 27
Hart, Moss, 99, 121, 222
Harvard University, 122
Hatchard's bookstore, 307
Hawn, Goldie, 127, 159
Hayes, Gabby, 116
Hayward, Susan, 211, 212
Heaven Can Wait, 38
Hecht, Ben, 38
Heller, Joseph, 252
Hemingway, Ernest, 128
Hepburn, Katharine, 78
Hillary, Edmund, 300
Hillside Cemetery, 85, 207
Hitchcock, Alfred, 89
Hoffman, Dustin, 97
Holly Soloman Art Gallery, 177
Hollywood, Calif., 87, 92, 211
  social life and parties in, 113–14, 125, 127–29
Holocaust, 217

Hope, Bob, 38–39, 122–24
Hopkins, Anthony, 96
House of Lords, British, 307
Hughes, Barnard, 21
Huizinga, Rob, 320, 323
Hyams, Nessa, 166, 169–70

Ibsen, Henrik, 31, 75, 121
I Do, I Do (Schmidt and Jones),
    291
Importance of Being Ernest, The
    (Wilde), 252
India, 178, 179
Indian Wants the Bronx, The (Horvitz),
    22
Ionesco, Eugene, 20
I Ought to Be in Pictures (film), 157
I Ought to Be in Pictures (Simon),
    153–57, 196
Ireland, 166–71, 173
Italy, 76–78, 85, 97, 121, 139

Jackson, Glenda, 75
Jake's Women (Simon), 171, 282–87,
    329
    Alan Alda in, 287
    autobiographical content of,
        282–87
Japan, 213–14
Jaws, 112
Job, Book of, 64–65, 248
Joe Turner's Come and Gone (Wilson),
    318

Jolson, Al, 207
Jordan, Glenn, 164

Kaufman, George S., 20, 99, 121
Keaton, Diane, 141
Keitel, Harvey, 82–84
Kelly, Gene, 89
Kennedy, John F., 300
Kennedy Center, 317
Kerr, Walter, 70
Kidd, Michael, 297
Kirkwood, James, 98–100
Kleban, Edward, 98
Klein, Ceil, 193
Klein, Martin, 193
Klein, Robert, 152
Klugman, Jack, 319
Koblin, Robert, 36–37
Korean War, 214
Kristofferson, Kris, 28

Lanchester, Elsa, 130
Lander, Bryn, *see* Simon, Bryn
    Lander
Lander, Diane, *see* Simon, Diane
    Lander
Laurents, Arthur, 128, 199
Lavin, Linda, 244
Lazar, Irving "Swifty," 38–39, 154
Leland, Andrew (grandson), 178, 270,
    271, 273
    education of, 299, 308
    Simon's London trip with, 305–11

Leland, John, 178–79, 270, 305

Lemmon, Jack, 20, 27, 34, 36, 266

Lenox Hill Hospital, 105

Levy, Marie, 193

Levy, Sol, 193

Liebman, Ron, 157

Life, 69

Lincoln, Abraham, 212, 302, 303

Lincoln Center, 192

Lion King, The (John and Rice), 197,
    318

Lithuania, 207–9

Little Me (Coleman and Leigh), 173,
    190, 298

Live, 320

London:
    Simon's visits to, 15, 87, 125–26,
        238, 267–68, 305–11, 327
    theater in, 152, 308, 309–11,
        327
    tourist attractions in, 307, 309

London Suite (Simon), 312–15
    picketing of, 314–15
    reviews of, 314, 315

Long Day's Journey into Night
    (O'Neill), 247, 266, 319

Loquasto, Santo, 293–94

Los Angeles, Calif., 33, 80, 86, 87–97,
    317
    Bel Air in, 91–97, 140, 185, 254
    Beverly Hills in, 89–95, 114, 115,
        202, 229
    Burbank Studios in, 122–23
    City Hall in, 249–50
    earthquake in, 107

hotels and restaurants in, 33–36,
    97, 163, 202, 232–33
opening of Simon's plays in, 104,
    114–15, 152, 193
Simon's home in, 93–97, 108, 125,
    140, 144–45, 176, 185–86, 254,
    261, 274, 280, 299, 320
Simon's move to, 96–97, 106–8, 173

Lost in Yonkers (Simon), 124–25, 171,
    263–70, 293
    autobiographical content of,
        263–66
    awards won by, 268–69
    casting of, 266–68
    reviews of, 268, 295

Lotus Club, 177

Lowry Field, 219–21

MacGraw, Ali, 41

MacLaine, Shirley, 127

McNichol, Kristy, 164

Madame Tussaud's Wax Museum,
    307

Mafia, 262–63

Maltese Falcon, The, 127, 150

Mamet, David, 160, 309–11

Manoff, Dinah, 153, 155–57

Mantz, Carol, 18–19

Mantz, Mark, 18

Manufacturers Hanover Trust, 27, 29,
    72–73

Mark Taper Theater, 153

Mason, Marsha, 22–23, 261, 267,
    276

Academy Award nominations of,
  73–75, 141, 148, 165, 293
character and personality of,
  45–46, 54, 62, 75, 76, 133, 140,
  145–48, 170, 176, 179
Eastern religion and philosophy
  interests of, 177–78, 179
first husband of, 51–52, 144
gall bladder operation of,
  105–6
physical appearance and charm of,
  28–29, 43, 47, 58, 72, 116
professional association of Simon
  and, 26–32, 43–47, 56–58, 73,
  76, 78, 97, 137–41, 163–65,
  171, 173, 293, 327
psychotherapy of, 180–81
separation and divorce of Simon
  and, 181–84, 186, 188, 200, 239,
  259, 275, 316, 324
Simon seen as "needy" by, 53–54,
  141, 184
Simon's relationship with, 26–32,
  43–59, 61–62, 72–78, 85–98,
  104–8, 125, 127, 135, 138–48,
  160, 166–70, 173, 176, 180–84,
  202, 204, 228, 254, 261, 274,
  327
stage and screen career of, 22,
  28–29, 30, 31, 56–58, 61,
  72–76, 77, 79–80, 86, 96, 104,
  108–12, 116, 137–41, 148, 152,
  164–65, 171, 183–84, 293, 295,
  327
as stepmother to Simon's

daughters, 46–53, 72, 74–75, 76,
  129, 141, 183
talent and star quality of, 44,
  56–58, 72–73, 116, 293, 327
three-year hiatus in career of, 76,
  140, 145
20th Century Fox contract of, 31,
  59, 72, 73, 79
whirlwind courtship and marriage
  of Simon and, 43–59, 143,
  251
Matisse, Henri, 17, 34, 90, 261
Matthau, Carol, 202
Matthau, Walter, 80–83, 84, 104, 157,
  202
Max Dugan Returns, 171
May, Elaine, 38
Melnick, Daniel, 80, 137
Metro-Goldwyn-Mayer (MGM), 23,
  60–61, 104, 137
Metropolitan Museum of Art,
  17–19
Midsummer Night's Dream, A
  (Shakespeare), 317
Miller, Arthur, 121
Miller, Glenn, 60
Mitchell, David, 193
Modern Times, 160
Molière, 252
Moore, Henry, 127
Moore, Robert, 134
Moreno, Rita, 225
Moriarty, Michael, 79
Morton's, 232–33
Muktananda, Swami, 178, 179

Murder by Death, 127, 129–37, 150
  cast of, 130–36
  Simon's original screenplay for,
    113, 122, 130–32

Napoleon I, Emperor of France,
  138
National Actors' Theater, 319
National Press Club, 302
Navy, U.S., 210–11
NBC, 122–24
Nederlander, James, 192, 222–23
Neil Bogart Memorial Labs, 300
Neil Simon Theater, 222–23, 314
Neiman Marcus (Beverly Hills),
  229–33, 237, 277
Newman, Mildred, 229
Newman, Paul, 75
New York, N.Y., 88
  Broadway theaters in, 43, 55, 60,
    67–68, 193, 222–23, 314
  garment district in, 262
  off-Broadway theaters in, 22, 161,
    312, 314–15
  Simon's Park Avenue apartments
    in, 125, 239, 271
  Simon's roots in, 125, 179, 187,
    194, 217
  Simon's 62nd Street home in, 14,
    37, 61–62, 85–87, 90, 96, 106,
    108, 113, 141, 145
  stores and restaurants of, 17, 74,
    85, 90, 114
  street life in, 113–14

  weather and seasons in, 114–15,
    120
New York Critics Circle, 199
New York Post, 199
New York Times, 66, 70, 74, 197, 198,
  199, 210, 222, 247, 295, 299,
  315, 318
New York University, 177, 212–13
  Film School of, 122
New York Yankees, 132
Nichols, Mike, 108, 110–11
Nicholson, Jack, 27, 202
Niven, David, 130, 133, 136

Odd Couple, The (film), 21, 38, 74
Odd Couple, The (Simon), 38, 87,
    125, 164, 172, 190, 191, 192,
    302
  all-women version of, *see Female
    Odd Couple*
  road company of, 84–85
  success of, 21, 70
Odd Couple, The (television series),
    152
Old Bailey courthouse, 307
Old Globe Theater, 215, 254
Olivier, Laurence, 133
"Ol' Man River" (Kern and
    Hammerstein), 322
O'Neill, Eugene, 20, 142, 247,
    266
Only When I Laugh, 164–65, 170
Our Town (Wilder), 192
Ovitz, Mike, 128

Pacino, Al, 22, 67, 75
Palm Springs, Calif., 205–6
Papp, Joseph, 97
Paramount Pictures, 23, 38–39,
    125
Paris, 15, 33, 100, 261
PBS, 276
People, 138–39
Peters, Bernadette, 292, 293, 294–95,
    297–98
Picasso, Pablo, 34, 128, 261
Picker, David, 166–70
Plaza Suite (film), 312
Plaza Suite (Simon), 97, 127, 190,
    217, 312
Plummer, Christopher, 21, 43, 56
Pollack, Sydney, 127
Pomona College, 141
Ponti (dog), 107
Porter, Cole, 167
Pound Ridge, N.Y., 15, 51, 61,
    106
Pound Ridge Cemetery, 13, 144
Price, Frank, 163, 164
Princeton University, 270
Prisoner of Second Avenue, The (film),
    20–21, 32–34, 36
Prisoner of Second Avenue, The
    (Simon), 20, 97, 327
Private Lives (Coward), 31
Promises, Promises (Bacharach and
    David), 66–67, 134, 298
Proposals (Simon), 171–72, 316–19
    New York opening and run of,
    317–19

out-of-town tryouts of, 317, 319
reviews of, 317, 318–19
Public Theater, 97

racism, 217–18
Radio City Music Hall, 199
Radio City Music Hall Productions,
    192
Radner, Gilda, 139
Raft, George, 202, 242, 243, 244
Ragtime (Flaherty and Ahrens), 318
Randall, Tony, 319
Reagan, Ronald, 128
Redford, Robert, 67, 116
Reilly, Charles Nelson, 66
Reiner, Carl, 87
Reuhl, Mercedes, 266–67, 268
Rev-Meter, 220–21
Revolutionary War, 215
Rewrites (Simon), 70, 328
Rich, Frank, 198, 199, 210, 222,
    247–48, 268, 318–19
Richards, David, 245
Richard III (Shakespeare), 79–80
Robards, Jason, Jr., 266
Rogers, Roy, 116
Rogers, Wayne, 193
Rose, Billy, 38
Ross, Herbert, 80, 83–85, 104, 127,
    154–57
    Goodbye Girl directed by, 115–18,
    137, 141, 267
Rostand, Edmond, 31
Roundabout Theater, 298

Rumors (Simon), 254, 255–56
Russell, Rosalind, 125

Sager, Carole Bayer, 150–51, 291
Saks, Gene, 193, 195–96, 242–43,
    255–56, 266–68, 291, 294,
    296–98
Salem witch hunts, 300
San Francisco, Calif., 86, 91, 105,
    193, 197, 305
Santa Fe, N. Mex., 173–76, 305, 308,
    311
    Simon's home in, 174–76, 179–80
Sargent, John Singer, 17
Saturday Night Live, 139
Scarlet Pimpernel (Wildhorn and
    Knighton), 318
Scorsese, Martin, 109
Scott, George C., 67, 109
Seattle Repertory Theater, 314, 315
Secret Service, 128, 302, 303
Seems Like Old Times, 159
Segal, George, 28–29, 30
Sellars, Peter, 130, 133–36
Shakespeare, William, 64, 75, 173,
    196, 198, 216, 301
Shaw, George Bernard, 75, 121
Short, Martin, 292, 293, 295–98
Shubert Organization, 192
Shubert Theater (Chicago), 294
Shubert Theater (New Haven),
    55–57, 69–70
Side Show (Krieger and Russell),
    318–19

Simon, Bryn Lander (daughter):
    beauty and charm of, 235, 325
    childhood and adolescence of,
        233–39, 246, 249, 251, 258,
        277–79, 288–90, 320–21, 324,
        325, 326, 327
    Simon's adoption of, 288–90
    Simon's relationship with, 235–36,
        237, 260–61, 288–90, 325, 326,
        327
Simon, Danny (brother), 106, 193,
    204
    characters in Simon's plays based
        on, 144, 240, 241, 247
    comedy writing taught by,
        224–25
    divorce of, 144, 274
    Simon's relationship with, 87, 144,
        224–25, 247, 269, 320
Simon, Diane Lander (wife),
    229–39
    character and personality of,
        234–35, 237–38, 246–48, 250,
        277, 299, 300–301
    charitable and political work of,
        234, 299–304
    family and religious background
        of, 235, 238, 280, 301
    magazine writing of, 234, 320
    marriages of Simon and, 249–51,
        280–81
    motherhood of, 233–39, 278,
        288–90
    prenuptial agreement of Simon
        and, 258, 315

separations and divorce of Simon
   and, 258–61, 275, 316, 319,
   324–27
Simon's relationship with, 233–39,
   244–51, 254–61, 274, 275,
   276–81, 288–90, 299–304,
   315–16, 320–21, 323–27
weight gain of, 276–77
Simon, Ellen Marie (daughter),
   177–79, 183, 229, 282
adolescence of, 13–16, 21, 23,
   24, 25, 32, 41–43, 46–48,
   53, 55, 58, 72, 74–75, 76, 86, 88,
   96, 104, 106–7, 129, 141, 191
dance aspirations of, 177
education of, 88, 96, 141, 177
marriages and motherhood of,
   178, 184, 270–73, 275, 299, 305,
   308, 311, 324
Nancy Simon and, 15–16, 41–43,
   47, 48, 74, 141, 273
Simon's relationship with, 15, 229,
   270–71, 275, 319
spiritual search of, 177–78
Simon, Irving (father), 262
absences and final departure of,
   172, 193, 240–41
characters in Simon's plays based
   on, 193–95, 241, 243, 245,
   263–65
heart disease and death of, 171,
   184
Mamie Simon and, 187, 193, 240,
   243, 245
Simon's relationship with, 209, 213

Simon, Joan Baim (wife), 87, 178,
   271
artistic and decorating interests of,
   15, 17–18, 76
as characters in Simon's plays,
   62–63, 171, 172, 282–87, 317
illness and death of, 13–15, 17–20,
   24, 32, 36–37, 40, 41, 45, 46, 54,
   59, 62, 63, 77, 105–6, 142, 172,
   176, 182, 184, 200, 207, 239,
   259, 273, 274, 282, 316,
   323–24
Simon's marriage to, 55, 251
Simon's meditative
   communication with, 24–25,
   51, 76–77, 274, 324
Simon's mourning for, 13–19,
   24–25, 36–37, 53, 62, 105–7,
   141–42, 144–45, 207, 274,
   275
Simon's relationship with, 15,
   17–18, 21, 24, 43, 55, 61–62, 76,
   106, 121, 142, 176, 228, 261,
   274, 300
Simon, Mamie Levy (mother), 106,
   201–9
character and personality of, 201,
   202–4, 205–6, 207–9
characters in Simon's plays based
   on, 202, 240–42, 243–44, 245
Eastern European Jewish heritage
   of, 206, 207–9
eightieth birthday of, 204–5
George Burns and, 202–4
illness and death of, 201, 205–7

Simon, Mamie Levy (mother),
    continued
    Irving Simon and, 187, 193, 240,
        243, 245
    Simon's relationship with, 172,
        193, 201, 202–9, 213
    social dancing of, 202–4, 205
Simon, Nancy Elizabeth, *see*
        Florimbi, Nancy Elizabeth
        Simon
Simon, Neil:
    Academy Awards nominations of,
        74, 104, 141
    adolescent fantasies of, 211,
        212
    antidepressant medication of,
        322–23
    Army Air Force service of, 208,
        210, 213–22, 240
    art collection of, 37, 111, 261, 326
    bachelor life of, 17–19, 40–43,
        184–89, 200, 228–39, 274–75
    brooding moods and depression
        of, 85, 129, 189, 201, 319–24
    business losses of, 92, 100, 152–53,
        298, 319
    career slumps of, 189–91, 193
    celebrity of, 254–55, 286, 316
    childhood and adolescence of, 13,
        18, 91, 128, 129, 172, 179, 187,
        192, 193–95, 207–14, 217,
        262–63, 276, 308, 317
    compulsive nature of writing to,
        120–21, 149–50, 158–61, 171,
        172, 328

on critics and reviews, 197–99,
        256, 294–95
Democratic political affiliation of,
        232, 234, 300, 302
"Doc" nickname of, 121, 125
documentary film on, 276
Dramatists Guild award of, 199
dry wit of, 232, 234–35, 278, 302
education of, 210, 211, 212–13
energy and restlessness of, 150,
        179–80
European trips of, 15, 76–78,
        125–26, 166–71, 238–39,
        305–11
fatherhood of, 13–16, 21, 23, 25,
        32, 41–43, 46–48, 86, 260–61,
        270–71, 273, 274–75, 282,
        288–90
fiftieth birthday of, 202–4
functions of memoir writing to,
        176–77, 201
grandchildren of, 178, 270, 271,
        273, 275, 282, 299, 305–11
gun incident and, 185–86, 189
heroes of, 127–28
honorary degree and tributes of,
        122, 124–25, 222–23
illness of, 19, 33–37, 172, 245–46,
        317, 319–23
interviews with, 138, 302
Jewish heritage of, 64–65, 206,
        207–9, 217, 280
loner image of, 120, 121, 128
on love and sex, 228, 316, 327,
        328–29

on marriage and divorce, 104, 183,
    200, 228–29, 238–39, 246, 274,
    280–81, 288–89, 316, 324, 327
marriages of, *see* Mason, Marsha;
    Simon, Diane Lander; Simon,
    Joan Baim
media coverage of, 69–70, 138–39,
    244, 248
New York Critics Circle Award
    of, 199
on pain and loss, 259–60, 273, 316
personal insecurities of, 121–24,
    129, 171–73, 184
pet dogs of, 107, 129, 184–86, 277,
    321
promptness and discipline of,
    25–26, 233, 321
psychoanalysis of, 124, 193,
    322–23
public and television appearances
    of, 122–25, 138, 177
Pulitzer Prize of, 269
rare writer's blocks of, 182, 184,
    190–91
recurring nightmare of, 67
rotator cuff injury of, 326–27
safety represented by work to, 121,
    172, 239
seventieth birthday of, 320
social life and dating of, 40, 41–43,
    113–14, 125, 127–29, 186–89,
    228–39, 254–55, 261, 274–75
Stage Hands Union picketing of,
    314–15
suicidal impulses of, 322

tennis playing of, 149, 179,
    186–87, 261, 274, 319
theater named for, 222–23, 314
Tony nominations and awards of,
    149, 164, 222, 268
White House visit of, 302–4
working routine of, 19–20, 21, 54,
    61, 108, 119–21, 149–50,
    160–61, 263–64, 328
on writing farce, 252–54
youthful jobs of, 211–12
Simon, Neil, works of:
abandonment theme in, 171–73,
    317
amateur and school productions
    of, 256
autobiographical content in,
    143–48, 171–72, 192, 193–95,
    215, 240–44, 258, 262–66,
    282–87, 317
early comedy writing in, 211–12
foreign production of, 217
humor mixed with pain in, 20–21,
    63–66, 164, 172–73, 192, 241
idiomatic dialogue writing in,
    216
independent life of characters in,
    20, 119–20, 121, 124, 263–64
musical books, 66–67, 134,
    150–52, 173, 190, 291–98
off-Broadway experiment, 312,
    314–15
process of writing and producing
    plays, 119–21, 124–25, 149,
    263–64, 328

Simon, Neil, works of, *continued*
  prolific output of, 119, 120,
    149–50, 153, 158–59, 172
  reviews of, 20–21, 59, 70, 104,
    115, 152, 164, 172–73, 197–98,
    245, 247–48, 256, 314, 315,
    317–18, 319
  rewriting process and, 69–70,
    119–20, 123–24, 150, 155,
    255–56
  screenplays, 20–21, 32, 34, 36, 38,
    50–51, 74, 112, 113, 122,
    130–32, 137, 141, 150, 159,
    164–65, 254
  television comedy writing,
    210
  three common themes in,
    171–73
  translation of, 216–17
  see also specific works
Simon, Paul, 122
Simpson, Alan, 245–46
Six Degrees of Separation (Guare),
  268
60 Minutes, 69–70
Skelton, Red, 59–60, 80
Smith, Maggie, 75, 130–32, 133, 136,
  312
Sondheim, Stephen, 151, 199, 295
Sovern, Michael, 269
Spacey, Kevin, 266, 268
Spielberg, Steven, 297
Spinoza, Baruch, 63
Stapleton, Maureen, 164
Stark, Fran, 128

Stark, Ray, 127–36
  film producing of, 37–39, 127,
    130–36, 139
  as friend and mentor to Simon,
    39, 93–94, 127–29, 133, 153,
    261
Starr, Amram, 276
Starr, Mannya, 276
Star Wars, 130, 134
Stein, Gertrude, 33
Sternhagen, Frances, 21
Stewart, James, 78, 125
Stone, Peter, 199
Stoppard, Tom, 121, 308
St. Paul's Cathedral, 309
Streisand, Barbra, 27, 38, 75, 125,
  127, 186
Struthers, Sally, 225
Subber, Saint, 107
Sullavan, Margaret, 78
Sullivan, Dan, 314
Summer Wishes, Winter Dreams, 75
Sunset Boulevard, 89
Sunshine Boys, The (film), 38–39,
  201–2
  Academy Award nominations and
    win of, 104–5, 202
  casting and rehearsal of, 59–61,
    80–85
  direction of, 80, 84
  filming of, 79, 80–85
  reviews of, 104
Sunshine Boys, The (Simon), 38–39,
  82, 190
  revival of, 319

Supreme Court, U.S., 301
Sweet Smell of Success, 153

Tammany Hall, 314
Tate Gallery, 307–8
Taxi Driver, 109
They're Playing Our Song (Hamlisch and Sager), 150–52, 291
Thin Man, The, 130
Three Sisters, The (Chekhov), 56–57
Time, 244, 248
Tolstoy, Leo, 104, 142
Tony Awards, 27, 157, 256, 318
   Simon's nominations and wins of, 149, 164, 222, 268
Touch of Class, A, 75
Tower of London, 307
Tracy, Spencer, 78
Turner, Lana, 211, 214
Turning Point, The, 127, 141
20th Century Fox, 31, 59, 72, 73, 79
Twister, 164

UCLA Hospital, 321
Union Square Theater, 314–15
United Artists, 166
USO, 211

Van Patten, Joyce, 155, 157, 196
Variety, 111, 134–35, 152
Vidal, Gore, 121

Walker, Nancy, 130
Wallace, Mike, 69–70
Warner Brothers, 20, 23, 108, 111, 137
War of 1812, 249
Washington Post, 245, 246
Wasserstein, Wendy, 199
Watergate scandal, 246
Wayne, John, 211
Way We Were, The, 37, 75, 128
Wellbutrin, 322–23
Welles, Orson, 132–33
Wells, Frank, 111
Wender, Phyliss, 22–23, 26, 29–31, 57
Westlake School for Girls, 104, 141, 177
Westwood Horizons Hotel, 204–5, 207
Who's Afraid of Virginia Woolf?, 108
Wilde, Oscar, 252
Wilder, Billy, 38, 127
Wilder, Thornton, 192
Willard Hotel, 302
Williams, Tennessee, 20
Williams College, 122, 177, 179
Wilson, August, 318
Wimbledon tournament, 308–9
Woman in Black, The (Malatratt), 308
Woodward, Joanne, 75
World War I, 249

World War II, 210–11, 213–14, 219, 263, 279
  bombing of Hiroshima and Nagasaki in, 213
  German prisoners of war in, 214, 219, 220
  patriotic films of, 211
Worth, Irene, 267–68

Yale University, 55
Young, Loretta, 90
Your Show of Shows, 87, 210

Zeno, Mabel, 277, 279
Zippel, David, 291–92, 295–98

PHOTO CREDITS

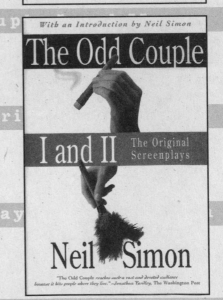